AF556038

Educational Sociology

Educational Sociology

Javed Shaikh

RANDOM PUBLICATIONS
NEW DELHI (INDIA)

Educational Sociology

ISBN 978-93-5111-413-0

Published in 2014 in India by

RANDOM PUBLICATIONS

4376-A/4B, Gali Murari Lal, Ansari Road
New Delhi-110 002
Phone : +91-11-43580356, +91-11-23289044
e-mail: randomexports@gmail.com, sales@randompublications.com,
info@randompublications.com

Reprinted 2021

Type Setting by : Keystoneprintads, Delhi-110051
Digitally Printed at : Replika Press Pvt. Ltd.

Preface

The sociology of education is the study of how public institutions and individual experiences affect education and its outcomes. It is most concerned with the public schooling systems of modern industrial societies, including the expansion of higher, further, adult, and continuing education. Education has often been seen as a fundamentally optimistic human endeavour characterised by aspirations for progress and betterment. It is understood by many to be a means of overcoming handicaps, achieving greater equality and acquiring wealth and social status. Education is perceived as a place where children can develop according to their unique needs and potential. It is also perceived as one of the best means of achieving greater social equality. Many would say that the purpose of education should be to develop every individual to their full potential and give them a chance to achieve as much in life as their natural abilities allow. Few would argue that any education system accomplishes this goal perfectly. Some take a particularly negative view, arguing that the education system is designed with the intention of causing the social reproduction of inequality.

A systematic sociology of education began with Émile Durkheim's work on moral education as a basis for organic solidarity and that by Max Weber, on the Chinese literati as an instrument of political control. It was after World War II, however, that the subject received renewed interest around the world: from technological functionalism in the US, egalitarian reform of opportunity in Europe, and human-capital theory in economics. These all implied that, with industrialization, the need for a technologically skilled labour force undermines class distinctions and other ascriptive systems of stratification, and that education promotes social mobility. However, statistical and field research across numerous societies showed a persistent link between an individual's social class and achievement, and suggested that education could only achieve limited social mobility. Sociological studies showed how schooling patterns reflected, rather than challenged, class stratification and racial and sexual discrimination. After the general collapse of functionalism from the late 1960s onwards, the idea of education as an unmitigated good was even more profoundly challenged. Neo-Marxists argued that school education simply produced a docile labour-force essential to late-capitalist class relations. The present book deals with the teachers' role, possessing the vast knowledge of socialization, social class influences, the teaching ethics, new technologies, research perspective, use of internet, television, management and professional accreditation in information technology etc.

I thank all members of my team who have helped in the preparation of the book. My special thanks go to "Random Publications" who have published the book.

– *Javed Shaikh*

Contents

1

Introduction

Education to Gandhiji was thus fundamentally a process of life building, or training in the art of living. It is the art of putting all things in the right order so that all functions, interests or activity which have a contribution to make to the good life may find their appropriate place in the scheme of life as a whole.

The labour which men contribute to Society demands the lion's share of their best hours. Accordingly it ought to make a substantial contribution to the culture, development, and satisfaction as well as well-being of those who contribute it. One of the functions of Basic Education is to give human labour a spiritual and cultural content. Basic Education is a process of learning through doing. 'It is a tragedy of the first magnitude,' says Gandhiji, 'that millions have ceased to use their hands as hands. Nature is revenging herself upon us with terrible effect for this criminal waste of the gift she had bestowed upon us as human beings.' (*Young India:* 17.2.1927).

'We are destroying the matchless living machine, *i.e.*, our own bodies, by leaving them to rust and trying to substitute lifeless machinery for them.' (*Young India:* 8.1.1925). The main purpose of the Gandhian experiment, explained Mashruvala, one of the ablest interpreters of Gandhiji's teaching, was 'from the hand and the senses to the brain and the heart, and from the school to Society and God, and it aimed at bringing out the moral, rational, and physical capacities of the child through the industry taught.' Basic Education recognises the organic connection between the fingers, the senses, and the mind, and the greater vitality and retentiveness of knowledge that is gained by doing and making things than by merely reading books or listening to lectures.

Gandhiji discovered that children love to do and make things and this is the most effective way to teach them. This can be done by imparting the whole art and science of a craft through practical training and thereby imparting the whole education. To break the fatal distinction between manual and intellectual work was one of the issues of Basic Education. 'If the future citizens are to build a sure foundation for life's work,' he wrote in *Harijan* on 11 October, 1937, 'the modulation of the voice is as necessary as the training of the hand. Physical drill, handicrafts, drawing, and music should go hand in hand in order to draw the best out of children and create in them a real interest in their learning.' To this process of education, Gandhiji maintained, there was no end. One can pass from human designs to that of nature, from human to divine qualities, to meditation and religion. Accordingly he started 'Ashram Schools' in every village. It was his conviction that Basic Education was a vital part of the social regeneration that was the essence of his concept of truth and non-violence.

'I would begin the child's education by teaching it a useful handicraft and enabling it to produce from the moment it begins its training. I hold that the highest development of mind and soul is possible under such a system of education'[5]. Basic Education is a way of life, a method of learning and living, of learning through living, an art which from infancy trains human beings to live humanly as members of small, vital communities, and through personal and co-operative action to satisfy their common needs, to organise their own economic life, and on its foundations build a beautiful and vital spiritual life. In such communities every person may live vitally, satisfyingly, and well. There is no limit to the spiritual possibilities of living on this plane, while communities trained in its ways would possess an inward strength and their strength would be manifest in all their works.

We are thus brought to the vital principle involved in what Mahatma Gandhi called Basic Education or Education for Living. *In the exercise of all man's powers in purposive, social living, which is essentially co-operative living, Gandhiji discovered a unifying principle by which the human person might become a whole person, who must be the foundation of integrated families, integrated communities, and of a peaceful world.*

In his book *Education for Peace,* Herbert Read discusses the immense possibilities of decentralization as the essential pre-requisite of building up a reintegration of the personality, a healing of the social consciousness in the West. We feel that he envisages the underlying principles of the Gandhian Basic Education when he makes a plea for Education in Things and says, 'In a life which is otherwise fully occupied with creative activities, by which I mean simply making things, doing things—when what we do is the exercise of human skill and imagination in every department of human work, then the distinction between work and play, between art and industry, between vocation and recreation...all these false distinctions disappear. Man becomes a whole man, and his way of life a continual celebration of his strength and imagination.'[6]

In this remarkable parallelism between East and West, we hear two prophets advocating the same faith in the redemptive power of work. Herbert Read deplores the 'partitive' system of education which tends not to unite but divide, and Gandhiji bases his whole educational experimentation on the principle that work is man's basic activity, the means by which all his material needs are satisfied. He says that it is also the major means of exercising and developing all his powers and of enabling him to experience the joys of self and social fulfillment[7]. The moment a person handles any raw material with the object of giving it a serviceable function in the life around him, he becomes a creator and develops an inward strength and a self-reliance which spur him on to greater fulfillments. Here, then, we have a life-principle of high value. To make something in the external world correspond to something in the spirit is to add beauty and value of life and quality to human personality.

Even a casual visitor to the Hindustani Talimi Sangh, the centre of Basic Education Experiment at Wardha in Central India, will be struck by the rich harvest reaped by carrying out the objectives underlying the Gandhian Education Scheme—'Nai Talim'. Creative opportunity and community cooperation are but the mean of developing whole, self-reliant persons and neighborly communities, conscious of their unity and inward strength. Work is that natural redemption which humanises the world and makes man divine. Accordingly in the Basic Schools, periods of silence for meditation come as naturally as sleep and waking, while meditative spinning symbolises the sacredness of every common task. In this latter act, we have found the same principle at work which during the Medieval Ages in the West was expressed in the words 'to labour is to pray'.

Creative activity, however, need not be the monopoly of any one particular educational philosophy. 'It is not another subject study. It is an attitude towards all subjects—a way of using the mind, the feeling, and the imagination while depending not so much on books as upon the student's own much neglected mental and spiritual resources[8]. What claims our attention to the Gandhian Philosophy of education is the mental and moral temper that Gandhiji wishes to impart through craftwork. He imparts through Basic Education his philosophy of non-violence and truth which represent one abiding aspect of Oriental culture. Concen-tration of purpose, steady and sustained effort, secrenity of mind, a voluntary submission of the self in the creative activity—all this indeed constitutes an experience which is nearer to Gandhiji's ideal of non-attached work or 'Nishkama Karma' as described in the *Bhagavad Gita.*

THE GANDHIAN EXPERIMENT

It is in such a setting that we must consider the teaching and practice of Gandhiji's Basic Education which is synonymous with the art of living. This mode of education is basic because it is a way of life and not a creed, a process of developing inward strength by Self-giving. Self-giving is the most potent force which lies within man's power, and on it the pioneers in Basic Living will have to rely to the utmost. Gandhiji's basis of the whole scheme is founded on a 'Living faith.' He says, *'Once we realise the necessity for reorientation of our educational philosophy, the means for giving effect to it will be found without much difficulty...only everyone must have a living faith in it as I have. Such faith can only grow from within. Nothing great in this world was ever accomplished without a living faith.'* [9]

Gandhiji's educational objective was based on the acknowledgement of the higher quality of life which is to be found in spiritual relationships and values. In the 90th Psalm of the Christian *Bible,* we find that same 'living faith' in the spontaneous activity of man. 'Let the beauty of the Lord God be upon us; and establish thou the work of our hands, yea the work of our hands establish thou it.' It is noteworthy that it not a prayer to 'establish thou the work of our heads.' The work of our heads is not likely to last unless the work of our hands confirms and establishes it. Education today has sadly underestimated the work of our hands; that has been the common failing of East and West and in both the hemispheres there are attempts made to supplement the diet of the soul with this essential vitamin.

In every man there is an urge to create with his hands, whatever that may be. The hand at work should not be trained in isolation from the whole body of which it is an integral part. 'A trained and skilful hand on an untrained and unskilled body is a most unpromising combination. If a body as a whole is untrained in balance, poise, natural self-control, the economy of movement and energy, we do not see how it is possible to get good results in the handicrafts by the training of the hand alone.' Thus Basic Education as the foundation of a nation's schools provides the quintessence of integration in spontaneous activity, which promotes the harmony of man's outer and inner self, man's unity with nature and fellow men.

In this connection we find a strong link in the Eastern doctrine of inward expansion through activity, with the Western doctrine of Grundtvig's philosophy of education. When we were at the Asked Folk High School in Denmark, we discovered the close affinity of that school and schools of her type, with the 'Ashrama' schools, like Hindustani Talimi Sangh at Wardha and Santiniketan—not in the pursuit of the activity curriculum alone but more so in the dynamic spirit of service that actuated the pupils who lived there. Here at last was a basic philosophy of education integrated in practice, where East and West were in intimate and enriching partnership. The great, Nordic Christian Philoso-pher Grundtvig (1783-1872) and Mahatma Gandhi sought to revive the power of religious tradition, both in the nation and in the individual, and thus to rekindle moral force. The Christian spirit of charity in one and the Hindu-Buddhist spirit of non-violence (ahimsa) in the other made them love the poor.

'Social justice for the needy classes and the defence of inward as of an outward freedom were the Alpha and Omega of his teaching.'[11] That was Grundtvig whose educational work was based on 'the spirit of the people' and 'the living word', which meant for him that personal inspiration can pass from teacher to pupil and kindle a living flame that shall be reflected in all his activities. In the concept of the 'spirit of the people', Grundtvig saw the whole inspiration and obligation of youth. Seldom, it has been said of him, has an educationist been imbued with so sure a sense of the reality of his aim and methods. It is in his plea for the integration in the education of the child that he and Gandhiji meet.

Both of them saw the futility of training the mind of the child in the class apart from manual work; the hand and eyes in manual work apart from the mind, and the heart in art and religion apart from the mind and action. The success of both their schemes depended largely on the fine quality of teachers. *Such teachers do not so much need training as they need conversion. They need to be turned right round mentally, to look at their work from a new point of view—teachers who express in themselves the ideational inheritance of the East-West culture, of the concept of man as a synthesis of Body-Mind-Spirit.*

Grundtvig conceived the idea of the Folk High Schools for the vast majority of the children from the peasant families in Denmark, for their living together and being educated for life with the 'living word' of the Teacher and the 'spirit of the people'. Practical training in life is the firm foundation of the agricultural education in Denmark and there are unmistakable signs of the success achieved in the quality of living both inwardly as well as in the quality of production and corporate living.[12] Life and learning are interwoven and in East and West we see this determined effort to raise the quality of the 'raw material', the people, to the most valuable level of spontaneous unfoldment. The educational problems in Denmark and India and Ceylon are vastly differently. The social, economic, and political set-ups are totally and entirely different. Yet in the search for a supreme aim in education, Mahatma Gandhi and Grundtvig worked with the same basic principles. If man does not use his tools in accordance with their true nature and his, they will soon begin to use him. Therefore it becomes the duty of the educators to instill this right attitude to activity among children in the schools.

This 'New Education' is based upon the belief that every human being needs to *make,* needs to *know,* and needs to *love.* In basic education the child is directed to discover for himself not only facts but the laws of investigation and thinking. He acquires the habit of scientific thinking. The knowledge so acquired becomes a part of himself. Vinoba Bhave, the faithful interpreter of Gandhism, insists that there should be no narrowness in our vision of 'Nai Talim' (New Education). 'Let us spend our lives in the villages but let us nourish them on the culture of the whole world. This can only come about by you yoking together of ahimsa and science. "Nai Talim" means the partnership of ahimsa and science.' We believe that a scientific comprehension of the essential processes is possible by practical application of these processes in the simplest forms of daily life, as envisaged in the craft-centered educational activity.

The fundamental thing today is that 'Easternism' should recover its own philosophy of life and ethic of work. The training of the specialist for his work and training the specialist and non-specialist alike to be thoughtful citizens, in other words, skills in work and citizenship, according to Gandhiji, are included in the growth of the human spirit. The significant ends of man's being are the ever expanding knowledge of the situations of living, an increasing fulfillment of a obligation to know and to do the right, and a deepening reverence for the spiritual realities of existence.

The material, physical and practical aspects of man's existence on the earth are not denied thereby. Gandhiji affirmed that all these things and their true fulfillments in the spiritual ends of living. Said Gandhiji: "Mankind will never reach perfection, but it may approach perfection and as it does so, its inward or spiritual strength will be its protection—the greatest and completest protection that is possible to man...Should it fail, life itself must fail and Good be proved to be weaker than evil, which is a denial of the basic truth that has survived the ages."[13]

If education strengthened the foundations of the essential unity of *man*, there could be no conflict between the individual and Society, nor between the 'type' and the growth beyond the type. Mahatma Gandhi clearly foresaw that Truth enshrined in the individual exercised its authority over the social order as well. 'I do not believe that an individual may gain spiritually and those that surround him suffer. I believe that if one man gains spiritually, the whole world gains with him, and if one man falls, the whole world falls to that extent.'

Such was Gandhiji's concept of the human personality and it reveals the place of 'non-violence' and Truth both as necessary conditions in the educative process by which the sanctity of Personality is achieved and as necessary quality of Personality itself. That the fragmentary man, the divided self, the supreme Group-Person, gives place to the essential wholeness of Personality is the quintessence of his Educa-tional Philosophy.

In one of his last prayer meetings in December 1947, he summed up his whole quest to find in Truth, a form of authority which would save and guarantee the wholeness of Man. 'Nai Talim' was popularly and correctly described as education through handicrafts. This was part of the truth but the root of this education went much deeper. It lay in the application of Truth and Love in every variety of human activity, whether in an individual lie or a corporate one. *The notion of education through handicraft rose from the contemplation of Truth and Love permeating life's activities. Love required that true education should be easily accessible to all and should be of use to every villager in his daily life.*

Mahatma Gandhi's greatness as an educational thinker and teacher lies in the fact that he created an ideological background not for the upper and middle classes only but for the nation at large. It will not be possible for any intelligent educational administration of the future to think of education only for the 'selected few' or to envisage the primary school as mainly a place of passive book learning, unrelated to the existing socio-economic situation of the country.

His 'New Education' was not merely a new educational technique but a distinctive philosophy, based on the ancient faith in the creative spiritual nature of man. The ultimate 'good' of the individual and of Society can only be secure if they conform to the very nature of things, if they are based upon truth and non-violence. *The essence of education is to help the growing child to feel and respond to the claims of this absolute code of Truth.*

In presenting his new Educational Experiment to his countrymen, Gandhiji reminded the educators of his day of their supreme role. 'What we need is educationists with originality, fired with true zeal, who will think out from day to day what they are going to teach their pupils. The teacher cannot get this knowledge through musty volumes. He has to use his own faculties of observation and thinking and impart his knowledge to the children through his lips, with the help of a craft. This means a revolution in the method of teaching, a revolution in the teacher's outlook...The new teacher will say, "I have done my duty by my pupil if I have made him a better man and in doing so I have used all my resources. That is enough for me".

2

Basic Education Inside the Poverty Cycle

PATTERN OF BASIC EDUCATION

Although there are local exceptions to the pattern of basic education in the rural areas of low-income countries sketched above, opportunities for basic learning are generally inadequate to help rural dwellers to break out of the poverty cycle. This lack of basic learning opportunities is both a contributing cause and an effect of rural poverty. It is part of what the International Fund for Agricultural Development calls the 'interlocking logjam' of disadvantages. Rural people are poorer partly because they are likelier to live in remote areas, to be unhealthy and illiterate, to have higher child/adult ratios and to work in insecure and low-productivity occupations.

They may also experience discrimination as members of ethnic minorities (IFAD, 2001). These several disadvantages tend to overlap (e.g. poor, illiterate, malnourished women belonging to an ethnic minority in a remote rural area) and cumulate so as to reduce their access to education and any possibilities of escaping from poverty or helping their children to escape. Basic education by itself is unlikely to break this vicious circle, but it should be a key part of a rural poverty-reduction strategy.

Given the oft-reiterated commitment of governments to reducing poverty, why is there not greater investment in basic education in rural areas The main reason seems to be that developing country governments have other priorities that absorb their attention and resources. Public expenditure patterns reveal that most countries' real priorities favour urban development rather than rural development.

This reflects an understandable concern to deal with the many problems associated with the relentless process of urbanization, but it is also a response to the growing political power of the urban population. "Where resources have to be divided between rural and urban spending on, for instance, health and education, outlay per head is normally less in reaching rural areas, even though rural people have lower initial health and literacy. So higher spending in rural areas should normally improve outcome more than higher spending in urban areas" (IFAD, 2001). Thus this urban bias in public expenditure is not only inequitable, it is not cost effective, nor does it contribute to a country's sound, overall development. The poverty and political weakness of rural populations are cited as main causes of rural neglect in a recent report issued by UNESCO's International Research and Training Centre for Rural Education: "... governance in developing countries bypass [sic] the politically voiceless – those who suffer multiple deprivations on account of their income, ethnicity, gender, religion and because they live in rural areas ... The poor in general and religious, ethnic and cultural minorities, in particular, bear disproportionately the burden of deprivation from essential public services including education [...]. The facts clearly are that the social sectors, especially the priority items of human development and education for the politically inarticulate and invisible rural poor, have been crowded out from government budgets by such items as heavy military expenditures, keeping afloat loss-making public enterprises in urban areas, subsidies that do not often reach the poor and external and internal debtservicing" (INRULED, 2001).

Basic education thus suffers neglect for reasons that apply to all forms of social investment in rural areas, but there are also other reasons specific to its nature. As seen above, the vast, unmet basic learning needs in rural areas cannot be satisfied through schooling alone. Much effort and investment is needed to reach out-of-school children, adolescents and adults. Most developing countries make little provision in their education budget for such programmes, nor do they have the administrative capacity to manage them. Although the 1990 World Conference on Education for All stressed the importance of providing basic education for all children, *youth and adults*, governments (and donors) have tended to focus exclusively on universalizing primary education– an ambitious goal in itself. Consequently, the provision of basic education for youth and adults, as well as out-of-school children, has been left largely to NGO and private initiatives.

Even when government recognises the imperative need to invest more in rural areas, it must sort through many competing demands and fix reasonable priorities. For some countries, prior disappointing experiences with agricultural education and with adult literacy campaigns raise legitimate questions about how best to proceed. For instance, how can primary school curricula be made relevant to local needs and conditions? What kind of adult basic education programmes will be most effective? Attempting to deal with these issues through a centralised education bureaucracy is fraught with problems and few governments have so far found a formula that allows sufficient flexibility and accountability.

Meanwhile, indecision and hesitant initiatives prevent any serious increase in resources allocated to basic education in rural areas. Finally, the very enormity of the needs in rural areas may have sometimes discouraged investment. According to one analysis, the generally dismal picture of education in rural areas tends to reinforce a 'deficit view' that lowers expectations, overlooks options, and reduces enthusiasm among those who could initiate and carry out improvements (World Bank, 2000*a*: 5). The question for them becomes: Why invest scarce resources in a less promising, if not hopeless, part of the education system? However, the next section examines a number of positive experiences that suggest that this 'deficit view' is unduly pessimistic.

VALUE BASED EDUCATION

The word for 'Education' in many Indian languages is vidya. The root vid, from which vidya is derived, represents a homology meaning, 'to know' and 'to exist' from which words like vidwan are derived nanya pantha vidyate anyanaya. Thus, the word vidya translated into English means 'To learn is to exits', 'Existence is knowledge or learning to be'. Every living organism is prewired for the capacity to learn, to remember and experience. Therefore, neither can there be life without education nor can there be education divorced form life.

Vidya becomes a-vidya when education initiates a process where wisdom is lost in knowledge and knowledge in information, where materialism divorced from spiritualism seeks pleasure and comfort which distort perception of reality and where complete lack or distorted vision of inter-connectedness leads to alienation, isolation and anomie. When this happens, one's responsibility to oneself, to one's neighbours, country and the world becomes the premium.

Melvin J. Lasky, in his book Utopla and Revolution points out how utopia ends in revolution, revolution turns into dogma, dogma provokes heresay which in turn triggers revolution. This cycle enslaves the minds of intellectuals in such a way that they become victims of a new cycle. In the words of Nietzsche "........life no longer resides in the whole. The word becomes sovereign and leaps out of the page, and the page comes to life at the expense of whole, the whole is no longer a whole".

In ancient India, life was measured in terms of fullness. Since fullness is such a concept that the product of all the four mathematical operations is fullness there was no space for emptyness, isolation and alienation when Vasudhaiva Kutumbakam and Yadum ure yavarum Ke ½ir "the world is my village and every person my kinsman", how can one become lonely? When God is so pervasive that one can accept and surrender, reject and deny, or doubt and question, how can one escape God?

Thus, God being a presence even in refusal and rejection, a person cannot, but be aware of interconnectedness, environmental, social and cosmic, value education must, therefore, begin with awareness of one's connection with the immediate eco-culture, with fellow beings in society and with cosmic laws and forces which bind the particular with the universal. The creative interdependence among the three has become all the more essential in face of modern science and technology, which is based on the triple principles of self destructive competition, materialistic acquisition and emphasis on commodity values.

Rabindranath Tagore made a distinction between Mukhos 'mask' and Mukhashree 'natural glow of the face'. That distinction is all the more important to remember today, when education tends to teach the use of mask rather then helping the natural inner glow to be reflected. School is not an extension of home, it has become either a substitution or rejection of home. The school does not treat the child as a resource.

The child is treated as an object to be fashioned in the image of the elders by knowing textbook lessons doing social work pre-determined by curriculum makers. There is no effort at relating knowing and doing with being and becoming. That explains why modernity is not rooted in tradition and seeking of status and affluence through grossly improper measures of excellence gets precedence over professional excellence and idealism to fight against untruth, injustice and inequality or to seek the causes of all of these.

The denial of the child and the refusal to treat the child as and independent layer of social science concern finds expression in the rejection of the child's home language in formal schooling. The teacher's lack of cognition of the processes of language acquistion and processes of reading and writing on the one hand and the teacher's belief that there is a single standard and correct form of language is responsible for this rejection. The dialects and the minority languages are also rejected on this count.

Whether it is the child or the non-standard 'dialect' speaker, (s)he is not perceived as a human being, but a human becoming. With the waves of educational theories since World War II, the focus of concern has moved like a pendulum from the subject matter to the child and vice versa, but the medium has been taken for granted. That is why curricular reform has meant change in textbooks and methods of approaching them, but has seldom concerned itself with modes of language use, communicability of languages used in textbooks and linkage between home language and school language on the one hand and first, second and further language on the other.

Intellect, emotion and will are the basic faculties of human psyche and all three are integrally related to language development. By rejecting, suppressing, supplanting, or denigrating the mother tongue, not only creativity and innovativeness is curbed, but the resultant intellectual mediocrity and emotional sterility distorts the perception of life as an integrated whole. Take for example English medium education for Indian language speaking children. Lack of words in English for the familiar flowers, fruits, plants, trees, birds, beasts, rains, winds results in an imbalanced relation between the child and the environment. Neutralisation of the three dimensional kin terms by terms like uncle, aunt and cousin result in distortion in the perception of societal relations. Lack of transmission of the myths and other cultural symbols leads to the creation of cultural perception blind spots which affect appreciation of literature, plastic and performing arts and architecture which use such myths and symbols. All these lead to disintegration of society and culture. All these erodes the values the culture holds high.

Value is not mask to be worn, but is a glow permeating culture. It is manifested in the personal, societal, psychological, cultural, educational, economic and political behaviour. As the seminar on the New Education Policy and Moral Education convened by the Bharatiya Vidya Bhavan, rightly observes, "A society wallowing in luxury, conspicuous consumption, obscenity, dissipation, corruption, disparities, exploitation, rivalries, hatred and violence can never achieve any real progress howsoever vast and well planned the efforts of Government may be for its economic development." It is unfortunate that neither social scientists nor agencies engaged in the study of development have undertaken trend measurement is respect of values among the youth both in school and out of school.

Let me share with you my perception of changes in values which have taken place during my life time. When I was young, money was not the defining criteria of success and respectability. Family tradition was a major factor. A Complex set of factors explained respectability of family and cut across castes and class. Joint family was still the norm and naturally family ties were cohesive and dense which absorbed a lot of socio-economic shock and tension. Marriage was arranged by the family, where informally the son or daughter's consent was obtained, family traditions were checked and the whole society participated in celebrations.

There was a work ethic. A person who did not work was criticised. Today a person who works is criticised. We were then told that, early to bed and early to rise, keeps a man healthy, wealthy and wise. The present day youth addicted to late night TV shows or nocturnal violence wakes up late from an alcoholic slumber. For him/her to be lazy, corrupt and inefficient is to be healthy, wealthy and wise.

In my young days, a person who did not take loan was respected. Now a person who does not take loan is considered foolish and one who gets away with the loan is considered clever. There has been a movement towards "deauthoritisation" as a result of which there is lessening of obedience to authority of law, the police, the government, the principal in an educational institution and the boss in a work situation. In my young days a sense of patriotism led us to movement of disobedience to an alien authority. The present trend appears to have no respect of the traditional concept of patriotism. The un-critical acceptance of Marxian dogma that labour has no country and the capitalist dogma that capital has no country has made the Indian intellectuals rootless and abettors of ruthless exploitation. Uncritical acceptance of liberalised sex modes without reference to the individual and social values has created a class of people who are neither Indian nor Western. The present day Indian youth is taught in a dilemma. Their values are not a synthesis between what is good in traditional and in modern values, but an antithesis of traditional values. It is primarily due to ignorance of tradition and its distorted representation as seen through Western eyes. Ideologically, they are opposed to a purely economic society bound in daily routines and which has no care for others, but practically they seek security in money which leads them to support an undering society. Neither organised religion nor organised schooling has been able to present a synthesis of life which would help deal with opposites and steer a course which would make a person to be Indian as well as universal without losing many identities which link the local with the universal.

In the past Hinduism was a cover term for all those who practised their own religion, without disrespect for other religions. Thus Hinduism encompasses monism, dualism, triad, transcendentalism, immanence, worship of 23 millions of gods including nature, idea and object gods as well as those challenging the existence of god. This was not a religion in the narrow sense of the term, but Dharma which binds together apparently disparate elements. In a single thread by which one perceived one self as a part of cosmic whole. Unless the core value of respect for different is emphasized in all disciplines and in all modes of behaviour, the thurst of Western values incompatible with the India, will continue to erode the value base of the Indian society and threaten its very existence.

At the time of doubt and despair, Buddha's message to his discipline, was Attadipo bhava. This has been variously translated as "make yourself a light' and 'look inwards of light', At a time when we are uncertain and afraid of our own identities and confused about the road to take, there is greater ne4ed to emphasize an integrated life and value based education. Therefore, all of us, young and old, who are victims of identity crisis, disbelief, dismay, and resultant paralysis of thought and action join together in involving the cosmic principle.

3

Higher Education: Meeting Challenges in 21st Century

ERA OF GLOBAL COMPETITIVENESS

The 21st century propelled by a new economy–an economy indisputably driven by knowledge, information and technology. With intellectual capital underpinning unprecedented prosperity, colleges and universities must play a pivotal role in addressing the challenges of the future and sustaining America's pre-eminence, as well as New Jersey's leadership role within it. The era of global competitiveness has spawned historic economic progress. Technological advances and innovations are stimulating high rates of productivity growth.

In the six-year period from 1994 to 1999, the national rate of growth in jobs doubled the rate in the previous decade; high-tech industries account for 1 million of the 19 million new jobs created. As a result of the nation's significant job growth, unemployment has dipped to a 30-year low. The unemployment rate in New Jersey during the first six months of 2000 was equal to or below the national rate and in June 2000 the number of unemployed state residents was the lowest since June 1989. The trend towards higher incomes and an improved standard of living is expected to continue, but the dynamic economy and globalization present formidable challenges as well. The gap in access to computers and the Internet between the highest and lowest income levels continues to grow.

In addition, inequality in the labour market has escalated as high-paying jobs have increased and well-paid low-skilled jobs have become more difficult to find. Strength and manual dexterity no longer suffice to ensure employment and a comfortable standard of living. As employers increasingly require verbal, mathematical, organizational, interpersonal, critical thinking, problem solving and high-tech skills, higher education opportunities must be extended to a segment of the population that could once prosper with a high school diploma or less. Further, as a result of globalization, low-skilled jobs that remain are often filled by low-paid workers from other parts of the world, leaving less-skilled Americans at a disadvantage. Thus, although the trend towards increased inequality in the labour force showed signs of reversing in the late 1990's, the gap in earnings is currently much larger than it was 20 years ago. Like the job market, the demographic landscape in America has changed dramatically and will continue to do so.

According to the U.S. Department of Labour, by 2050 the country's population is expected to increase by 50 per cent, with ethnic minority groups making up nearly half the population. At the same time, the population of older Americans will continue to grow, more than doubling in 50 years. These changing demographics will be closely reflected in the make-up of the workforce.

Beyond these challenges, passing our civilization on to the next generation is a fundamental role of education – primary, secondary and post-secondary. Higher education has a unique job in that regard, because it not only polishes the thinking, quantitative and communication skills of students, it is also responsible for transmitting the civic and social values of our society.

ADDRESSING THE CHALLENGES

To prosper in the new millennium, America must aggressively address the challenges inherent in the new economy while seizing opportunities to enhance the nation's economic capacity and technological growth. New Jersey is well positioned to do that, boasting abundant human, geographical, commercial and industrial assets. Its public and independent higher education institutions are integral to expanding those assets and assuring the economic future of the state. The nation's economy is more dependent than ever on the knowledge and skills of its workers.

THE EDUCATION AND CONTINUAL UPGRADING

With its diverse population and changing demographics, the United States can capitalize on its multiracial, multi-ethnic society to compete successfully – domestically and in the global marketplace. To do so, all citizens must be equipped with the skills and knowledge they need to succeed in and contribute to the new economy. The country is facing a shortage of workers prepared to meet the needs of the competitive marketplace and the economy will surely suffer if that shortage is not addressed. This is particularly true in New Jersey and other states where industries are intensely knowledge-dependent. The education and continual upgrading of the workforce and citizenry to sustain the economy and quality of life are dependent to a large degree on higher education.

Colleges and universities prepare entry-level workers, middle management and corporate executives, while providing essential civil and social foundations. Enrolment in higher education across the nation is increasing and the trend is expected to continue. More Americans are graduating from high school and according to the U.S. Department of Labour, in 1998, 57 per cent of the high school graduates entered college the following fall. In the past 50 years, enrolment in U.S. higher education institutions has grown from 2.5 million to more than 14 million. Here in New Jersey, college and university enrolment increased 160 per cent since 1965, rising from 127,000 students to over 330,000.

More than one-third (123,000) of these students are enrolled in two-year community colleges. Over 140,000 attend senior public institutions, with 62,000 at the three research universities and 78,000 at the state colleges and universities. About one-fifth (67,000) of the students attend independent colleges and universities, including 14 public-mission institutions, 3 proprietary institutions and 8 theological institutions. Since 1965, graduate enrolment in New Jersey doubled from 25,000 to 50,000, undergraduate enrolment grew from 100,000 to 280,000 and part-time enrolment grew from 58,000 to 1,41,000.

The growth of the nation's population certainly explains part of the increase in participation in higher education. Enrolment growth, however, is influenced also by labour market requirements, which have increased steadily. Put simply, the information-based economy is skills-intensive and knowledge is essential for growth. High-tech industries account for a significant portion of the new jobs being created across the nation. In New Jersey, technology is the fastest growing sector, requiring specific skills and ongoing training and development.

Nationally, occupations that require a college degree are growing twice as fast as others and the value of those degrees continues to increase. In 1979, the average college graduate earned 38 per cent more than the average high school graduate; by 1999, it had jumped to 71 per cent more. While the fastest growing jobs do require a college degree, many jobs being created require specific skills but less than an associate degree. For individuals with training and those with a degree, life-long learning to upgrade skills and prepare for multiple careers over a lifetime is now a standard expectation.

The dynamic economy and global marketplace have significantly increased the demand for higher education and training at New Jersey colleges and universities. The institutions are expanding their capacity to meet increasing enrolment and needs, enhancing flexibility to serve students effectively through non-traditional means and strengthening parity among all minority groups in respect to enrolment, academic performance, faculty retention and graduation rates. As colleges and universities strive to provide both access and success for all potential students, government support for institutions is crucial. Given the key role higher education plays in preparing future citizens and leaders and sustaining the economy and well-being of the state, the return on investment in colleges and universities is high. Operating support from state and local governments provides the very foundation on which New Jersey's 31 public institutions exist; the state also provides financial support to the 14 independent institutions with a public mission. The state's targeted support for student assistance; higher education facilities, technology and equipment; special programmes; and research and development is also fundamental to sustaining a higher education system prepared to meet the challenges of the future.

ACCESS TO KNOWLEDGE AND OPPORTUNITY

In FY 1999 New Jersey made a commitment to significantly increase funding for its 19 community colleges. The commitment is consistent with the state's long-range plan for higher education, which calls for an increase in the state's share of operating costs for public institutions to better balance the funding partnership. New Jersey students were paying considerably more to attend community colleges than their counterparts nationally, even after adjusting for cost of living.

As a result of the state's annual funding increases, average tuition increases at the two-year colleges have been minimal since FY 1999 and several institutions have frozen tuition. The state's share of operating costs increased from 24.8 per cent in FY 1998 to 28 per cent in FY 2000. The additional funding provided in the current year and in FY 2002 will continue to increase the state share.

Increased state funding is working to help the community colleges rebalance the partnership among students, the state and counties. But, it takes time and a commitment from the institutions to moderate both expenditure and tuition increases. It also requires a commitment from all county governments to move towards their one-third share of operating expenses. Currently support from counties varies considerably, with some paying well above one-third and some paying much less. The average percentage share for countries has decreased, however, from 34 per cent in FY 1995 to 31 per cent in FY 1999.

Shares of Operating Aid

While all students benefit, the minimal increases in community college tuition since FY 1999 have had the greatest impact on the state's most disadvantaged, low-income students. For them, access to higher education is particularly dependent on reasonable tuition levels, which better enable students to complete their degrees expeditiously and to move into the workforce or to a four-year college. Continued effort to reduce the student share of the partnership to one-third will help attain the desired parity in enrolment and opportunity. New Jersey's community colleges strive to provide a convenient and efficient transfer route for baccalaureate seekers, reducing overall tuition outlays. They are often the only route to higher education for many economically and academically disadvantaged students, as well as many older returning students who seek to upgrade their skills. The community colleges are also a principal source of human capital at the technical level, which is highly desired by the state's high-tech industries. Like the community colleges, the state's 12 senior public institutions play a major role in preparing students to contribute to the workforce and society.

The state's three public research institutions comprise the land grant university, the comprehensive health sciences university and the technology research university. In addition to preparing future members of the workforce, these institutions play a significant role in research and development. The state is also advantaged to have nine state colleges and universities that collectively prepare a major portion of the state's workforce at the baccalaureate level.

Each of these nine institutions has a distinctive mission, encompassing a variety of educational emphases, including science and technology, education and teacher preparation, service to urban populations, adult and continuing education and undergraduate and graduate programmes in the liberal arts, fine arts and business disciplines. The state's long-range plan for higher education calls for a two-third state share of operating costs for the senior public institutions, with student tuition covering the other one-third. Preliminary figures for FY 2000 indicate the state's share was approximately 57 per cent.

The long-range plan also stresses the need for institutions to be increasingly diligent in holding down costs, enhancing instructional and research productivity and collaborating with their peers, as well as in raising external funds to assist in meeting some non-recurring costs. External funds have increased somewhat at the senior public institutions. On average the institutions also have held down expenditure increases over the past five years while taking steps, when necessary, to meet the demand for new students, expand and improve offerings and facilities and upgrade technology and library collections.

The percentage increases in expenditures from FY 1994 to FY 1999 are indicated below. Salaries account for approximately 72 per cent of these increased expenditures, with contractual salary increases, which are negotiated by the state in most cases, as the primary driver. The state should strongly consider a significant increase for the senior public institutions in FY 2002 to cover inflationary and salary programme increases and assist with improvement efforts and growth to accommodate the increasing numbers of students seeking to enrol.

Additional funding will move the state closer to the desired two-thirds share of state support, reduce the need for tuition increases to cover increasing operational and debt service expenses and have a significant impact on the continued affordability, adequate capacity and overall quality of the public four-year institutions. Restraint in tuition increases in this sector will also enhance access to higher education opportunities for citizens, reduce time to degree completion and expedite entrance into the workforce. At the same time, additional state funding will assist the colleges and universities in developing a high-tech workforce to support New Jersey's industry, economy and societal needs.

The state's colleges and universities must be competitive with the best in the nation. They require excellent faculty who are equipped with the latest technology and other resources to prepare students for the rapidly changing workforce that fuels the economy. Additional state support for the 12 four-year public colleges and universities will help them to meet these challenges without relying on students to pay an increasingly larger share of operating and debt service costs and without limiting access and opportunity for middle- and low-income students.

It will also assist the institutions in further enhancing their reputations and attracting more students from within and outside New Jersey. In order to help maintain a strong sector of independent institutions that offers both access and choice, New Jersey's Independent College and University Assistance Act (ICUAA) provides state funding to the 14 independent institutions with a public mission.

The act reaffirmed the state's commitment to the development and preservation of a planned and diverse system of higher education that encompasses both public and independent institutions. Subject to the availability of funds, the ICUAA calls for state aid to this sector based on the number of full-time equivalent New Jersey undergraduates enrolled multiplied by 25 per cent of the level of direct support for the state college and university sector.

This support recognizes the major contribution of the independent colleges and universities to the state's citizens and economy. These 14 institutions enrolled more than 56,000 students in 1999 and over 75 per cent of their undergraduates were from New Jersey. Approximately 14 per cent of New Jersey's undergraduate students and 34 per cent of its graduate students attend public-mission independent institutions.

Like the public two- and four-year colleges, the independent institutions also require high-quality faculty and infrastructure to help fuel the economy by preparing leaders and a labour force to meet the challenges of the future. In 1995, the Commission's report on funding higher education called for the state to move towards full funding of the ICUAA statute.

Consistent with that goal, the Commission recommends an FY 2002 appropriation for the independent institutions that will move the state towards the statutorily prescribed funding level for ICUAA, thereby strengthening the public-private partnership and the institutions' contributions to New Jersey.

Equitable Access and Student Support

Given that minority groups will make up nearly one-half of the population and immigration is expected to account for almost two-thirds of the population growth, the nation cannot afford to underutilize any segment of the talent pool. All must be integrated into the workplace, recognizing issues of equity and the shortage of skilled workers at all levels. Diversity is undoubtedly the nation's greatest opportunity for the future.

Among the industrialized countries in the world, the United States is a leader in providing access to higher education. However, less educated workers of all racial groups continue to fall behind in earnings. All Americans must be equipped with the skills and knowledge needed to succeed. Endeavours to achieve this goal and expand access to higher education and the opportunities it offers must be intensified. The demand for increased skills and life-long learning require even greater efforts to include workers who have been left behind and not shared in the prosperity.

Nationally, educational attainment is rising, but gains vary considerably across racial and ethnic lines. According to the U.S. Department of Labour, 1997 was the first time the high school graduation rate for African Americans was statistically on par with the graduation rate for whites. However, the high school graduation rate for Hispanics, the fastest growing segment of the population, was more than 20 per cent lower, with little increase shown in the 1990s. Programmes designed to achieve parity in higher education enrolment, academic performance and graduation rates are central to capitalizing on the nation's diversity. New Jersey has a highly educated and diverse populace. Demographic reports indicate that the state is and will continue to be one of the most diverse in the nation. Approximately 87 per cent of the residents over age 25 have a high school diploma and close to 31 per cent have obtained a bachelor's degree or higher. This is well above the national average of 25 per cent.

The attainment rates among New Jersey minority groups exceed national averages. Minority enrolment in college has increased steadily over the past 20 years, consistent with the national trend. Following a brief decline in the early 1980's, African American enrolment increased from 9.6 per cent in 1986 to 12.5 per cent in 1999. Hispanic enrolment grew from 4.4 per cent in 1979 to 11.3 per cent in 1999 and Asian enrolment grew from 1.2 per cent in 1979 to 7.1 per cent in 1999. While more students from all racial groups are attending college, African Americans and Hispanics continue to lag behind in college attendance and transfer and graduation rates in New Jersey as they do nationally.

New Jersey has a long-standing commitment to state student assistance programmes that keep higher education affordable for all residents. The state is ranked second in the nation in the percentage of full-time undergraduates receiving need-based grant aid and in need-based dollars per student; it is sixth in financial aid of any kind as a percentage of total state higher education funding. A recent report in *Post-secondary Education Opportunity* cited New Jersey as one of the top three states in the nation in regard to providing opportunities for college enrolment for students from families with annual incomes below $25,000. The report acknowledges New Jersey as a state where a student's chances to attend college have significantly increased over the past seven years.

Tuition Aid Grants (TAG): The state's primary need-based aid is provided through the Tuition Aid Grant programme, which significantly reduces tuition costs for nearly one-third of all undergraduates attending public and independent colleges and universities in New Jersey. In FY 1999, nearly half of the 57,400 TAG recipients were from families with incomes under $18,000 a year. Without the support of TAG, along with Educational Opportunity Fund grants, most of these low-income residents would likely be shut out of higher education and the career opportunities it affords.

In FY 2002, increasing TAG to maximum current year tuition levels for full-time students will help ensure access and affordability and continue the state's long-standing commitment to need-based aid. In recent years, support has escalated to extend TAG to the most economically disadvantaged part-time students as well, without limiting funds for those who attend full-time. The Higher Education Student Assistance Authority completed a study on resources and needs of part-time students. After discussing that study, the Authority adopted a recommendation to support funding to extend eligibility under the TAG programme to part-time students in accordance with specific tenets established by the Authority. The Commission concurs with the Authority's recommendation and supports their intention to consider award values, funding and expenditures for a part-time TAG programme separately from the same considerations for the full-time TAG programme.

EDUCATION OPPORTUNITY FUND (EOF)

Although minority enrolment continues to increase, the state must ensure that all New Jerseyans are able to contribute to and participate in our economic prosperity. The Educational Opportunity Fund Programme exemplifies the state's commitment to higher education access and success. Since 1968 the programme has assisted students who must overcome economic and educational disadvantages in order to achieve their academic potential. Recognized as one of the nation's premier state programmes to enhance higher education access and opportunity, EOF provides supplemental financial aid to help defray college costs and expenses as well as campus-based academic support services.

In FY 2001, student grants were increased, providing an additional $100 per student at public institutions and $200 for those attending independent colleges and universities. Considering the academic and social hurdles EOF students must overcome, EOF's counselling, tutoring, academic, career exploration, pre-freshman and other support programmes are also absolutely vital to their success at the college level. It is the link between financial aid and intensive academic and student support services that distinguishes EOF from other student assistance programmes. The EOF programme has demonstrated significant achievement, easing access to college for roughly 12,400 students annually and improving short-term student retention.

For example, third semester retention rates among EOF students at the state colleges increased from 64 per cent in fall 1986 to over 80 per cent by fall 1998. Given New Jersey's growing number of immigrants and minorities and the increasing importance of a college degree in our high-tech economy, EOF must build on this success to help more students overcome disadvantaged backgrounds to succeed in college and achieve their educational goals. As we begin the 21st century, the EOF community is committed to narrowing the gap between transfer and graduation rates for low-income and minority students and those who do not face educational or economic disadvantages. Addressing this challenge will not only ensure a brighter future for more New Jerseyans, but will also enhance the state's overall economic prosperity and quality of life by narrowing the gap between the "haves" and the "have-nots."

To this end and consistent with the recommendation of the Fund's Board of Directors, increased state funding to strengthen the capacity of campus EOF student services is a top priority for FY 2002. State Article IV funding for the campus-based support programmes requires a partnership with institutions, which must provide at least a dollar-for-dollar funding match. An increase in state Article IV programme support will enable the individual campus programmes to enhance student support services and have a greater impact on transfer and graduation rates.

The Fund's Board of Directors also stresses the ongoing challenge to ensure that finances are not a deterrent to college attendance for EOF students. While Article III academic year grants did increase in FY 2001, some students and their families continue to face extraordinary costs relative to their incomes, even when EOF, TAG and federal Pell grants are considered.

College Bound: Efforts directed towards the educational advancement of disadvantaged children prior to entering college have proven effective across the nation. New Jersey's College Bound Grant Programme was established in 1986 to address the educational needs and aspirations of disadvantaged, at-risk youth in grades six through twelve. Without a funding increase in the past 10 years, this exemplary programme has supported pre-college enrichment activities to help students in Abbott school districts complete secondary school and successfully pursue a Post-secondary education in the sciences, mathematics, or technology. Like EOF, the programme has proven to have an enduring effect on participants' future academic and career pursuits.

The College Bound programme currently serves approximately 2,100 students in 15 programmes run by New Jersey colleges and universities. Students from low-income families face many barriers to attending college. Nationally, only about one student in four from a low-income family background makes it to college at all between the ages of 18 and 24 years. To help New Jersey students overcome these obstacles, the College Bound programmes reinforce the state's school reform efforts in Abbott districts. The per student cost of College Bound is significantly less than comparable programmes at the federal level. In FY 1999, the state's contribution to the programme was $1,381 per student, whereas the federal government's contribution to Upward Bound was $4,164 per student. Nevertheless, the College Bound programmes have achieved success; over 80 per cent of the seniors participating in the programme in 1999 attended college upon high school graduation.

An increase in FY 2002 will increase and improve services, allowing for additional campus-based programmes and expanding the number of Abbott district students served. Further, it will provide for an adequate investment in the computer hardware and software and scientific equipment needed to support high-quality pre-college exposure and enrichment in the sciences, mathematics and technology. According to a 1999 U.S. Department of Commerce report, the gap in Internet access between those in the highest and lowest income levels grew by 29 per cent from 1997 to 1998. College Bound helps to bridge that gap with after-school, weekend and summer programmes that allow students to understand and benefit from the Internet and become skilled in the technology that drives the future.

When College Bound helps disadvantaged, at-risk students stay in school, do well and go to college, New Jersey reaps vast benefits. These students will become part of the state's educated citizenry. They will be more employable, earn higher incomes, pay more taxes and contribute to their communities.

Increased investment in College Bound also will enable the programmes to leverage funding from other sources, such as the federal government, foundations and corporations. Last year the state appropriation for College Bound and institutional contributions provided a match to enable the Commission to obtain a five-year $10 million federal GEAR UP grant.

CAPITAL AND RELATED SUPPORT

Establishing and preserving a safe and adequate physical plant are critical to educating the populace, recruiting and retaining students, fostering research and development and enhancing the overall quality of higher education. Colleges and universities across the nation are faced with the challenge of keeping facilities and equipment current in order to prepare students for the rapidly changing workplace and to contribute to the research and development that underlies the nation's economy and future.

Funding for institutional facilities, technology infrastructure and other equipment is essential to the nation's success in the information-based economy. To meet the challenge of maintaining modern facilities and providing students with access to world-class instruction and technology, New Jersey currently supports five targeted capital programmes for higher education: In this book for community colleges, the Higher Education Facilities Trust Fund, the Equipment Leasing Fund, the Technology Infrastructure Fund and the newly created Capital Improvement Fund to address deferred maintenance and renewal at the four-year institutions. Each of these programmes helps to keep the colleges and universities current, competitive and responsive to student and research needs. The state's recognition of the need to renew and possibly expand these programmes as needed is vital.

The FY 2001 commitment to renew the $100 million Equipment Leasing Fund allows institutions to make significant new investments to keep up with the fast-paced emergence of new equipment and technology. Recognizing the need to continually replace and upgrade today's high-tech equipment, consideration should be given to raising the cap on this fund and issuing an additional $100 million in bonds within the next two to three years. The need for increased assistance in procuring equipment is driven by high-tech workforce needs and rapidly obsolescing equipment and staggering the availability of dollars from the Equipment Leasing Fund will avoid the six to seven year lag in availability of state assistance. The return on the state's investment in capital programmes is considerable. A noteworthy example is the $50 million Higher Education Technology Infrastructure Fund, which was established in 1997. The 45 eligible institutions expeditiously moved to enhance their campus technology infrastructures, enabling advanced student and faculty connectivity and growth in distance learning capabilities. A centralized electronic library (VALE) was established to allow the colleges and universities to share full-text, reference databases and provide access to journals, business directories and government publications. Perhaps most important, an unprecedented collaborative effort was undertaken to establish a broadband, systemwide telecommunications network, which is close to realization.

Support for these enhancements to campuses are crucial to institutional quality and economic advancement. However, an annual appropriation to assist the state's senior public institutions with capital maintenance and renewal is also a necessary and sound investment that will benefit students and the state. New Jersey is located at the heart of the nation's most prosperous and culturally rich marketplace. The state is a global pioneer and leader in science and research, communications, pharmaceuticals, computer technology and biotechnology. Clearly, the state's prominence contributes greatly to the robust economy and the resulting good it produces. On the other hand, such prominence also carries with it responsibilities and challenges relative to higher education's role in the economy. Continued investment in facility and equipment infrastructure is essential to developing the workforce and research required to meet the high-tech, rapidly advancing needs of employers.

Investment in Excellence

New Jersey's system of higher education aspires to be among the best in the world, embracing excellence, access and affordability. The 1999 update of the long-range plan for higher education cites the considerable progress made since 1996 in addressing the critical state issues around which the plan is designed. It also calls for more deliberate planning and bold action to achieve the goal of being among the best.

Over the past several years, many states have significantly increased investments in higher education institutions, recognizing that knowledge is the principal engine of economic growth and societal well-being. Initiatives designed to enhance excellence within the colleges and universities while directly addressing statewide economic development and societal goals provide dual dividends: students benefit from the enhanced quality of programmes and the state benefits from higher education's efforts to address critical state needs. Annual state investments targeted to such needs will strengthen New Jersey's overall competitiveness in the global economy.

High-tech Workforce Excellence Grants

The FY 2001 $165 million economic development package, *New Jersey Jobs for the New Economy*, is designed to increase the state's competitiveness in the creation of high technology jobs and ensure that all citizens share in the state's technology advances and economic success. Recognizing the central role higher education plays in advancing technology and economic growth, the initiative includes a High-tech Workforce Excellence Grant programme, which build on the strengths of New Jersey's colleges and universities.

As a result of the $15 million competitive grant programme, nine outstanding high-tech education projects received funds to create a pipeline of graduates to meet future workforce needs. At the same time, the top quality technology-related programmes will help to create, attract and retain high-tech companies and jobs in New Jersey. The nine programmes, ranging from sophisticated engineering and biomedical programmes to improved training for math and science teachers, demonstrate the synergy that exists between higher education and New Jersey's high-tech workforce. An appropriation for a second round of grants in FY 2002 will further develop outstanding high-tech academic programmes that are essential to meet the demands of New Jersey's highly competitive marketplace.

The excellence grants are consistent with *New Jersey's Plan for Higher Education: 1999 Update*, which calls for state resources to assist institutions in the pursuit of excellence in areas that coincide with state priorities. There is great promise that in addition to spurring the economic well-being of the state, higher education excellence grants will significantly help to move New Jersey's colleges and universities into the upper echelon nationally. As the excellence programme evolves in future years, other academic disciplines that are related to state goals should be targeted. The grant programme has the potential to attract students and faculty to New Jersey institutions by enhancing programmes in a wide range of academic disciplines. For many students and faculty, the strength of disciplines and programmes, the quality of faculty and institutional reputation play a primary role in choosing a college or university.

By investing in excellence at selected colleges, the state will help them become institutions of choice for more New Jersey resident students and attract those from out of state. Similarly, it will attract talented faculty and enhance institutional prominence among the business and government communities. The excellence grants will provide a significant return on investment over time.

TEACHER PREPARATION AND DEVELOPMENT

The preparation of the state's future leaders and workforce begins at an early age and is influenced enormously by teachers from preschool through high school. Teacher quality is recognized as important across the nation. However, after more than a decade of school reform efforts, the nation still has not succeeded in making systemic improvements in teaching and learning. Reform efforts have focused primarily on addressing core content standards, student assessment and other equally important areas, with little attention to teacher preparation, professional development, or teacher standards.

Over the past three years, however, there has been an unprecedented convergence of opinion on the need to improve teacher quality in order to effect true school reform. The National Commission on Teaching and America's Future reported in 1996 saying, "What matters most as Americans prepare for a new century is the quality of teaching in American schools." The American Council on Education recently stated that the nation will effectively adapt to the new economy only if the quality of teachers entering the profession improves. And the American Association of State Colleges and Universities called upon higher education institutions to accept responsibility for ensuring they produce excellent teachers.

As states across the nation and the federal government place teacher quality at the top of the agenda, colleges and universities face an enormous challenge and responsibility. The consensus around the need to renew teacher education programmes and ensure the quality of all teachers comes at a time when the nation estimates the need for more than two million new teachers over the next decade to meet enrolment increases, fill vacancies due to retirements and replace thousands of teachers who leave each year in search of new careers. Higher education must therefore prepare more teachers and ensure that they are prepared to effectively undertake their role as educators in a new economy that depends more than ever on knowledge and its application.

The level of need for new teachers will vary among states; New Jersey's population is not expected to increase as much as many other parts of the nation. Nevertheless, the state will experience a significant demand for new teachers. While there will be comparatively modest enrolment increases, there will be large-scale retirements and continuing resignations. In addition, New Jersey faces the need for large numbers of new teachers for three- and four-year-olds to meet the state's Supreme Court mandate growing out of the *Abbott v. Burke* decision. In fact, the effort to improve the quality of education in the state's most disadvantaged school districts will require more and better-prepared teachers in all grades in the Abbott districts. Like other states, New Jersey also faces pressures to decrease class sizes in the early grades and to address shortages in bilingual education, foreign language, special education and math and science. The state also faces aggressive recruiting competition. Many states are already offering signing bonuses and recruiting aggressively beyond their own borders.

Concurrent with this increased demand are the findings of a number of large-scale studies that provide evidence that the most significant factor in student achievement is the quality of the teacher. There is widespread agreement that teachers must be well prepared in subject areas, understand their students and what they need and master the professional skills required to make learning come alive. Unfortunately, this is not always the case as evidenced by the significant inequities in teacher quality that currently exist. Recent studies show that poor and minority children – those who are most dependent on their teachers – are more likely to have ineffective teachers, which contributes mightily to the achievement gap between poor and minority children and others.

The challenge, then, goes beyond preparing two million new highly qualified teachers. The nation must also aggressively overcome inequities in teacher quality – deepening knowledge of subjects and how to teach them. The recent report from the American Council on Education, *To Touch the Future,* calls upon the institutions to transform the way teachers are taught. New Jersey's future prosperity is inextricably linked to its success in preparing high-quality teachers who can provide all citizens with the learning foundation to be productive members of society. State efforts are under way to improve teacher quality in several ways:

- The State Department of Education (DOE), working with the P-12 and higher education systems, is in the process of reviewing and revising the state regulations for teacher education programmes and certification of educational professionals.

- The grade-point average necessary for teacher certification was recently raised to 2.75.
- The DOE is engaged in state-supported teacher recruitment efforts.
- A two-year beginning teacher-mentoring programme is getting under way.
- Teachers are now required to complete 100 hours of approved professional development every five years.
- Professional development schools received additional state funding to expand existing and establish new P-16 partnerships.
- The state continues to implement an NSF Statewide Systemic Initiative (SSI) grant to improve science and mathematics instruction.
- Individual colleges continue to undertake various initiatives to enhance teacher preparation and professional development programmes.

Higher education plays a role in most of the above initiatives – in some cases a very significant role. Each of these initiatives is important in building a quality teaching corps. Additional efforts must be considered to expand the capacity of colleges and universities to prepare high-quality teachers; expand the recruitment and retention of minority teachers; address the critical teacher shortages in preschool, special education and mathematics and science; recruit and retain effective teachers in disadvantaged areas; and raise the overall desirability of teaching as a profession.

The New Jersey Commission on Higher Education and Department of Education are working jointly to develop a series of related initiatives to comprehensively address these teacher quality and shortage issues. Much of the responsibility for improving the quality of the educators in our nation's schools depends heavily upon the strength and effectiveness of teacher preparation and development programmes provided by colleges and universities in collaboration with the elementary and secondary schools. In many states, special support is now directed specifically to teacher preparation and professional development programmes to assist the colleges and universities as they address the challenge of training and retraining more and better-prepared teachers for the 21st century.

With overall enrolment growth in higher education and widely ranging responsibilities and concerns, the state is working in tandem with the institutions to ensure that teacher quality resides atop the state's educational agenda. A special state appropriation in the FY 2002 budget would help colleges and universities that have teacher preparation programmes to construct a comprehensive approach to change, with a focus on four primary goals.

1. Moving the education of teachers to the top of institutional agendas and articulating the centrality of teacher preparation to the roles and missions of institutions, with a focus on the role of arts and sciences faculty.
2. Increasing the state's capacity to produce highly effective teachers to fulfil ever- growing demands and shortages.
3. Improving teacher preparation and professional development in a manner that links knowledge and performance expectations for teachers with the content standards for P-12 students.
4. Expanding collaborative efforts with P-12 schools in areas such as curriculum development, mentoring, induction and professional development.

Such an initiative would strike at the very core of teacher quality by assisting the institutions in their move towards comprehensive programme improvement and increased capacity to prepare highly effective educators. It has the potential to become the linchpin programme in the state's efforts to improve teacher quality, which in turn will lay the groundwork for parity in educational opportunity and workforce preparedness for all racial, ethnic and socio-economic groups.

Recognizing the diversity among the institutions, a state incentive grant to be used over one to three years should be provided to each college or university with a teacher preparation programme. The Commission and Department of Education are working with the state colleges and universities and representatives from other institutions that have teacher education programmes to define criteria that will guide disbursement and use of the grant funds. Each institution will develop a plan to address the above goals and funds will be available for use following a review by the Commission, in consultation with the Commissioner of Education. Special emphasis should be placed on implementation of practices and programmes proven to be effective and enhanced efforts to facilitate the smooth transfer of teacher candidates from two- to four-year colleges should also be a priority. Ongoing state support for senior public institutions is recommended through additional state-funded positions that are necessary in order to increase the institutions' capacity to meet the growing demand for more teachers. In addition, the senior public institutions may request that a portion of their grant funds be included in their base budgets to assist in supporting ongoing salaries for new faculty hired to increase capacity.

The Department of Education is working with representatives from the state colleges and universities and with the Commission to shape two related initiatives. The first is a targeted effort to recruit highly qualified, undergraduate and post-baccalaureate teacher candidates of colour, as well as highly skilled candidates for areas of shortage such as math, science, special education and preschool. The Department, in consultation with the Commission, would oversee a programme to provide bonuses for such candidates who teach in Abbott school districts. The programme could have an immediate effect in FY 2002 by placing more highly qualified new teachers in disadvantaged schools. It could also have a long-term effect by enticing more students of colour and students interested in math, science, special education and preschool to complete teacher preparation programmes and teach in an Abbott district.

The second related initiative is focused on teacher retention and quality. The Department, in consultation with the Commission, would provide grants to the six state colleges and universities that prepare the majority of new teachers in the state. The institutions (The College of New Jersey, Kean University, Montclair State University, New Jersey City University, Rowan University and William Paterson University) would establish Professional Development Academies. These six academies would be learner-centred, content-based and tied to the Core Curriculum Content Standards. They would provide two- to three-week paid summer sessions for current teachers, as well as ongoing seminars during the school year. Elementary and secondary students could participate in summer Learner's Academies on campus, which would provide academic enrichment for students and a laboratory setting for teachers to try out new strategies and ideas.

Together, these three, targeted initiatives have the potential to significantly advance school reform efforts and meet state needs. They will positively impact schools statewide and play a particularly important role in the effort to provide parity in the state's Abbott school districts. High-quality educators are among the state's most precious resources and the investment in these initiatives will reap significant returns. However, the issue of an adequate number of high quality educators extends beyond preschool to grade 12. In future years, planning efforts should consider a means to better recruit, retain and develop high-quality diverse faculties for colleges and universities as well, recognizing that a large turnover is expected in the first decade of the 21st century.

4

Women in Higher Education in India

WOMEN IN HIGHER EDUCATION

The data on enrolment (a) of women and men in higher education, (b) of women across faculties/ disciplines or subjects, (c) across levels/stages, viz, undergraduate, graduate/post-graduate and doctoral/research level. It also highlights the difference in their enrolment in general and professional education. The period covered is 1950-51 to 2002-03. For specific examples, statistics of 2001-002 have been used because of the non-availability for later year.

The enrolment statistics for the 1990s are the focus of discussion while the data for the preceding four decades is used to indicate trends and shifts. Starting from 1950-51 when the proportion of women was 10.9 per cent to 40.04 per cent in 2002-03, the increase has been significant. In other words there were, 14 women per 100 men in 1950-51 which increased to 67 in 2002-03. Thus, the proportion of women entering higher education today has increased rapidly from 1,685,926 (—%) in 1991-92 to 40 per cent (3,695,964) of all students. There have also been shifts in women's choice of disciplines in higher education. There are also wide disparities in enrolment by region, caste, tribe and by gender. These differences impact on women from the disadvantaged groups.

EMPLOYMENT IN GENERAL AND PROFESSIONAL EDUCATION

The programmes in higher education are divided into those of general subjects such as arts which includes social sciences and humanities; and pure sciences, on the one hand, and the professional courses such as engineering (which includes architecture), medical science, teacher education, agriculture, law etc, on the other. They are also divided into masculine and feminine disciplines. For example, arts, social sciences, humanities, teacher education have been viewed as feminine disciplines. On the other hand, commerce, law, engineering are masculine disciplines. Medical Science has not been a masculine discipline in India unlike in the western countries. In India as in the rest of South Asia, the practice of female seclusion enjoined the treatment of women patients by women doctors. This necessitated training women doctors thereby enabling women to enter the medical profession.

The proportion of women in some of the masculine disciplines was miniscule soon after independence and remained so till the 1980s with the exception of commerce. For example, the proportion of women in commerce was 0.5 per cent in 1950-51 and increased to 15.9 per cent in 1980-81. Thereafter it has been going up steadily and now stands at 36.7 per cent in 2002-03. In Engg./Tech courses, their proportion was 0.2 per cent in 1950-51; 3.8 per cent in 1980-81 and is now 22.3 per cent. In law, their proportion has increased from 2.1 per cent to 20.8 per cent. In education women were 32.4 per cent even in 1950-51 and are now 50.6 per cent. In medicine their proportion was 16.3 per cent in 1950-51 and is now 44.7 per cent.

In science the proportion of women decreased from 33.3 per cent in 1950-51 to 28.8 per cent 1980-81. This was the period when natural science was at a premium, especially physics and chemistry. Till the eighties they were the first choice for men students and while competing with men women were pushed out. It is also possible that science was not, in any case, the first preference for young women whose parents perceived marriage as a priority over higher education. An undergraduate degree, of any kind, only helped in the marriage market by raising the social status. A science degree required a longer investment of time and other resources, therefore, was not desirable. The young women were also socialized to perceive higher education from that view point.

Nowadays, research in natural sciences is not –– preferred by men because it does not lead to high – salary profession. Besides, it requires several more years than an engineering, IT or a management degree. Thus, more women are staying on to do research in natural sciences. Therefore, the proportions of women and men have almost become equal in 'sciences' during the last one decade. The differential importance of general science for women and men over time has to be understood as a background to shifts in disciplinary choices in the recent past.

The Proportion of Women

The proportion of women in 2002-03 in arts was 44.2 and has been increasingly steadily since 1970-71. The proportion of men, on the other hand, has decreased gradually during the same period from 83.9 per cent to 54.6 per cent. In teacher's education, another feminine discipline the proportion of women has gone up from 32.4 to 50.6 per cent. Science, a masculine discipline, provides an interesting insight on disciplinary choices of young women and men. For example, in science the proportion of men which was around 80-90 per cent till 1980-81, has come down to 59.8 per cent in 2002-03. These days young persons both men and women are impatient with just pursuing 'studies'. They like to earn as soon as they can, even while in school. The revolution in values cuts across strata, *i.e.* young persons even from the upper and middle strata want to earn as early as possible. The daughters of city based professional parents, especially if they do not have brothers, have really undergone a sea change in their socialization.

The parents are giving the best education to their daughters and expect them to be independent and follow careers. This revolution in values contrasts with those values which dominated prior to the nineties, *i.e.* education and its linkage to the job market early on in life, was only for those men who needed jobs and was certainly not for women. In this changed situation, the priorities of women have also changed. They too want professional education and are, therefore, entering the so called masculine disciplines. This can be better understood if one were to look at their percentage distribution in different disciplines.

PERCENTAGE OF WOMEN AS PROPORTION OF TOTAL ENROLMENT OF WOMEN IN HIGHER EDUCATION

The percentage of women as proportion of total enrolment of women in higher education is an interesting dimension. In other words, out of every 100 women students who take admission in higher education, how many enroll for which subjects? It is noteworthy that fewer women per hundred women in higher education are opting for teacher's education or for medicine. For example, in teacher's education, considered to be a women's profession, the percentage has decreased from 3.1 per cent in 1950-51 to 1.8 per cent in 2002-03.

As noted earlier, the number has also somewhat declined during the last one year. In medicine too, there is a decline from 5.8 per cent to 3.6 per cent. In commerce, the growth chart is interesting. Their percentage has increased from 0.4 per cent in 1950-51 to 11.8 per cent in 1980-81. In fact, most of the expansion seems to have taken place during the 70s, a period when it begins to become a stepladder to management, chartered accountancy etc. After 1980-81 it grows steadily to 16.5 per cent in 2002-03. In engineering and technology too, there is a significant increase from less than one per cent in 1950-51 to 4.2 per cent in 2002-03 and in law from 0.7 per cent to 4.2 per cent.

There are two simultaneous trends of clustering/concentration and dispersal that can be seen in the participation of men and women in higher education. During the first three decades while women tended to be clustered in the general disciplines of arts and sciences (nearly 90 per cent); men's participation was characterized by both clustering in arts and sciences disciplines but also significantly dispersed in others such as commerce, engg/tech and law. Lately, however, women's participation too is marked by clustering as well as dispersal.

WOMEN ENTER HIGHER EDUCATION AT THE UNDERGRADUATE LEVEL

Once women enter higher education at the undergraduate level, do they move on the next two levels, namely, the graduate and research? In other words, their transition from one level to another will highlight their staying power. Table 4 shows the distribution of men and women by level/stage of education.

In 1991-92, 14,79,231 women were enrolled for undergraduate programmes which increased to 3,285,544 in 2002-03; 169,267 women were enrolled for graduate programmes in 1991-92 as compared to 355,893 women in 2002-03; from and 19,894 in 1991-92 to 23,609 in 2002-03 for research programmes. During these years their proportion has also increased from 32.8 per cent to 39.9 per cent in undergraduate programmes; from 34.7 per cent to 42.0 per cent in graduate level progammes; and from 37.1 per cent to 38.0 per cent in the M.Phil and Ph.D. programme Their proportion is highest at the graduate level while their proportion in research programmes has marginally declined from 39.2 per cent in 1995-96 to 38.0 per cent in 2002-03. Until 1950-51, only 20.2 women had enrolled for research degrees which increased in the next three decades to 8,780 in 1980-81. Their number nearly doubled to 15,018 in 1988-89. Now it stands at 23,609 in 2002-03.

The slightly higher percentage at the graduate level indicates that more women are transiting from undergraduate to the next higher level courses. It may also have something to do with the popularity of masters programmes in management, computers and IT, media, advertising, fashion technology etc. which are popular in the metropolitan cities. But in the absence of statistics it is difficult to come to a conclusion.

Division of the Indian Union Reflects

The division of the Indian Union reflects, to some extent, social, cultural and economic differences and, therefore, the growth and expansion of women's education has varied over time across different provinces. These disparities have been referred to, time and again, by the official committees and commissions. For example, the Committee on Women's Education 1956-58, the first one to look comprehensively on women's education, highlights the fact that the four southern provinces of Karnataka, Tamilnadu, Andhra Pradesh and Kerala were better than the northern Hindi speaking provinces in female literacy and education. *Towards Equality, the Report of the Committee on the Status of Women, 1974,* also mentions that regions and cities with high populations of SC/ST and Muslims were marked by low literacy rates.

Unfortunately, these trends are continuing and the enrolment of women varies from province to province. Kerala has had the highest enrolment and even now it is 60 per cent *i.e.* there are more women than men in higher education. Apart from pro-women cultural traditions and values, which I can not explain here, the migration of young men to the middle east may also have caused this gender imbalance. The other states where they are more than half the proportion are: Goa (58.5), Punjab (52.68); Andaman and Nicobar Islands (57.77); Chandigarh (55.5) and Pondicherry (52.60). Those with the lowest proportion are also the most backward; namely, Bihar (23.81); Jharkhand (30.40); Chhatisgarh (36.70); Rajasthan (32.33); Uttar Pradesh (38.40); and Madhya Pradesh (37.20). In these provinces the proportion is less than the all India average of 40.05 per cent. The link between province and professional education is very close.

For example, the regional variation can also be seen in the growth of engineering and technology courses in the four southern states. In 1991, out of 70,481 students in degree courses 4,419 (6.3) were women which had increased from 3.9 per cent in 1983 (IAMR 1995). A majority of women students were from the southern (1,989) and western (608) region. Even in 2001-02, the enrolment in undergraduate degree programmes BE/BSc. (Engg.)/B.Arch was highest in the four states in which the maximum number of private colleges have been established. The number of women is also the highest in these states, *e.g.* Maharashtra (24,710); Karnataka (22,287); Andhra Pradesh (22,615); Tamilnadu (10,722) which works out to 20.6, 20.1, 30.4 per cent and 18.7 per cent of total enrolment in the subject. Similarly, in medicine Maharashtra has the highest enrolment followed by Tamilnadu, Andhra Pradesh, Gujarat and Karnataka. Women's enrolment too is high in these provinces. In Maharashtra, the proportion of women is 48.0 per cent (17,471). It is 38.4 per cent (6,206) in Tamil Nadu; 46.3 (6,066) in Andhra Pradesh; 37.8 (4,173) in Gujarat, and 33 per cent (2367) in Karnataka. Though the number of students in MBBS is nearly the same as in Karnataka, Uttar Pradesh and Bihar, the proportion of women in the last two provinces is lower at 23.6 and 16.6 per cent respectively.

In commerce, too, the highest enrolment is in the same states alongwith some others. For example, the highest enrolment in commerce is in Maharashtra, West Bengal, Andhra Pradesh, Gujarat, Bihar, Tamilnadu. The higher enrolment of women is also in the same provinces - 39.6 per cent in Maharashtra, 41.7 in Andhra Pradesh, 44.9 in Tamilnadu and 31.2 per cent in Karnataka. These states add to the increase in the proportion of women at the all India level. The same is true for the degree programmes in engineering.

The regional differences are due to several factors. One of them is the earlier start of formal education in the southern as compared to the northern region during the colonial period. Moreover, a large number of private engineering colleges have been established here even in contemporary period. Third, the socio-cultural practices and positive attitudes of parents towards the higher education of their daughters also impact on women's access to professional education. This difference is, to a large extent, due to the practice of female seclusion in the north and the absence in the south which I have discussed elsewhere.

Caste, Class, Gender and Region

In 2001-02, the proportions of SC/ST students were as follows: Scheduled Castes 11.5 per cent (1,016,182) SC men 8 per cent (7,06,769) and SC women 3.5 per cent (309,813). The ST students constituted 4 per cent (351,880) of total enrolment; men 2.7 per cent (240,495); women 1.3 per cent (114,168). In M.Phil/ Ph.D. programmes, there were 53,119 students all over the country. Of these 36.3 per cent (19,299) were women; 5.9 per cent (3,133) SC students; and 1.80 (951) ST students.

There were 824 SC women and 344 ST women, *i.e.* 4.3 per cent and 1.8 per cent respectively of all women research students. It is quite well known that inspite of a very well formulated policy of positive discrimination, the representation of SC/ST students is not adequate and the proportion of women is negligible. They generally join general education courses and are denied access to elite/courses and institutions.

Case of Scheduled Caste/Scheduled Tribe Students

Further, disciplinary choices are affected by socio-economic factors especially in the case of Scheduled Caste/Scheduled Tribe students whose representation remains marginal in higher education. But they, too, are better represented in states in which women have better representation and in which higher education facilities have expanded in recent years. For example, the proportion of Scheduled Caste women to total SC enrolment is 34.1 per cent in Maharashtra; 39.7 in Tamilnadu, 32.2 per cent in Andhra Pradesh, 24.5 per cent in Karnataka.

Similarly, the Scheduled Tribe women are 29.4 per cent in Maharashtra; 22.6 per cent in Karnataka; 32.0 per cent in Andhra Pradesh, 41.2 per cent in Gujarat; 33.7 per cent in Madhya Pradesh. This trend also continues in different disciplines. For example, in 2001-02, the proportion of all women students in BE/B.Sc. Engg. and B.Architecture courses was 24.8 per cent. The proportion of all SC students was 7.4 (38,935) and of STs was 3.5 per cent (18,644). Further, the proportion SC women was 1.9 of total and ST women was 0.4 (2035). The number of tribal women has increased from fourfold since 1995-96 when it was 575. If we look at the proportion of SC/ST women vis-à-vis total number of women in engineering courses, the SC women are 7.5 per cent and ST women are 1.6 per cent.

Proportion of SC Women

The proportion of women vis-à-vis the SC/ST students as a whole also reflect the same trend. For example, the proportion of SC women as part of total SC enrolment was 28.2 per cent in Andhra Pradesh, 29.2 per cent in Karnataka, 24.6 in Tamilnadu, and 39.4 per cent in Kerala. 61.6 per cent of SC women students in engineering courses are enrolled in Andhra Pradesh, Karnataka and Tamilnadu. If only the information had been available for Maharashtra, the proportion would be much higher. Similarly, the proportions of ST women are also high in the same provinces. For example, 23.4 per cent in Karnataka and 18.7 per cent in Andhra Pradesh.

If we look at the enrolment in the three states of Karnataka, Tamilnadu and Andhra Pradesh, 55.3 per cent of women are enrolled in engineering courses in the three provinces. In medicine too, the situation is similar, 60.8 per cent of SC women (4,035 out of 6,637) in medicine are in the four states of Maharashtra, Karnataka, Tamilnadu and Andhra Pradesh. In Medicine, 68.2 per cent (4,577 out of 6,849) ST women are enrolled in Nagaland, a tribal majority province in North-eastern India. However, the ST students, especially women, are very small in numbers and, therefore, the proportions have to be seen accordingly.

Disciplinary Choices and Career Options?

The relationship between availability of disciplinary choices and women's ability to access them are not directly related nor are they dependent on women's academic achievement. In India, girl's academic performance is generally better or at par with the boys when they finish school. At least, this is true of those who are at the top. Every year newspaper headlines highlight the better performance of girls at the school board examinations in different provinces. Yet when they join college, it is not necessarily the subject of their choice.

CAPACITY IN SPECIFIC ACADEMIC PROGRAMMES

While the shortage of seats or of intake capacity in specific academic programmes and lack of success at the entrance tests may be ostensible reasons for the lack of consonance between educational aspirations and disciplinary choices, these do not provide sufficient explanations. The fact is that a large majority of women may be deprived of exercising free options at the school level (*e.g.* being discouraged by family to take up science subjects) or not being sent to expensive private 'good quality' schools. After schooling they may not be provided the financial investment in coaching/tuition for entrance tests (*e.g.* there is an entrance test for coaching classes for IIT entrance tests) because they are very expensive and women, after all, are not socially expected to work and earn before marriage.

What are the implications of new discipline choices for the participation of women in the job market? Discipline boundaries not only limit choices, they are also dependent on the future options of "life chances" of women. For example, even though higher education for young women is taken for granted nowadays among the upper and middle strata in the cities, it is still not viewed as an immediate investment in their careers. Education is, among the majority, and investment to fall back upon in case of the daughter becoming a widow or being deserted (Chanana 1998). The poor parents have another problem even though they perceive the significance of education. Education is to provide immediate returns whereas professional education excludes the poor students because it requires several years of studentship and higher financial investment than the general education.

But general education does not assure a job. So general education is useless while the professional education is unaffordable. Besides, there is lack of role models and socialisation support at home. Women from these social categories are the most affected by the stratification of disciplines, programmes and institutions. Further, the social and economic disparities are reflected not only vis-à-vis caste and tribe but also at the regional level, *i.e.* in different provinces.

SOCIAL ROLE EXPECTATIONS AFFECT THE ASPIRATIONS OF WOMEN

Social role expectations affect the aspirations of women in other ways too. For example, in the patriarchal social structure, parents are not expected to use the income of their daughters. Therefore, even educated daughters are not encouraged to work and if they do so, it is for a short period before marriage. Its the right of the groom's family to decide whether she will work or not. Therefore, for a majority of young women in the academia higher education is not linked to careers.

This is the reason why women join arts and humanities because they are cheaper, softer, and shorter than the professional courses. But we have seen that the number of those who are entering the professional subjects is growing. In fact, there is a general trend of moving away from the general courses to the professional courses which lead to jobs and careers. Some of the popular new courses are not mentioned separately in the statistics.

There is also a big demand for vocational courses at the undergraduate level. Discussions with experts indicate that of the specializations offered in management, women seem to prefer human resource management (HRM) and development (HRD). It is likely that jobs involving public relations, personnel management, marketing, and advertising in the corporate sector, such as the banks, IT firms, BPO companies are becoming feminine jobs and specializations.

This leads to the question: are women moving from discipline choices to specializations within disciplines? The statistics display a trend which reflects the current interests of young women and men. One could treat post 1991 phase as a period which set forth a change which increased the social demand for specific kind of professional education, especially skill oriented undergraduate degrees which lead to a career and a job. Earlier an undergraduate degree, except in engineering and medicine, was a step to further higher education and was not a finishing degree. Young men and women were not expected to work and earn soon after finishing undergraduate education. Those who did so belonged to the lower middle strata and needed to work and to earn to support the family and themselves. The middle and upper strata, on the other hand, could postpone income generation until further education. This was more applicable to most women across strata, that is, they were not studying in order to earn and to take up jobs. It was an investment in their social status as well as an additional criteria for marriage.

Although this may still be true of a large majority of women and their parents, that is, they do not expect their daughters to earn after receiving a degree, there are changes in the expectations of parents and of young women in big cities. Therefore, parental expectations and young women's aspirations have been push factors in the shift of disciplinary choices in the mid 90s. It is related to the change in values as mentioned earlier and as a response to market demands in the post liberalization phase.

More women are enrolling in engineering and law but the preference for management degrees and computer related degrees and skills higher. These subjects are available in the fast expanding private sector which responds quickly to the unmet demand for specific skills. Informal discussions with key persons reveal that computer applications and software computer engineering as compared to other specializations are popular among women. It will, therefore, have to be seen if women are getting professional training which leads to jobs and careers?

There are hardly any micro studies for macro data to fall back upon to answer this question. There are now differences in the specialisations within disciplines which have career implications. For example, HRM requires interaction with the public and there are several others of this kind. In the last few years women have become visible in the call centres; telemarketing; front desk jobs in the multinational/private banks, hospitals, hotels, etc. Quite a few of these jobs are short term and contractual and, therefore, suit the social role expectations of women.

So far as teaching is concerned, the latest statistics for colleges and universities are only for 1993- 94 when the proportion of women teachers in higher education was 18percent— 21 per cent in affiliated colleges and the 11.6 per cent in the universities. The proportion in distance education is no better in 2001-02 where it ranges from 18 to 21 per cent. Their presence as teachers is much less than their presence as students and research which is close to 39 per cent. Moreover after they joined, they still face barriers which inhibit gender equity in the universities. This is true of the social sciences as well as of natural sciences. It is also anticipated that the private institutions which offer contractual, low paid, short term jobs may have, in the long run, substantial number of women faculty leading to the feminisation of teaching in the private higher education.

Study of Women Scientists in Biological Sciences

A study of women scientists in biological sciences in the central universities and the national laboratories also concludes that there are fewer permanent women faculty in comparison to those who obtain research degrees. It is argued that the researchers join as faculty members when they are in their early thirties, a time when women are either married or have to be married soon.

They need a break to raise a family and after the break cannot compete with men in research and professional experience. Again, more women than men are holding junior faculty positions. The presence of women students in technology and engineering has also increased but a study of women engineers by Parikh and Sukhatme showed that the most preferred specialisations of women were: electronics, electrical and civil engineering. Computer science, chemical and mechanical engineering followed in that order.

They also mentioned that there are fewer women students in the elite institutions such as the IIT's and the regional colleges of engineering. Again, management is a professional discipline which is being offered in the expensive private institutes and women are joining them. The question that one would like to ask is why do they acquire these degrees? In the absence of any study, I would like to give the example of a women's college in Chennai, Tamilnadu, which I visited a few years back.

This is a private unaided self-financing college which offers programmes in arts and management. Every year about 60 students are admitted in the undergraduate and graduate management programmes. At any time, nearly 250-300 students are on the rolls. Informal discussions with the college principal and some students indicate that only about 30 per cent have career goals. For others, this degree improves marital prospects or provides a waiting period before marriage. This is because higher education, that is, at least the first degree, has become the taken for granted qualification for young women and would be brides among the urban middle and upper strata. In such a situation counselling for subjects choice and career options is either not available in the institutions or is not gender sensitive.

Therefore, shifts in disciplinary choices seem to reinforce tradition through the acquisition of modern skills and education. The new disciplines which are offered in the public and private sector higher education, though exclusively in the latter, seem to meet the aspirations of a minority of young women and their parents in metropolises to be professionally qualified, to have a career, to earn to be independent. This means that there is now social acceptance of a career before marriage. Here gender and class overlap in overcoming the traditional barriers to women's education.

Wrap Up in Higher Education

Even though higher education has been inexpensive or almost free during the first four decades, yet access has not been easy for women. In fact, it has been denied to the disadvantaged groups and especially women from these groups because of social and economic reasons. Therefore, when higher education has become self-financing what is the gendered impact of the higher cost?

I wanted to explore the access and participation of women students in the public and private institutions of higher education. I also wanted to compare them with the public institutions. There were two very pertinent reasons for this. First, these institutions offer mostly 'masculine' subjects. Second, they are very expensive and a longstanding understanding of the social situation of women indicates that a majority of the parents are reluctant to invest in the education of their daughters whose education does not have a production value because her income goes to the groom's family. Would women be joining them and in what proportions and in which subject and specialisations?

I have not been able to answer these questions directly in the absence of relevant data. Instead I have put together information which highlights the changes in higher education and the place of women in it. The statistics on higher education in India are very poor. The private institutions lack in transparency and do not provide any statistics. Additionally, there is as yet no separate information on private self funded unaided institutions. Again, there is hardly any effort to document systematically either the extent or the shape of the changes that are changing the universities' work culture or to look at the kind of impact, gendered or otherwise, that the changes may be having on the teachers, staff, students. Nevertheless, the private sector has met the unmet demand for specific subjects and increased the intake capacity in the most sought after disciplines though at a cost.

Therefore, there has been expansion and the number of students has increased. It is very noticeable in engineering. Women seem to have been the beneficiaries of this expansion, though it is difficult to come to this conclusion without separate gender based enrolment data for private and public institutions and for each and every discipline and academic programme separately. One is reluctant to give credit to private institutions because they are too expensive and parents may be unwilling to spend on the education and the dowries of their daughters.

Moreover, pure sciences, social sciences, arts and humanities remain confined to the public institutions. It seems that the earlier trend of concentration of women in these disciplines is expected to have been reinforced. Additionally, even though women are enrolling in professional education in larger numbers, it is not clear which subjects and specializations do they take up. Which institutions are they joining and in what proportions? The unbridled and unregulated expansion of expensive private institutes is also disturbing. The problem with most is that they do not offer good quality education and are very expensive – the best institutions are still in the public sector. Unfortunately, the issues of social access and equity or of quality receive little attention in the private sector. Would parents spend on the higher education and dowries for their daughters? The policy implications of the current situation of women suggests the imperative of creating a broad-based database on higher education which is gender sensitive.

At present, the first problem is of a very scanty database and the second is that it is not gender sensitive. It is a sad state of affairs that a country which boasts of very large higher education system should not have considered it necessary to collect data on higher education which will provide information about students, faculty and staff in the public and private institutions. Information on students, namely, their enrolment and outturn by level, discipline, specialisation and institution are imperative for any understanding of the system. A framework will have to be evolved to decide what are the questions that need to be answered and what parameters are necessary to provide an understanding of the system and what happens to women who enter it. It would also help in charting out the future course of action and the research policy.

Secondly, research on higher education deserves support so that a quantitative database can be supported by qualitative inputs. For this availability of funds earmarked for research programmes and projects on higher education will go a long way. Issues of equality, social access, and quality of education have been pushed into the background at a time when only seven per cent of the relevant age group have managed to enter the system. The government must have a vision that encompasses the governance of the public and private sectors and keep in focus the gender concerns. The present ad hoc approach without a conceptual framework is fraught with negative implications for women's access to HE.

HIGHER EDUCATION, ACCESS AND EQUALITY: POLICY FRAMEWORK

Higher education was entrusted with the responsibility of protecting the constitutional provisions for positive discrimination. The commitment to broaden the student base was reflected in the financial incentives provided to SC/ST students, namely, hostels, post-matric (high school) scholarships, etc. In addition, special cells/administrative units were set up in universities to monitor the entry/progress of Scheduled Caste and Scheduled Tribe students, staff and teachers. In course to time and as a result of political interventions, the reserved categories have been expanded to include people with disabilities, other backward castes or OBCs. There is no gender-based positive discrimination in education or employment although some provinces or institutions may have made a separate provision for them. Since higher education was entrusted with the responsibility of promoting social change until 1991 there has been a continuous refrain in most policy documents on education that universities must develop scientific and technical knowledge and encourage its application to eliminate hunger, disease and ignorance. These are the important parameters of 'social development' which is being increasingly linked to literacy and primary education. The state owned full responsibility for the growth and development of higher education and kept the private sector out of its purview. Since reform in the social situation of women was central to the movement for independence, the development strategy in independent India in the 1950s included women, especially their education, in the Five Year Plans. The *Report of the Committee on the Education of Women, 1959,* made extensive recommendations which led to a more focused thrust in the subsequent plans. But disparities in the education of men and women continued. These were substantiated by the Report of the Committee on the Status of Women, 1974. This led to a broader perspective and the Sixth Plan linked education to the participation of women in the development process. There was a shift from a welfare approach to making women active partners in the development process. The National Policy of Education, 1986 underscored the role of education as an instrument of women's equality and empowerment. The National Perspective Plan, 1988-2000 AD reiterates this point of view and states that women themselves must overcome their handicaps. Thus, there has been a careful articulation of education for equality for women which is reflected in the educational policy discourse in post-independence India.

TRENDS IN THE ENROLMENT OF WOMEN IN DIFFERENT FACULTIES AND DISCIPLINES

The latest trends in the enrolment of women in different faculties and disciplines. Simultaneously, it also attempts to see if there are any shifts in the disciplinary choices of women during the last 50 years. In addition, the data on the marginal groups such as the dalits and tribals are also given. The regional disparities are as crucial as those of the general population and the marginal groups. Therefore, attention is also given to this dimension mainly to reflect on trends in the different states of India. While the disciplinary choices are the main focus, the participation of women at different levels, namely, undergraduate, post-graduate and research levels has also been highlighted. This way it is possible to focus not only on women's entry into the system of higher education but also to see what happens to them after they enter the system. What are the chances of their staying on and progressing from one stage of higher education to another stage?

5

Educational Administration and Organized Planning

Every person concerned with health and physical education needs to understand the principles of administration. The chairman or head of the department must use technical information as the basis of the organized planning, analyze problems according to their functional relationships to other affairs of the school and community, and plan a programme which begins with the situation as it exists and moves forward towards the realization of broader and more comprehensive goals.

All members of the staff, including teachers and supervisors, have administrative functions to perform in the daily conduct of their work which contribute to the successful accomplishment of avowed educational outcomes. Thus mutual understanding and support of established administrative practices is the professional responsibility of each person employed in the programme.

The community has a right to expect of its teachers a broad background of preparation; of its supervisors, successful experience in addition to preparation. Teachers, supervisors and administrators must have personality, that intangible something which enables them to get along with people and to inspire confidence and respect. They must understand the philosophical, psychological, sociological, and political bases of general education. They must possess a philosophy of health and physical education which clearly indicates the function of this programme in the complete education of youth. They must have ideals, but temper these ideals by expediency. They must be able to plan intelligently, take the prog-ram where they find it, consider the needs and resources of the community, and, each in his own professional sphere, establish a working basis which gives direction to the programme for years to come. These are the essentials of administration.

A DEFINITION OF ADMINISTRATION

Administration means providing the necessary constructive leadership to direct the programme, and the establishment of such policies and procedures and enable the programme to function effectively. In a much narrower and more technical sense administration means organized authority.

BASIC BELIEFS OF HEALTH AND PHYSICAL EDUCATION

Every administrator must establish a *working philosophy* or a series of *basic beliefs* for his programme. These *basic beliefs* provide a foundation upon which the entire administrative structure is built. *Basic beliefs* for health education or physical education indicate the contributions of these special fields to all education and to life. But first, the administrator needs to have a *philosophy* of education which to him seems acceptable and satisfactory. Second, he needs to establish *basic beliefs* for his special programme which coincide with the general *philosophy,* and which show precisely how his special programme functions in the life of the child.

There are two reasonably easy ways of formulating *basic beliefs*. Some persons prefer to follow one method, some the other. The first method is to describe a youth, at a given age or grade level, who is health educated or physically educated. What does he look like? What does he know how to do? What ideals, attitudes, skills and appreciations has he formed? In this description one is sure to reflect his philosophy of education and the contribution which health education or physical education makes to complete education. The second method is to write: "My Philosophy of Physical Education," or "My Basic Beliefs About Physical Education." Under this caption follows, "I believe that...," and the writer indicates what he does believe or stand for in his profession.

Policies and Procedures—After the list of basic beliefs has been prepared, the administrator is ready to establish *policies and procedures* for his programme. In fact *policies and procedures* flow naturally out of his basic beliefs. Administrative *policies* of health and physical education are general concepts or goals applicable to and consistent with all education. *Policies* reveal a person's ideals and hopes; ideals which he hopes to attain some day. One might, for example, select the general accepted *policy:* "A programme of physical education that meets the inherent and individual needs of each child." Many administrators would approve another *policy:* "Credit towards promotion and graduation for health and physical education awarded on a basis comparable to academic education."

Some persons do not believe in credit for health and physical education and would, therefore, exclude the second example. *Policies* are used in administration for the same purpose that aims are employed in constructing the course of study. A person may be guided and influenced by study but his basic beliefs and *policies* are his own, carved from the foundation of his biological and social inheritance and fashioned after the pattern of his education.

Administrative *procedures* are interpretations of policies in terms of time and place. Administrative *procedures* adapt policies to meet local conditions; the expedient thing to do for the present; plans which lead towards the fulfillment of policies. *Procedures* in administration are like objectives in curriculum building. A person might, for example, willingly accept the policy of providing a programme of physical education to meet the needs of each child, but putting this policy into practice would involve *procedures* affecting the entire school system. Is the school organization of traditional type or does it follow the principle of individual needs? Were the teachers of physical education prepared in colleges or universities which emphasized formal gymnastics and calisthenics, or were they trained in schools using a more informal programme? Are students assigned to physical education classes on the basis of reasonably homogenous groups and in small numbers, or do the wide range of interests and abilities and huge class size restrict consideration for individual needs? Numerous factors relating to the local situation must be learned and taken into account in listing the *procedures* to be followed which lead to the accomplishment of the administrative policy.

Survey Technics—The *survey* is used to obtain information relative to existing local conditions and to provide the basis for intelligent future planning. First, all pertinent data are collected; these may be designated as the *findings* of the surveyor. Second, proposals are made for improving conditions found; these are the *recommendations* of the surveyor. The *findings* tell what the conditions are, and the *recommen-dations* disclose what the investigator believes should be done to improve the situation.

Surveys may be classified into two types; the *general survey*, and the *special survey*. The *general survey* includes all parts of the programme such as facilities, personnel, finance, courses of study, health examinations, instruction, and others. The *special survey* is confined to one aspect of the programme. At the beginning the *general survey* is superior to the *special survey* because it gives a broader picture of the entire programme with interrelationships and implications shown in perspective. Later the *special survey* may be used to advantage for detailed study of one or more administrative activities.

Some years ago *survey* technics consisted of collecting pertinent information about affairs in the local situation, and comparing these data with established standards. Recommend-ations were based on such comparisons. For example, the findings might show that each school nurse supervised 4000 children. Since a generally accepted standard is 1500 to 2000 school children per nurse, it would be recommended that the number of nurses be increased.

A more recent development in survey technic directs greater attention to the functional operation of the programme than to statistical comparison. Instead of comparing obtained data with established standards, the attempt is made to determine how well the school is accomplishing its avowed purposes. Followers of this plan believe that it is more significant for administrators to establish policies and procedures on a local functional basis, and to evaluate success in terms of the degree to which these goals are attained, than merely to compare conditions in the local situation with standards based principally on the law of averages. If the avowed purposes of the programme are adequate in meeting the needs of children the plan appears highly commendable.

In either case the technics of colleting information are essentially the same. Surveying is a continuous process. Change is inevitable, and change in one school activity brings modification in others. The *continuous* survey conducted in one form or another provides the professional nourishment out of which the administrator's *basic beliefs, administrative policies, administrative procedures, and onethree-five-year programme* become functional.

One-Three-Five-Year Programme—We have seen how the administrator at the work first establishes *basic beliefs* about health and physical education which are in accord with his philosophy of general education. He next prepares *administrative policies* which represent goals he would like to accomplish. Through the *survey* he interprets his *administrative policies* into *administrative procedures* which connect desired goals with existing conditions.

The next step is to arrange administrative procedures into three groups: the first-year group; the third-year group; and the fifth-year group. Into the first-year group will appear those procedures which may be completed during the first year. Those requiring more time will be assigned to the third- or fifth-year programme respectively.[1] Allocation of items to one year or another merely provides a definite plan for the administrator. Due to unforeseen developments certain items may be transferred from one year to another, either up or down the scale.

The question is sometimes asked, "How am I to know which year's programme best fits this particular item?" There are no hard and fast rules governing the assignment of procedures since the types of school organizations vary in different communities. Generally speaking items in the first-year programme will include those over which the department of health and physical education has control. Suppose, for example, the policy is established, "In-service training of personnel is a responsibility of the department." Let us further assume that the procedures are listed as: staff meetings; visitation; attendance at conventions and summer sessions; and others. Nearly all of these procedures could be effected by the department and hence belong to the first-year programme.

The third-year programme will include those items involving school interrelationships, *i.e.,* affairs beyond the administrative province of the department but confined to the school organization. The following policy is an example: "Supervision of elementary classroom teachers should be regulated by appointment from the central office and upon request by the building principal rather than by the rotation-inspection method." The procedures might be listed as: approval of change by school superintendent and board of education; approval by supervisors; approval by building principals; approval by classroom teachers; reorganization of courses of study; start with one school where the plan will function smoothly; and others. Administration of functions involving school interrelationships takes time; such items belong in the third-year programme.

The fifth-year programme will contain those items concerned with community interrelationships. The following policy is an example: "When school children are not using physical education facilities and equipment they should be available for out-of school recreational groups." Here the procedures include a wide range of people and interests. In establishing the procedures a number of questions must be answered.

Does the board of education have legal right to loan these facilities to out-of-school groups? Perhaps certain groups will be allowed to use the school premises while others will not; what basis will be used to accepts or reject requests? Shall outside groups be expected to provide adequate supervision of activities? Who will pay for or replace broken equipment? Administrative matters involving community interrelationships usually require a formulation of policy by the office of the school superintendent as well as by the department of health and physical education.

The one-three-five-year programme is an indispensable administrative aid. It gives direction to the programme. It requires serious preliminary thought followed by careful planning and organization. It is to be used as a guide. It is not to be followed slavishly, but reconstructed and organized in accordance with changes in the school or community. The successful administrator understands his community. He recognizes changes in the community and knows the reasons for these changes before they are apparent to the general public.

He adapts his one-three-five-year programme to meet these changing conditions sometimes postponing a first-year procedure because of unusual developments, sometimes coming forward with a fifth-year procedure for the same reason. The one-three-five-year programme means looking ahead, planning for the future; it means efficiency.

A DEFINITION OF PHYSICAL EDUCATION

Definitions change with the ideas that express people's notions of values, of importance, of measures, and of life. The ideas of the time and place have ever shaped and fashioned all parts of education. Thus, physical education has responded to dominant ideas. Perhaps the most influential ideas in shaping modern physical education in the United States are the concept of organismic unity, the doctrine of interdependence between organism and environment, and the clear recognition of social and emotional as well as physiologic outcomes of physical activities. As a result of these new orientations, physical education ceases to be merely a gymnastic technic, a series of steps, or a coordination; it becomes a rich and varied practice that has its focus not in the muscles but in the living of the individual. Although the physical is not neglected in this view, the chief outcome is not *always* perspiration; in some instances it may be the interests developed. The teacher of physical education can agree with other teachers who hope that young people will learn to like wholesome living.

From this point of view, "physical education is the sum of man's physical activities, selected as to kind, and conducted as to outcomes." Since physical education is to be considered as a means of education through physical activities rather than an education of the physical—how absurd the latter—the phrases "selected as to kind" and "conducted as to outcomes" assume considerable importance.

Selected as to kind implies at the very outset that activities differ, that there are kinds, and that a selection is indicated. Activities are of varying worth. What ones shall be chosen? Obviously some are better than others. A choice is required but, when one chooses, a standard is necessary. What standards should one have in selecting physical activities? The old ones of muscular development and strength are not to be discarded, but they need tremendously to be supplemented with skills and interests that not only contribute to wholesome leisure but also minister to the development of the personality in desirable ways. Any physical education that selects its activities on the basis of mere muscular development is doomed to disappointment and despair when the larger problems of social and individual adjustment in modern civilization are seriously faced.

It is the simplest matter of common sense to observe that individuals will carry into their free hours of leisure those activities in which they have found joy. Obviously, the school of tomorrow must enlarge tremendously its plant and facilities for leisure time education. A football field for a dozen boys and corridors and classrooms for the calisthenics of the school will be known for what it actually is—a tragedy and a despair. Physical education as a way of living requires then that we think of school days as days of opportunity for the education of youth in preferences for education in skills that bring joy as well as in skills that bring financial competence since man does not live by bread alone.

The second phrase, *conducted as to outcomes,* is equally significant. One is not to neglect the traditional outcomes in physiological results, in growth and developmental accruals, or in neuromuscular skills, but a proper emphasis in modern education is upon an education in interests and attitudes as well. It is precisely this emphasis that modern physical education is disposed to make. It is convinced that an education in physical activities may mean a real interest in whole-some recreation, that an attitude favouring play, dramatization, and art may touch lives that would otherwise be merely dull and dignified. This conviction is so real that we are ready to cast aside many of the traditional practices in physical education to the end that boys and girls may secure an education that will enrich and deepen life.

DEVELOPMENT OF THE TERM "PHYSICAL EDUCATION"

A changing terminology may reflect the vacillating moods of an interest that has no fundamental principles, or on the other hand, the growth and development of a movement that continually shifts to new grounds as it advances in its philosophy, technical achievements, and determined outcomes. The latter seems to be a fair explanation of what has taken place in health and physical education. The earliest efforts of physical education were primarily hygienic in character and the prophylaxis of a practical hygiene was the motive force behind the imitation of such departments in colleges.

Body building, body development, muscular symmetry were frequently mentioned, but these seemed justified by their advocates on grounds of health and general welfare. These motives that influenced the colleges to promote phases of health and physical education shaped the early purposes of the public schools in similar direction. As programmes developed and changing ideas altered the content and evolved new motives, the terminology was altered to express the new ideas.

In the early beginnings of health and physical education, the terms "physical culture and hygiene" were used quite independently. The former had more vogue than the latter partly because it was an expressive phrase and had activities to offer. Hygiene was promoted by different groups but received its chief impetus from the status legislation requiring, instruction in the schools regarding the "effects of alcohol and tobacco." The content of hygiene in the schools was enriched somewhat by the movement for medical inspection that began about 1894, but until after World War I, its status was essentially perfunctory, uncoordinated, and without vitality.

The activity programme at first was widely known as *physical culture.* This may be attributed to the influence of Delsarte, but in the colleges it parallels the use of the term, "culture," with respect to numerous other subjects of instruction. For example at Smith College in 1879, the catalogue lists courses in aesthetic culture, religious culture, social culture, physical culture, and intellectual culture.

In some institutions the term *physical training* began to be used and gained a wide acceptance due no doubt to the influence of the Land Grant Act of 1864. The German and Swedish systems of gymnastics that were introduced in the early part of the nineteenth century were military in character and promoted the training idea. During the period when programmes of activities were chiefly calisthenic and gymnastic in character, and were under the influence of foreign systems of gymnastics, the term "physical training" was appropriate. There were many forces in social and educational developments that led to the present term *physical education.* The change in programme, the recognition that education takes place in various ways, and the declaration of physical educators to serve the larger purposes of education were doubtless influential factors. In a few places, the term "physical training" is still employed although physical culture has passed entirely out of the schools. This shift, from physical culture through physical training to physical education is well shown by Elliott in her study of physical education in state universities. It should be noted that the term "physical education" was used before 1893 (Elliott gives data only on state universities). In fact, Lewis in the spring of 1861 established a training school for teachers in Boston which he called the Normal Institute for Physical Education.

IMPLICATIONS OF THE DEFINITION FOR ADMINISTRATION

The definition of physical education suggests three implications that need elaboration and discussion: (1) Physical education is an indispensable education; (2) physical education is an education *through* the physical rather than *of* the physical; and (3) physical education unifies school life.

PHYSICAL EDUCATION AN INDISPENSABLE EDUCATION

Physical education is indispensable in modern society. In the first place, aside from the influence of heredity and nutritive conditions, physical education is the sole source for the development of vitality. Organic power is dependent in large part upon the activities of youth and neglect of physical education in childhood produces abnormal adult types. Secondly, physical education is the sole organized means for the development of neuromuscular skills so essential for the proper functioning of the individual as a moving, motor mechanism. There are doubtless, also, vast contributions from these skills to the complete orientation of the individual as a thinking, feeling, and acting organism.

Thirdly, physical education is indispensable today as the most important agency to develop attitudes towards play and to combat the sedentary life and its associated evils. No subject in the schools and no agency outside the schools is so well prepared to promote the idea that play is a part of the good life. There is no need to argue the necessity for such teaching. Society today gives numerous signs that play and recreation are essential. To keep alive the play motive requires education of people in skills that will provide satisfactions in the activities of recreation. Dubs do not enjoy activities in which they falter. Some excellence is necessary. Fourthly, physical education is indispensable for setting up standards of sportsmanship. Games offer the laboratory where vital attitudes are formed and the teaching of these, so essential for sport, is equally demanded for the whole of life.

Physical Education an Education through the Physical.—No one can examine earnestly the implication of physical education without facing two questions. These are: Is physical education an education of the physical ? Is physical education an education through the physical ? It is clear that an education of the physical would have some concomitant learnings in addition, and also that an education through the physical would produce some distinct physical gains. Nevertheless, there are in these two questions two points of view, two emphases, two ways of looking at physical education.

Education of the physical is a familiar view. Its supporters are those who regard strong muscles and firm ligaments as the main outcomes. Curiously enough this restricted view is not heeded alone by physical educators but also by those who talk about educational values, objectives, and procedures. In effect, such a view is a physical culture and has the same validity that all narrow disciplines have had in the world. The cult of muscle is merely another view of the narrowness that fostered the cult of mind or the cult of spirit. The desire to focus human effort on well defined objectives may lead to partial views. In educational endeavor, whether secular or religious, the partial view frequently obtains.

The history of man is replete with records of special disciplines. Vestiges of the super sensual discipline that ruled Europe from the fourth to the fourteenth century remain in our Western world today. Speech, customs, beliefs, attitudes—all share in this heritage that found the only true reality in spirit. The cult of mind has never declared its principles so boldly, although its practice in schools and colleges for generations needs no descriptive statement. Probably the cult of muscle has been the most ridiculous of the three. Physical education in its newer role seeks no single justification for its service to man.

Army draft boards may reveal unparallel physical deterioration in our young men, but no modern physical educator, sensitive to the complex and varied needs of man will rush to the conclusion that strength is the sole value or that weight lifting affords an adequate programme. Neither "body" nor "mind" alone supplies an answer to the vexing problems of modern life. Science has taught too well!

Physical education views man as a unity. Not yet knowing the possibilities of the physical, it follows Aristotle in declaring also that we shall never know until the physical finds its true function as instrument for the whole of which it is an indissoluble part. Materialism consists not in frank recognition of the physical, but in assigning it to a spurious supremacy. "There can be no materialism in utmost emphasis upon physical education," writes MacCunn, "so long as 'Body for the sake of soul is, as it was with Plato, the presiding principle of educational action." This recasting of the scene for physical education is no superficial move but a tendency of deeper growth. It holds that we need to aim higher than health, than victorious teams, than strong muscles, than profuse perspiration. It sees physical education primarily as a way of living, and seeks to conduct its activities so as to set a standard that will surpass the average and the commonplace. There is in such a view something of the loftier virtues of courage, endurance, and strength, the natural attributes of play, imagination, joyousness, and pride, and through it all the spirit of splendid living-honest, worthy, competent.

AUTOCRATIC AND DEMOCRATIC ADMINISTRATION

Administrators differ in many respects. Some are efficient in office routine. Others excell in formulating policies, delegating to subordinates the execution of details. Some prefer to direct personally the affairs of the department. Others place the responsibility on staff members. If the administrator in an autocratic disciplinarian he dictates the policies and procedures, asserts that he, as the administrator, knows best what should be one, claims the responsibility of his, and contends that since he is to be held responsible by higher authority he will determine the course of action.

If he is imbued with the principles of democracy, the administrator shares responsibilities and conducts his department with greater freedom. Extreme examples of autocratic and democratic administration may be expressed as follows: Many years ago Jowett's advice to administrators was, "Never retract, never explain. Get it done. Let'em howl." A super-intendent in one of our largest cities has adopted the policy, "Administration should be organized in such a way that all persons affected by the decision shall share the responsibility in making the decision.

Many school superintendents, principals, or directors of health and physical education conduct their professional affairs according to one pattern or the other. Formerly the dictator type of administrator was most frequently encountered. In more recent years the trend has been in the opposite direction. Doubtless most administrators accept a middle-ground somewhere between the two extremes. One administrator may arrive at a decision, call a meeting of those persons affected by the decision, and try to get them to see his point of view.

Through his salesmanship or fear of consequences the subordinates accept the decision without question. At best this closely resembles the autocratic type of administration. Another administrator delays making a decision until the various interest groups have been given the opportunity to voice their opinions. After carefully weighing the evidence on all sides the administrator makes his decision which then becomes the departmental policy. Decisions arrived at by this method more closely approximate the democratic types of administration. The training, personality and ability of the administrator largely determine the course which he will follow. There is no one best type of administration, although contemporary educational thought turns away from authoritarian doctrines and moves towards democratic freedom. The administrator should experiment with many actual problems and choose the kind of administrative practice which seems most satisfactory to him. Unquestionably the plan employed by his superior officer, the superintendent or principal will guide him in making his decisions, since the conduct of affairs in health and physical education should follow the general plan of education established for the school system as a whole or by the principal as the chief executive officer of the building.

6

Physical Education in Schools

INTRODUCTION

Physical Education is the process by which changes in the individual are bought about through movements experiences. Physical Education aims not only at physical development but is also concerned with education of the whole person through physical activities. It would not be wrong if we say that Physical education is the play-way method of education.

Various Definitions of Physical Education are:

- Barrow defined Physical Education as an education of and through human movement where many of educational objectives are achieved by means of big muscle activities involving sports, games, gymnastic, dance and exercise.
- According to Webster's Dictionary Physical education is a part of education which gives instructions in the development and care of the body randing from simple callisthenic exercises to a course of study providing training in hygiene, gymnastics and the performance and management of athletics games.
- Jackson R. Sharman points out that physical education is that part of education which takes place through activities, which involves the motor mechanism of human body which results in an individual's formulating behaviour patterns.
- Charles A. Bucher defines physical education, an integral part of total education process, is a field of endeavour which has as its aim the development of physically, mentally, emotionally and socially fit citizens through the medium of physical activities which have been selected with a view to realizing these outcomes."
- Central Advisory Board of physical Education and Recreation defines Physical education as an education through physical activities for the development of total personality of the child to its fullness and perfection in body, mind and spirit.

AIMS AND OBJECTIVES OF PHYSICAL EDUCATION

AIMS

The ultimate goal is final end aim of physical education, it the way and achieved some certain objectives. The general education like aim of physical education is to develop human personality in its totality well planned activity programmes. In physical education aim at the all round development of the personality of an individual or some development of human personality and it includes physical, mental, social, emotional and moral aspects to make an individual a good citizen. The physical education means at making an individual physical fit, mentally alert, emotionally balanced, socially well adjusted, morally true and spiritually uplifted.

The objectives of Physical Education are steps considered towards the attainment of the aim and the particular and precise means to realise an aim. An aim is achieved it become an objective in the action that goal on continuing. There some objectives of physical education are the objective of physical fitness is essential to leading a happy, vigourous and abundant life. The second is the objective of social efficiency is concerned with one proper adaptation to group living and all these qualities help a person to make him a good citizen. Another objectives of physical education is culture, it aims at developing an understanding and appreciation of one own local environment as well as the environment and a person understand the history, culture, religious practices etc and the aesthetic values associated with these activities. So find the best step the ultimate goal in aims of physical education.

OBJECTIVES

Physical education is an important part of every school curriculum and a class every pupil awaits. Physical education is that segment of the daily timetable that every student eagerly waits to attend, as it is the only official time when the students can be on the grounds, engaged in their favourite sports. One of the main objectives of physical education is to bring in this element of joy to the academic orientation of schools. Physical education aims at dedicating a daily time for some physical activity for the students. The physical training class, as it is also called, involves sports, games, exercise and most importantly, a break from the sedentary learning indoors.

One of the other important objectives of physical education is to instill in the students the values and skills of maintaining a healthy lifestyle. Daily physical activity promotes an awareness of health and well being among students. It boosts them to engage in physical activities on a daily basis. It promotes them to lead a healthy life in adulthood. Physical education classes constitute programmes to promote physical fitness in students, train them in sports, help them understand rules and strategies in playing and teach them to work as a team. A very vital factor in physical education is to develop interpersonal skills in children. Sports aim at making them team players, developing a sportsman spirit in them and enhancing their competitive spirit. Sports that form a part of physical education classes help the students invest time in fruitful and competitive activities. One of the other important objectives of physical education is to inculcate in the minds of the students, the importance of personal hygiene and cleanliness. Physical education classes aim at teaching the students, the habits of personal cleanliness and the importance of the maintenance of personal hygiene in life. Physical education classes also impart sex-education to the students, help them clarify their doubts and find answers to all the questions that occur to their minds.

The sports, which are a part of the physical education class, help in developing motor skills in children. The ability to hold a racket or a bat, the ability to catch a ball and the ability to swing a bat are some examples of the motor abilities that can develop with the help of sports. The physical activity that is involved in physical education helps the students in bringing discipline to body posture and body movements.

Hitting a ball with a bat or a shuttle with a racket as also aiming a ball for a goal or catching it to get the opponent team out, are some of the commonly observed actions in sports and are extremely beneficial in improving hand-eye coordination. The very important objective of physical education is to encourage the upcoming sportsmen and women of the crowd. Physical education gives the budding sports people a platform to exhibit their talents. Those with a flair for sports get an opportunity to display their talent. Their small step on the school playground can eventually turn into a huge leap in the field of sports. Moreover, sports refresh the students' minds. Physical education class becomes enjoyable for the kids while proving helpful for their overall growth and development. Physical education is indeed one of the most fruitful activities of a school schedule.

NEED AND IMPORTANCE OF PHYSICAL EDUCATION

In the Present World of Space age and automation era, all human beings appear to be living a more and more inactive life. They ride instead of walk, sit instead of stand and watches instead of participants. Such type of inactivity or sedentary life is detrimental to mental and physical health. Thus, there is great need for physical education as a part of balanced living. Physical education which is commonly a part of the curriculum at school level includes training in the development and care of the human body and maintaining physical fitness.

Physical education is also about sharpening overall cognitive abilities and motor skills via athletics, exercise and various other physical activities like martial arts and dance. Here are some of the benefits that highlight the importance of physical education.

MAINTAINING SOUND PHYSICAL FITNESS

Physical fitness is one of the most important elements of leading a healthy lifestyle. Physical education promotes the importance of inclusion of a regular fitness activity in the routine.

This helps the students to maintain their fitness, develop their muscular strength, increase their stamina and thus stretch their physical abilities to an optimum level. Physical fitness helps to inculcate the importance of maintaining a healthy body, which in turn keeps them happy and energized. Sound physical fitness promotes, increased absorption of nutrients, better functioning of digestion and all other physiological processes and hence results in all round fitness.

OVERALL CONFIDENCE BOOSTER

Indulging in sports be it team sports or dual and individual sports, leads to a major boost in self-confidence. The ability to go on the field and perform instills a sense of self-confidence, which is very important for the development of a person's character.

Every victory achieved on the field, helps to boost a person's self-confidence. Moreover, the ability to accept defeat on field and yet believe in your own capabilities brings a sense of positive attitude as well. Thus participation in sports, martial arts or even dance and aerobics, is always a positive influence on a student's overall personality and character and works wonders for his/her self-confidence.

AWARENESS ABOUT IMPORTANT HEALTH AND NUTRITION ISSUES

Physical education classes are about participating in the physical fitness and recreation activities, but they are also about gaining knowledge about the overall aspects of physical health. For example in today's world the problems of obesity, or anemia and bulimia are rampant amongst teenagers. Physical education provides an excellent opportunity for teachers to promote the benefits of healthy and nutritious food and cite the ill effects of junk food.

INCULCATING SPORTSMANSHIP AND TEAM SPIRIT

Participation in team sports, or even dual sports helps to imbibe a sense of team spirit amongst the students. While participating in team sports, the children have to function as an entire team, and hence they learn how to organize themselves and function together.

This process of team building hones a person's overall communications skills and the ability to get along with different kind of people. Thus participating in team sports instills a sense of team spirit, which is a great value addition to anyone's personality and helps a lot in all the future endeavors.

DEVELOPMENT OF MOTOR SKILLS

The ability to concentrate, the ability to swing the racket just at the right time are some of the examples of development of motor skills in the physical education classes. Participation in sports and several physical education activities helps to sharpen the reflexes of the students. It also brings order and discipline to the body movements and helps in development of a sound body posture as well. The hand-eye co-ordination improves as well.

IMPORTANCE OF HYGIENE AND SEX EDUCATION

Physical education classes also include sessions about the importance of personal hygiene and importance of cleanliness. Thus the physical education classes help the students to know the important hygiene practices that must be practiced in order to maintain the health and well being throughout the life.

In addition to this, the physical education classes also cover an important aspect that the children have to deal with at the age of puberty. Physical education classes also impart sex-education and hence help the students deal with their queries and doubts about the subject of sexuality.

ENHANCING OVERALL COGNITIVE ABILITIES

Physical education classes help to enhance the overall cognitive abilities of the students, since they get a lot of knowledge about the different kinds of sports and physical activities that they indulge in. For example a person who is participating in a specific type of martial arts class, will also gain knowledge about the origins of the martial art, and the other practices and historical significance associated with it. Thus physical education helps to enrich the knowledge bank of the students.

ENCOURAGING BUDDING SPORTSMEN

Physical education classes are an excellent opportunity for all the budding sportsmen and sportswomen who wish to make their mark in the world of sports. Physical education classes allow the budding sportsmen and sportswomen to explore and experiment with several areas until they find what interests them. After this, physical education classes also allow the students to indulge the sport of their choice and then go ahead to participate in several tournaments and competitions, which help to give the students an exposure to the competitive world of sports.

A STRESS BUSTER AND SOURCE OF ENJOYMENT

In addition to the health benefits and the knowledge benefits that the students get from the physical education classes, one important aspect of it remains to be recreation. Students, who are busy with their other subjects in the curriculum, often get exhausted with the listening, reading and writing pattern of studying and need a recreational activity as a source of recreation. Sports and other physical fitness activities offered in the physical education class are a welcome break for the students.

PROMOTING HEALTHY LIFESTYLE IN ADULTHOOD

Children, who learn the importance of health and hygiene in their early ages, tend to grow up to be responsible and healthy adults who are well aware of the benefits of a healthy lifestyle. Thus the overall physical education programme, that includes different types of physical activities and sports and also provides important information about hygiene and overall health, helps in creating well-informed pupils. A well-balanced and all-round physical education class helps to create responsible adults who know the importance of a healthy lifestyle.

AIM AND APPROACH OF THE CURRICULUM

The aim of physical education is to enable all students to enhance their quality of life through active living. The Physical Education 11 and 12 curriculum builds on and expands the curriculum developed for Kindergarten to Grade 10. Physical Education 11 and 12 provides opportunities for students to experience a variety of recreational pursuits, career interests, and activities that promote lifelong, healthy living. Students focus their learning in areas of personal interest and participate in activities that promote social interaction, community responsibility, and skill development.

In Physical Education 11 and 12, teachers work with students to develop programmes to meet student needs and interests. Programmes are structured so that the duration, intensity, and frequency of activities motivate students to meet their individual goals. Students participate in a balance of activities from the movement categories.

PHYSICAL EDUCATION CURRICULUM

The Physical Education 11 and 12 curriculum focusses on promoting healthy attitudes and regular physical activity as important parts of each student's lifestyle. It emphasizes analysing and improving physical competence, maintaining personal fitness, developing effective leadership and sports-management skills, and planning for careers.

In senior physical education programmes, students:

- Apply the concepts of a balanced, healthy lifestyle to design programmes for themselves and others
- Apply the elements of movement and knowledge of fitness to improve personal functional levels of competence in a variety of activities and environments
- Demonstrate an appreciation of the needs of various groups and adapt activities for them

- Recognize an activity's impact on the environment
- Integrate safety practices and the prevention and management of sports injuries in a variety of physical activities and environments
- Apply knowledge and skills from certification programmes
- Model and apply leadership skills and positive personal qualities in volunteer work and physical activities at school and in the community

CURRENT PHYSICAL EDUCATION CURRICULA

As in the past, the present curriculum focusses on the unique and significant contributions of physical education in the development of every student. The previous curriculum (1987) organized important goal statements under three domains: affective (attitude), cognitive (knowledge), and psychomotor (skills).

The prescribed learning outcomes of the new curriculum are grouped under three curriculum organizers: Active Living, Movement, and Personal and Social Responsibility. In each organizer, the prescribed learning outcomes incorporate learning from the three domains.

In addition, the previous curriculum provided seven movement categories, while the new curriculum has only three.

Nature and Scope of Physical Education, Exercise Science, and Sport:

- What is "contemporary physical education?"
- How do different areas of physical education relate to the field overall?
- What is the importance of creating your personal philosophy of physical education, exercise science, and sport?

Goals for Physical Educators

- Access to physical education and sport for all, regardless of: age, gender, race, ethnicity, sexual orientation, disability status, income, educational level, geographic location and ability.
- Prevent disease and positively contribute to health and well-being of all participants.

Expansion of Physical Education, Exercise Science, and Sport:

- Moved from the traditional school setting to:
- Community
- Home
- Worksite
- Commercial and Medical Settings
- Corporations.

Who says Physical Activity is Good?

- National Reports:
- "Physical Activity and Health: A Report of the Surgeon General"
- "Healthy People 2010"
- "Promoting Better Health for Young People through Physical Activity and Sports".

Definitions: Physical Education

- Physical education....
- An educational process that uses physical activity as a means to help people acquire skills, fitness, knowledge, and attitudes that contribute to their optimal development and well-being.
- Contributes to the development of the whole person.
- Education
- An on-going process that occurs throughout our lifespan.

Definitions: Exercise Science

- Exercise Science...
- The scientific analysis of exercise or physical activity through theories from many different disciplines such as biology, biochemistry, physics, and psychology.

Definitions: Sports

- Organized competitive activities governed by rules that standardize the competition and conditions so individuals can compete fairly.
- Competition against oneself or opponent(s).
- Strategy and skill play a significant role in the determination of the outcome.

Definition: Athletics

- Highly organized, competitive sports
- Skillful participants.

Our Physical Activity Challenge

Improve Participation of Populations with Low Rates of Physical Activity: Current Participation Patterns:

- Women are generally less active than men at all ages.
- African Americans and Hispanics are generally less active than whites.

- People with low incomes are typically not as active as those with high incomes.
- People with less education are generally not as active as those with higher levels of education.
- Adults in the Northeast and South tend to be less active than adults in the North Central and Western States
- People with disabilities are less physically active than people without disabilities.
- Participation in physical activity declines with age. By age 75, one in 3 men and one in two women engage in no physical activity.

U.S. Department of Health and Human Services. Healthy People 2010: Understanding and Improving Health. Washington, DC: U.S. Government Printing Office, November, 2000.

The Field (More than a Playing Surface!)

- Field.... "a combination of a well-established discipline and one or more professions that deliver a social service and are focused on common goals." (Corbin)
- Discipline ..."organized body of knowledge embraced in a formal course of learning." (Henry).

Physical Education, Exercise Science and Sport: The Profession

- Profession...
- An occupation requiring specialized training in an intellectual field of study that is dedicated to the betterment of society through service to others.
- Some examples of professional organizations:

Organizing the Profession

- With developing technologies, knowledge, and methods of enquiry from other disciplines in the 1960s, physical education, exercise science, and sport broadened its horizons to incorporate the fields of psychology and sociology.
- The result:12 subdisciplines.

Sub-disciplines

- Exercise physiology
- Sports medicine
- Sport biomechanics

- Sport philosophy
- Sport history
- Sport psychology
- Motor development
- Motor learning
- Sport sociology
- Sport pedagogy
- Adapted physical activity
- Sport management.

Exercise Physiology

- Impact of exercise and physical activity on the human body.
- Short-and long-term adaptations of the various systems of the body.
- Effects of physical activity and exercise on the health status of different populations.
- ACSM:

Sports Medicine

- Medical relationship between physical activity, sports-related injuries, and the human body.
- Prevention-the design of conditioning programmes, fitting of protective equipment, and counseling regarding proper nutrition.
- Treatment and rehabilitation-the assessment of injuries, administration of first aid, design and implementation of rehabilitation programme and treatment.

Sport Biomechanics

- Applies the methods of physics to the study of human motion and the motion of sport objects.
- Study the effects of force on the body and sport objects.
- Mechanical analysis of activities (production of power, leverage, and stability)
- Analysis of effectiveness and efficiency of movements.

Sport Philosophy

- Study of the nature of reality and values of movement for all participants.
- Debate critical issues, beliefs, and values relative to physical

education and sport (i.e.What is the relationship between the mind and the body?).

- Influences thoughts, actions, and decisions in our professional endeavors and personal lives.

Sport History

- Critical examination of the past with a focus on events, people, and trends that influenced the direction of the field.
- The "who, what, when, where, how, and why of sport" is examined within the social context of the time.
- Looking into the past provides greater understanding of present events and insight with respect to the future.

  NASSH: North American Society for Sport History publishes the Journal of Sport History.

Sport and Exercise Psychology

- Uses principles from psychology to study human behaviour in sport to enhance performance.
- *Sport Areas:* achievement motivation, arousal regulation, goal setting, self-confidence, leadership, and team cohesion
- *Exercise Areas:* exercise addiction, adherence, motivation, and satisfaction.

Sport and Exercise Psychology

- Sport areas:
- Achievement motivation
- Arousal regulation
- goal setting
- Self-confidence
- Leadership
- Team cohesion
- Exercise areas:
- Exercise addiction
- Adherence to exercise
- Motivation
- Satisfaction
- Uses principles from psychology to study human behaviour in sport to enhance performance.

Motor Development

- Interaction of genetic and environmental influences on movement and lifespan motor development.
- Use theories of development to design appropriate movement experiences for people of all ages and abilities.

Motor Learning

- Study of factors that influence an individual's acquisition and performance of skills, such as practice, experience, use of reinforcement, and condition of learning environment.
- Progression through stages of learning from a beginner to a highly skilled performer.

Sport Sociology

- Study of the role of sport in society.
- "What is the influence of society on sport?"
- "What is the influence of sport on society?"

Centre for the Study of Sport in Society at Northeastern University publishes the Journal of Sport and Social Issues.

Sport Pedagogy

- Study of teaching and learning.
- Creation of effective learning environments, instructional strategies, outcome assessment, and relationship of instructional process to learning.
- Development of effective practitioners through the analysis of the behaviours of teachers/coaches and students/athletes.

Adapted Physical Activity

- Providing individual programmes and services that encourage participation to the fullest extent by those with disabilities.

Sport Management

- Encompasses the managerial aspects of sport and sport enterprise.
- Facility and personnel management, budgeting, promotion of events, media relations, and programming.
- The Journal of Sport Management is the official journal of the North American Society for Sport Management (NASSM).

A New Name for the Field

- Physical Education-traditional, but too narrow; does not reflect the expanding nature of the field.

- Kinesiology-study of human movement, but the public is not familiar with the term.
- Exercise and Sport Science-reflects the broad emphasis of the field and easy to understand.
- Physical Education and Sport-traditional, familiar, and includes sport as a vital part.
- No common agreement as to the name of the field, but there is a growing central focus: Physical Activity.

Allied Fields

- Health:
- Health Instruction
- Health Services
- Environmental Health
- Recreation
- Dance

These fields share many purposes with physical education, exercise science, and sport, but the content of the subject matter and methods to reach their goals are different.

Definition of Terms

- *Health:* A state of positive well-being associated with freedom from disease or illness.
- *Wellness:* A state of positive biological and psychological well-being that encompasses a sense of well-being and quality of life.

Definition of Terms

- *Holistic Health:* The physical, mental, emotional, spiritual, social, environmental, and genetic factors' influence on an individual's life. (similar to wellness)
- *Quality of Life:* overall sense of well-being that has a different meaning for each individual.

Definition of Terms

- *Physical Activity:* any bodily movement produced by the contraction of the skeletal muscles that increases energy expenditure above the baseline level.
- *Exercise:* physical activity that is planned, structured, and repetitive with the purpose of developing, improving, or maintaining physical fitness.

Definition of Terms

- Physical Fitness: the ability to perform daily tasks with vigour and without undue fatigue, and with sufficient energy to engage in leisure-time pursuits, to meet unforeseen emergencies, and the vitality to perform at one's fullest capacity.
- Health-related and Performance-related physical fitness: what are the components of each?

Physical Fitness

- Health-related Fitness
- Cardiovascular endurance
- Body composition
- Flexibility
- Muscular endurance
- Muscular strength
- Performance-related Fitness
- Agility
- Speed
- Coordination
- Power
- Reaction time
- Balance.

Philosophy

- "The love of wisdom" (Greek)
- A set of beliefs relating to a particular field.
- A system of values by which one lives and works.
- Helps individuals address the problems that confront them through the use of critical thinking, logical analysis, and reflective appraisal.

Branches of Philosophy

- Metaphysics-the ultimate nature of reality; what is real and exists.
- Epistemology-the nature of knowledge
- Logic-Examines ideas in an orderly manner and systematic way.
- Axiology-the nature of values
- Ethics: issues of right and wrong, responsibility, and standards of conduct.
- Aesthetics: the nature of beauty and art.

General Philosophies

- *Idealism:* The mind interprets events and creates reality; truth and values are absolute and universally shared.
- *Realism:* The physical world is the real world and it is governed by nature; science reveals the truth.
- *Pragmatism:* Reality and truth is determined by an individual's life experiences.
- *Naturalism:* Reality and life are governed by the laws of nature; the individual is more important than the society.
- *Existentialism:* Reality is based on human existence; individual experiences determine what is true.
- *Humanism:* Development of the full potential of each individual. Emphasized meeting the needs individuals' needs.

Philosophical Approaches

- "Education of the Physical"
- Focus on fitness development and acquisition of skills; the development of the body.
- "Education through the Physical"
- Focus on the development of the total person: Social, Emotional, Intellectual, and Physical development.

Sport Philosophy

- Study of the true meanings and actions of sport and how sport contributes to our lives.
- Eclectic philosophy of education (1875-1950)
- Comparative Systems Approach (1950-1965)
- Disciplinary Approach (1965-present)
- Sport philosophy offers us guidance in addressing inequities in physical activity opportunities experienced by underserved populations.

Why Develop Your Own Philosophy?

- Assists in the development and clarification of beliefs and values that guide your behaviours.
- Aids in decision-making.
- Helps determine goals, objectives, and methods of instruction and evaluation used in physical education programmes

EDUCATION IN INDIA: SPORTS AND PHYSICAL FITNESS

If a career in sports and physical fitnsess holds your fancy, there are three main options you can choose from. Pursue the sport or game on a full time basis generally with sponsorship from an employer/promoter Become a trainer/instructor/coach for a game or sporting event. Finally use the experience acquired over years as a sportsperson to work in a related field, such as, sports journalism, sports goods manufacture/marketing or as commentator. To be a sports person one needs to be physically fit, energetic and enthusiastic. If aspiring to become a trainer or manager, a graduate degree in physical education can be pursued after Class XII (any stream with physical education).

Physical Fitness

General Fitness: In a more general meaning, physical fitness is a general state of good somatic health and abilities. A handicapped person may nevertheless be physically fit. Fitness helps them to compensate disability. Physical fitness is usually a result of regular physical activity, *e.g.*, physical exercise, and proper nutrition. Cardio is a type of fitness designed to improve cardiovascular strength.

Task-oriented Fitness

A person may be said to be physically fit to perform a particular task with a reasonable efficiency, for example, fit for military service.

Military-style

In recent years, Military-style fitness training programmes have become increasingly popular among civilians. Courses are available all over the US and Europe. They are usually taught by ex-military personnel. Very often the instructors held highly regarded positions within various military organizations. Often times the instructors were formerly Drill instructors, Special Forces Operatives or held otherwise distinguished positions. These courses always have some common elements. They often focus on military style calisthenics and group runs. The courses are often held very early in the morning and will meet in almost any weather. Students can expect push-ups, sit-ups, pullups, and jumping jacks, as well as more obscure drills such as flutter kicks, sun worshippers and flares. Almost invariably a workout will include short runs while longer runs are more scheduled. Special forces are renowned for their level of fitness and intensity of their workouts.

Personality Traits

- Sports persons are required to be energetic, enthusiastic and physically fit.

- All professionals in this field must be absolutely committed to the profession and the game.
- Coaches and instructors have several years of experience and training.
- Patience, perseverance and a sporting spirit are required to excel.
- In allied areas of work, communication and business skills are gaining importance and value.
- A sportsperson's work needs psychomotor and physical conditioning.

Courses/Training

Courses:

- Class XII-any subject with physical education
- Graduate degree in Physical education; Postgraduate degree in Physical education. Jobs as Physical education trainers/ educators/ therapists/coaches.
- Graduation in Physical Education followed by Post graduation for Trainers and Managers
- Graduation/ Post graduation in Physical Education and B.Phy.Ed for teachers.

Admission Procedure: Sports can be pursued at any age, hence the trajectory gives information on the schemes for promoting talent. Sports talent can be spotted at the school level.

The Sports Authority of India has been constituted at the National level to encourage and develop acumen in sports. SAI has State level branches to organise, manage and conduct a host of schemes intended to promote sports facilities and assistance for the talented. Sports Authority of India (SAI) is responsible for training coaches, R&D in sports, physical education, R&D in physical education, sports promotion, nurturing talent, and training of athletes.

- *Age 9-12 National Sports Talent Scheme:* Talent in swimming, athletics, gymnastics as well as ball and net games which include tennis, hockey, basketball, table tennis, football, volleyball, badminton and wrestling are supported under this scheme. Students in the 9 to 12 age can qualify tests conducted by the Sports Authority. The tests check general and specific physical skills required for each of the disciplines. Selected students undergo sports training along with school education in one of the SAI sponsored schools. The sponsorship includes all expenditures including tuition fee, boarding, lodging, incidental expenditures, sports kits maintenance allowances, medical facilities, travel etc. Coaches provide the necessary training to students selected under this scheme, conduct evaluation tests and maintain performance records.

- *Age 16-20 years Students:* Can benefit from the Hostel scheme in sponsored institutions. Special Area Games Schemes operate for identifying and nurturing talent from all regions in the country.
- *Army:* Regimental training centres have schools where students with sporting talent from neighbouring areas are enrolled. Education, training in sports, and military training completes the curriculum.
- *Scholarships at Colleges/universities:* Students participating in national championships, inter-university tournaments are eligible for the Sports Talent Scholarship awarded by the Government of India, Department of Youth Affairs and Sports. Candidates are selected on the basis of merit, ascertained by a duly constituted Selection Committee.
- *Private Sponsorships:* SAI has six regional sports centres. Coaching facilities in popular sports such as badminton, tennis, hockey and cricket are provided. The facilities provided are of international standards. Special Sports Academies/Federations provide similar facilities. These are often privately sponsored and sportspersons with proven talent are supported by these academies.

DEVELOPMENT OF PHYSICAL EDUCATION IN THE SCHOOLS

Until recently in the history of the United States, physical education has not been recognized as an important part of the educational process. Many factors were responsible for this social flag. The attitude towards play as exemplified by the Puritans who thought of it as being the work of the devil and that as such it should be shunned and the belief among the early schools in America that play was a frill and something which should not be included in a curriculum with the classics and the three R's are two such factors. The belief in scholasticism with its stress on book knowledge, the lack of adequately trained teachers, and the belief that money should be spent on aspects of the school plant other than gymnasiums and swimming pools were also cogent factors in retarding the progress of physical education.

More recently in our history, however, there has been a rapid advancement of physical education as a result such events as the introduction of the Swedish and German systems of gymnastics into the United States, the industrialization of the country, the increased number of children going to school, the recognition of the importance of training the "whole" child, the mushrooming of teacher training institutions, and the growth of athletics in colleges with the secondary schools aping the higher educational institutions. These factors have resulted in an increased number of physical education buildings being added to school plants, legislation being passed providing for physical education in the schools, training of teachers of physical education, and an upgrading of the requirements of such teachers.

Physical education has taken its place alongside the other major subjects in the curricula of schools. No longer is it considered a frill, and no longer is it believed that physical education consists only of exercises done to command.

Instead, it has a major contribution to make in the growth and development of all youth. By reason of this fact, physical education personnel hold positions of high respect and prestige on school faculties and in community life.

CONTRIBUTIONS OF PHYSICAL EDUCATION TO GENERAL EDUCATION

A fuller description of the role of physical education in the educational process is needed at this point. For purposes of organization is seems that such a discussion may be grouped under four headings, which the Educational Policies Commission lists as being objectives towards which education is striving.

These are: (*i*) the objectives of self-realization, which are concerned with developing the individual to his fullest capacity in respect to such things as health, recreation, and philosophy of life; (*ii*) the objectives of human relationship, which refer to relationships among people on the family, group and society levels; (*iii*) the objectives of economic efficiency, which are interested in the individual as a producer, a consumer and an investor; and (*iv*) the objectives of civic responsibility, which stress the individual's relationship to his local, state, national, and international forms of government. Physical education, as a phase of the total educational process, contributes to each of these objectives.

THE OBJECTIVES OF SELF-REALIZATION

The objectives of self-realization are aimed at developing the individual so that he realizes his potentialities and becomes a well-adjusted member of society. This development means much more than the accumulation of knowledge. It means that the individual in the process of constant interaction with his environment has achieved his rightful place, that a proper relationship has been established, and that he recognizes and associates with what is best in his culture. It means that education is interested not only in shaping the individual for his future role, as a member of society but is interested also in his development and growth as he progresses towards adult life. Physical education contributes to the objectives of self-realization by contributing to: (*i*) an enquiring mind, (*ii*) development in reading, writing and speaking, (*iii*) knowledge of health and disease, (*iv*) a desirable attitude towards family and community health, (*v*) skill as a participant and spectator in various sports, (*vi*) resources for utilizing leisure hours in mental pursuits, (*vii*) appreciation of beauty, and (*viii*) ability to purposefully direct one's life. An enquiring mind is essential to the educated person. Only through curiosity is it possible to probe into the make-up of one's environment. The motor mechanism of the child enables him to explore, to cruise and to see his environment. It stimulates his curiosity. He wants to see what is on the other side of the fence, how hot the stove is, what happens when he pulls the light cord, what is in the box with the cover, how people react to certain situations and the like. Motor activity helps develop the enquiring mind and aids in the solving of problems, which at times thwart the individual. As one grows older, physical education activities open up new fields of curiosity.

The student seeks to discover the answers to such questions as why a vigourous workout and a shower are exhilarating and why exercise improves his appetite, circulation, respiration, stamina and endurance; why Jim can lift his own weight in the air and Dick cannot; why Henry can wield a tennis racquet with great skill; and why Sally can swim so gracefully. A new and interesting phase of living is opened to the individual through activity. His enquiring mind is active and he seeks the answers to his health and physical problems.

Physical education, through the various activities that it sponsors, helps an individual to speak, read and write with more effectiveness and clarity. Through the development of a healthy and physical fit body one has better poise to command the attention of one's listeners. Francois Delsarte, a French teacher of voice and dramatics, pointed this out when he developed a special system of physical exercises which were aimed at more effective dramatics and singing. This system spread to America where it was received with a great deal of interest. Many teachers of oratorical public speaking were in accord with his (Delsarte's) methods, combined them with their own ideas, and developed a system of exercises which contributed to health, poise, grace and beauty of face and figure. The ability to speak is recognized as being very worth while when it is realized that approximately 90 per cent of all communication is carried on via this method—through face-to-face conversation, telephone, radio, television, motion pictures and the like. In order to realize one's potentialities and achieve a satisfactory relationship with one's environment, the ability to speak effectively is imperative.

The ability to read efficiently is important to an individual's development. It has been pointed out that there are three types of illiterates. First, there are those who cannot read; second, those who have mastered the mechanics of reading but do not use this acquired art; and, third, those who read material of insignificant value. Physical education contributes to discrimination in reading by pointing out scientific materials, which are available in regard to the maintenance and promotion of one's health and physical fitness. It discounts the literature of health and physical culture "faddists", quacks, quick-cure artists, and medicine men who are exploiting the public. It refers students to sources of information where scientific information may be obtained. It develops in the student a critical attitude towards quick health cures and other misleading advertising that is chronicled daily in newspapers and magazines and broadcast over radio and television. Through this medium of discriminatory reading, physical education contributes to self-realization.

Physical education aids an individual to write effectively. The ability to express one's views in a clear, concise manner is a medium, which contributes immensely to the solving of problems. In the presentation of physical education reports on activities, in health lessons, and in the writing of examinations there should be a constant alertness on the part of the physical education teacher to see that acceptable standards of written work are adhered to. This work should not be the sole prerogative of the English profession. Instead, it is the duty of all educators to utilize every "teachable moment" in the improvement of the writing ability of their students.

KNOWLEDGE OF HEALTH AND DISEASE

The educated person has an understanding of the facts that are pertinent to health and disease. To a great degree, a person's success is dependent upon his health. His state of health and physical fitness will determine to a great extent whether or not he succeeds in realizing his potentialities. An individual cannot expect to be a top executive in the business world if he is sick and stays away from work two or three days a week.

One cannot expect to achieve stardom in professional athletics without a physically strong and healthy body. One cannot aspire to a high-salaried position in radio, engineering, the ministry, education, advertising, law, medicine, or dentistry unless his body can stand the rigours of long hours of study and work. One cannot expect to achieve happiness in living unless he is in good health. A knowledge of health and disease, therefore, is a contributing factor to self-realization so that health obstacles, handicaps and strains may be guarded against. Physical education contributes to this knowledge by instructing the individual as to the importance of nutrition, exercise, rest and sleep; by informing him of the preventive and control measures that exist to guard against disease; by providing opportunities for vigourous out-of-doors activity; by motivating the formation of wholesome health attitudes and habits; by following up the correction of defects; by stressing safety factors for the prevention of accidents; and by establishing various health services. Through the experiences and knowledge provided by a physical education programme, the objectives of self-realization are brought much closer to attainment. Family and Community Health: The educated person protects his own health, his dependent's health, and the health of the individuals within the community where he resides. The educated person has a knowledge of health and disease and applies these facts to himself, to his family, and to his community. He sees that his body is cared for in the manner prescribed by the authorities on health and disease and has periodic health examinations. He obtains adequate amounts of exercise, rest and sleep; eats the right kind of food; engages in activity conducive to mental as well as physical health; and sees that others also have the same opportunities to maintain and improve their health in accordance with his standards. He realizes that health is a product that increases in proportion as it is shared with other individuals and knows that health is everybody's business.

Physical education provides a programme of activity to improve the physical and mental health of the individual, his family, and the entire community. In the schools a planned programme of physical activity is offered as an essential to the optimum body functioning of youth during this developmental period of their lives. It enables them to experience many pleasurable emotions and to develop organic power, which is essential to a healthy, happy and interesting existence. The groundwork for adult years is laid during this formative period. Recreational programmes provide facilities and opportunities for the adult to continue, after leaving school, adapted physical activity so essential to health maintenance. They offer adults the opportunity to lose themselves in wholesome activity and thus be relieved of some of the tension experienced in modern-day living. Such a programme is essential to the health of all.

SKILL AS A PARTICIPANT AND SPECTATOR IN SPORTS

The educated person participates and observes sports and other pastimes. The stress of modern-day living with its quest for material possessions, its machine-type labour, its sedentary pursuits, and its competitive nature has implications for all who would enjoy some of the simple, natural, and wholesome forms of activity. Modern-day man has been bitten by a bug, which has destroyed to some extent his sense of values in regard to entertainment. Many no longer wish to find entertainment through their own resources but, instead, desire to have professionals satisfy these needs. Too frequently they turn to the nightclub, to the horse races, or to some games of chance for amusement.

The educated person selects the manner in which he will spend his leisure time, with discretion and with regard for enriched living. Participating in a game of softball, tennis, or badminton or going for a swim not only provides an interesting and happy experience during leisure hours but at the same time contributes to mental and physical health. The development of physical skills in all persons rather than in just a few select individuals is an objective which is educationally sound and should be encouraged more and more by educators. The so-called recreational sports should receive greater emphasis so that activities may be better adapted to the older segment of the population.

Swimming, golf, tennis, camping and similar activities should occupy a prominent place in all physical education programmes. Physical education not only develops skill in the participant but at the same time develops an interest and knowledge of other activities which at times may be engaged in by individuals from the standpoint of a spectator. Although it seems the benefits from participation would outweigh the benefits of being a spectator in regard to physical activity, nevertheless, many leisure hours may be spent in a wholesome manner observing a ball game or some other sports activity. The wise person, however, discovers the proper balance between the amounts of time he will utilize as a participant and as a spectator.

The balance is destroyed if one fails to realize that being a spectator cannot result in the same values for an individual as being a participant. Physical education can help by supplying a knowledge of various sports so that the role of the spectator may be more meaningful and interesting.

RESOURCES FOR UTILIZING LEISURE HOURS IN MENTAL PURSUITS

The educated person has mental resources for the utilization of leisure hours. Recreation is not confined to sports and exercise. Instead, there is a whole gamut of activities, which are more inactive in their nature but which offer entertainment and relaxation after working hours for a great many people. Such activities as reading, photography, music and painting may be included in this group. Physical education contributes here in providing the material for interesting stories of great athletes, such as Bob Feller, Jackie Robinson, Glenn Cunningham and Ben Hogan.

These individuals, through the stories that have been written about them, allow others to live vicariously their struggles in attaining fame and fortune amidst obstacles that seemed almost insurmountable. Physical education offers photography and painting enthusiasts subjects for their pictures. All have seen works of art that were inspired through some sports event. Physical education also offers many hobbies. A sport such as fishing motivates a hobby such as teeing flies. Many other examples could be listed. Physical education acts as a stimulating influence in playing upon one's mental resources for the utilization of leisure hours. Furthermore, it provides trained personnel who supervise and direct many of these recreational activities.

The educated person has developed an appreciation of the beautiful. From the time of early childhood the foundation of an appreciation of beautiful things can be developed. Architecture, landscapes, paintings, music, furnishings, trees, rivers and animals should ring a note of beauty in the mind of the growing child and in the adult. Physical education has much to offer in the way of beauty. The human body is a thing of beauty if it has been properly developed. The Greeks stressed the "body beautiful" and performed their exercises and athletic events in the nude so as to display the fine contours of their bodies. Nothing is more beautiful than a human body that is perfectly proportioned and developed. Physical activity is one of the keys to a beautiful body. Also, there is a beauty of movement, which is developed through physical activity.

When one picks up an object from the floor, it can be done with a great deal of skill and grace, or it can be done crudely and awkwardly. When a football pass is caught, a basketball goal made, a high jump executed, a two and one-half somersault dive performed, or a difficult dance displayed, there can be included in the performance of these acts rhythm, grace, poise and ease of movement which is beauty in action. Anyone who has seen Wes Santee run, Ben Hogan drive a golf ball, Mickey Mantel field a fly in deep centre, Sammy Lee dive, Tony Trabert hit a tennis ball, Tom Gola hook a shot through the net, or Ted Williams hit a home run knows what beauty of performance means. Such beauty comes only with practice and perfection.

The educated person conscientiously attempts to guide his life in the proper direction. Upon the shoulders of each individual rests the responsibility of determining how he will live, what religion he will choose, the moral code he will accept, the standard of values he will follow, and the code of ethics he will believe in. This is characteristic of the democratic way of life. In a democracy man can in reality "half control his doom". Man must develop his own philosophy of life.

The way he treats his fellow men, the manner in which he assumes responsibility, the objectives he sets to attain on earth, and the type of government he believes in will all be affected by this philosophy. Through the philosophy that he has established man forms his own destiny. Physical education can help in the formulation of an individual's philosophy of life. Through the medium of physical education activities, guidance can be given as to what is right and proper, goals that are worth competing for, intrinsic and extrinsic values, autocratic and democratic procedures, and standards of conduct. The child is a great imitator, and the beliefs, actions, and conduct of the coach and the teacher are many times reflected in the beliefs, actions, and conduct of the student. In education, leadership is the key that unlocks the door to self-realization for many of our youth.

THE IDEAL PHYSICAL EDUCATION PROGRAMME PLACES HUMAN RELATIONS

THE OBJECTIVES OF HUMAN RELATIONSHIPS

Human relationships may be defined as the relationship that exists between individuals. Good human relations may be summed up in the Golden Rule: "Do unto others as you would have others do unto you". Good human relations imply that people live together, work together and play together harmoniously. Each individual appreciates the other person's viewpoint and attempts to understand his actions. Good human relations are found in families where brother and sister, mother and father, father and son, and mother and daughter live cooperatively and happily together. They are found among friends who are willing to help each other in time of need, among classmates who share responsibilities, among neighbours who thrill to the accomplishments of others, and among workers who help solve each other's problems. Poor human relations also exist. These occur when a business competitor seeks an unfair advantage, when a football player drives a cleated shoe into an opponent's face, when a boy shows disrespect for his parents, and when a fellow worker condemns a colleague.

The question of human relations is one of the most pressing problems of this day and age. Good human relations is the key to a happy and successful life and a peaceful world. Therefore, it is important that education play its role to the fullest extent in accomplishing the objectives of human relationships.

Physical education can make a worth-while contribution in this area of human relations. This can be done through the following means: (*i*) placing human relations first; (*ii*) enabling each individual to enjoy a rich, social experience through play; (*iii*) helping individuals play cooperatively with others; (*vi*) teaching courtesy, fair play, and good sportsmanship; and (*v*) contributing to home and family living.

The human being is the most valuable and the most important consideration of anything in this life. Nothing is more important than human life. One human life is worth more than a handful of diamonds or any other abundance of material possessions that could be accumulated. It rates at the top of all the values in the world. Such being the case, then human welfare should receive careful consideration in all walks of life. When a new law is passed by Congress, there should be due consideration for its effect on human welfare; when a machine is invented, we should take into consideration if it will affect human beings beneficially or adversely; and when an accusation is made, the effect on human welfare should be considered. The more human welfare is considered the happier the living for all.

The ideal physical education programme places human welfare first on its list. When an activity is planned, it takes into considered the needs and welfare of the participants; when a rule or regulation is made, the player's welfare is considered; when a student is reprimanded, his welfare and that of others are considered. The desire or convenience of the teacher is not the first consideration. The physical education programme takes into consideration the weak and the less skilled and makes sure adequate arrangements have been made for such individuals. It is a student-centred programme with the attention focused on the individuals for whom the programme exists. Throughout the entire procedure there is prevalent among students, teachers, and administrators the thought that the human aspects are the most important consideration. Through the media of precept and example, consideration of others is the keynote of the programme. When the student plays, he considers the welfare of others; and when the teacher plans, he considers the welfare of all. By placing human relations first, a spirit of good will, fellowship and joyous cooperation exists. Play experiences offer an opportunity for a rich social experience. This experience can help greatly in rounding out a child's personality, in helping him to adapt to the group situation, in developing proper standards of conduct, in creating a feeling of "belonging", and in developing a sound code of ethics.

Children need the social experience that can be gained through association with other children in a play atmosphere. Many live in cities, in slum areas, and in communities where delinquency runs rampant, where their parents do not know the next door neighbour, and where the environment is not conducive to a rich social experience. In such neighbourhoods the school is one place where children have an opportunity to mingle and physical education offers a place where they have opportunity to play together. The potentialities are limitless in planning social experiences through "tag" and "it" games, rhythms, games of low organization, and the more highly organized games. Here the child learns behaviour traits, which are characteristic of a democratic society. Because of his drive for play, he will be more willing to abide by the rules, accept responsibility, contribute to the welfare of the group and respect the rights of others.

The physical education programme should stress cooperation as the basis for achieving the goals an individual or group desires. Each member of the group must work as though he were a part of a machine. The machine must run smoothly, and this is possible only if every part does its share of the work. Pulling together and working together bring results that never are obtained if everyone goes his separate way. Former President Truman, in a speech delivered at Madison, Wisconsin, stressed the effectiveness of cooperation in our day-to day living, citing such examples as farm cooperatives, cooperative stores and the bringing of electricity to rural areas through cooperative means. He then went on to stress that world peace is possible only through cooperation among the nations of the world and that the problems confronting the nations of the world today will be solved only through working together.

A physical education programme that would teach individuals to play cooperatively should stress leadership and followership traits. The success of any venture depends on good leadership and good workers or followers. Everyone cannot be a captain on a basketball, relay, or soccer team. Everyone does not have leadership ability. Those who are good leaders should also be good followers. A leader in one activity might possibly make a better follower in another activity. These are a few of the points that should be brought out. The important thing to stress is that both leaders and followers are needed for the accomplishment of any enterprise. All contribute to the undertaking.

All deserve commendation for work well done. All should reap the rewards. The question might be raised as to the advisability of the practice that is sometimes followed of using the class cut-up, the bully, the "Mickey McGuire", as the captain of the team. This is one procedure that is sometimes utilized for eliminating a discipline problem. Leadership, it seems, should be earned as a result of eliminating a discipline problem. Leadership, it seems, should be earned as a result of contributing to a group, of earning the respect of a group, and of proving oneself a good follower. To place the "Mickey McGuire", in such a coveted position seems to encourage rather than discourage antisocial behaviour.

A physical education programme that would teach individuals to play cooperatively should stress cooperation as the first consideration, rather than competition. Competition is good, but it seems that cooperation is the first concern of education. Students in our schools compete for grades, to make the honour roll, to receive a bid to certain societies, to be a member of the squad, and to be an officer of their class. This may be good if conducted according to proper procedures; but in many of our schools it breeds discontent, cheating, and cliques and results in nervous breakdowns and personality maladjustments. The person who takes home the honours, accumulates the prizes, and grabs the headlines is too often the hero in the eyes of the public, whereas the diligent, hard-working, quiet individual who cooperates to his utmost for the success of a group enterprise receives nothing for his efforts. The success of the democratic way of life depends on cooperation among members of society and not on the exploits of a few who seek honour, prestige and glory. The "all for one and one for all" motto will accomplish much more than the "all for me" motto. In adult life people follow many of the objectives that were formulated in their youth. If competition rather than cooperation receives the main consideration in school, it will aggravate the competitive "survival of the fittest" existence that is so characteristic of modern-day living. Cooperation is the secret of successful living.

The amenities of social behaviour are a part of the repertoire of every educated person. They have developed as part of our culture just as the playing of baseball, eating "hot dogs", and democratic living have. Some individuals in our societies are referred to as "ladies" and "gentlemen", whereas others are called "hussies" and "rowdies". Many times such courtesies as saying "please" or "thank you", tipping one's hat, offering a lady your arm, and acting in a polite, quiet manner have made the difference in these labels attached to certain individuals.

Courtesy and politeness are characteristic of good family training just as fair play and sportsmanship are characteristic of good training in physical education activities. On the one hand, it reflects the character of the parent or guardian and, on the other, the teacher or coach. When a player kicks his opponent in the groin, trips him up, or does not play according to the rules, he reflects the spirit of his leader. Some coaches and teachers will use any means to win a game or achieve a goal. Others feel that winning is not the prime objective. Instead, their main objective is to provide an experience, which will help the members of a group realize values that will help them live an enriched life.

Courtesy, fair play and sportsmanship contribute to good human relations. The player who is a gentleman on the field is usually a gentleman off the field as well. Such an individual makes friends easily, builds good will, and inspires trust among those with whom he comes in contact. Others know that he believes in playing according to the rules, that he will not take unfair advantage, that he assumes responsibility, and that he is considerate of others. These characteristics should be developed in every child who visits a physical education class or tries out for any athletic team.

Physical education has a contribution to make to family and home living. The make-up of a child depends to a great extent on the type of family and home environment he lives in. Many times such an environment determines whether an individual is kind or mean, quiet or boisterous, or polite or rude. In view of the imprint of the home and family upon the child, the school has the educational responsibility to improve and nurture the child, to interpret society to him in its correct light, and to strengthen family ties. Physical education can assume part of this responsibility. The coach and the physical education teacher are many times individuals in whom a child puts his trust and confidence and whom he desires to emulate. The nature of physical education work and its appeal to youth probably are the causal factors of such practice. Consequently, physical education personnel should utilize their advantageous position to become better acquainted with the youth and his home and family life. Many times divorce and separation have affected children's lives. A change from rural to urban life with the difficulties of adjustment might be an experience through which a child is passing. There may be a lack of "belonging" or a protected existence, which causes anxiety and worry. By having knowledge of the whole problem, the teacher or coach will be able to help in the adjustment process and in making for better home and family living. This could be done through proper counselling and guidance, helping youth to experience success in play activities, talks with parents and home visitations.

The increased complications of family living, because of such factors as the prevalence of divorce, the desire for careers on the part of women, the turmoil of urban existence, and juvenile delinquency, place more responsibility upon education to help children make proper life adjustments. Physical educators, because of their programme in which children have a natural desire to engage and because children look to them for guidance and help, can contribute considerably in these adjustments.

PHYSICAL DEVELOPMENT AND CONDITION OF CHILDREN EDUCATION

SCHOOL PHYSICIAN

The second chief function of the school physician is the annual assessment of the physical development and physical condition of school children. Children present number of growth disturbances, developmental abnormalities, and remediable defects that should be detected and corrected. The relationship of physical defects to school attendance has been noted many times in the literature.

Experience shows that school attendance is more irregular among those children suffering from defects. In addition to the routine examination of all pupils, the school physician must examine boys and girls trying out for places on school athletic teams. The physician's decision in these cases should be accepted as final. Children seeking working certificates are required by law to pass a medical examination before the papers are issued. This examination is the duty of the school physician.

The physician should know the hazards of different occupations and be prepared to advise and decide accordingly. A third function of the school medical advisor is to plan a procedure for follow-up and treatment of cases of defect. The purpose of the examination is not the history of defects but the correction of remediable conditions. A policy regarding treatment of pupils should be established and plans evolved for handling indigent cases. As a general rule the school does not give treatments. This policy is perhaps justified since the school is not equipped for therapeutic services rather than because social effort of this kind is undesirable. As a matter of fact this policy is frequently violated. School physicians treat whole classes for ringworm, pediculosis, impetigo, and scabies[1] and are justified in doing so by the extreme contaguousness of these skin infections. Nevertheless, until a policy of socialized medical care is evolved that will win the support of public opinion, it is best for schools to refrain from treatments as routine procedure and to seek the enlargement of clinical services that will care for those children unable to secure private medical attention.

It is obvious that more than notification is required. Hence, there has developed the practice of following up these cases by the school nurse in home visitation. Success with this procedure is variable. Some communities yields as many corrections without home visitation as others do with it. The practice, however, has other justifications. Health and economic conditions are related. The nurse serves as an excellent contact for clinics and hospitals and is quite indispensable for those families that must rely upon charitable agencies. Close cooperation of the school physician's staff with social agencies is vital in this connection.

CORRECTION THROUGH PUBLIC HEALTH AGENCIES

This method, either free or at nominal cost, is an approved health service procedure. Through the school nurse these services are brought to the attention of families unable to pay for the attention of a private physician. The principle of ability to pay is exceedingly difficult to administer and requires the full cooperation of school, health and welfare authorities. In many instances the nurse aids in taking the child to the hospital or clinic, often makes the appointment, and is always ready to bring confidence to the unformed parent in matters of this kind. The hospital with a clinic service or a special clinic or health center comprises the usual type that furnishes free medical care. These may be endowed institutions operating on a budget supplied by private funds or public or semipublic institutions supported in whole or in part by public funds.

This is an admirable form of correction especially for certain types of defects. Its great advantage is the unity possible in the organization. Detection and correction go together. Examples of this type of correction are dental clinics, nutrition classes, special openair classes, and postural classes. The Cleveland Public Schools conduct an excellent Division of Mouth Hygiene in the Department of Physical Welfare. Dental clinics in many cities are conducted by the schools out of funds received from the city. In St. Augustine, Florida, a dental clinic for all children is an endowed institution with some support from the city through the funds of the board of education. Special classes for malnourished, and pretuber-cular children and special instruction for postural cases are common practices in many public school systems. In the former food is given the children as an aid in correction of the defects present. The practice of providing an organization within the school that will meet the needs of children is well established.

SUPERVISION OF THE HEALTH OF TEACHERS AND SCHOOL OFFICIALS

The fourth function of the school physician in the health service is the supervision of the health of teachers and school officials. This function should operate mainly, though not exclusively, in the selection and certification of teachers so that persons of good health will be admitted into the profession. The examination of all school officials should exclude cases of tuberculosis. To this end, the x-ray is increasingly used.

In addition to examining teachers for positions in the schools, the physicians should be available for periodic health examinations of teachers in service. Industry and business organizations find it profitable to conduct such examinations for employees and the time will soon come when such examinations for teachers will be a well-established practice. It is now required in some communities of all persons handling food in the school cafeteria.

Teachers and school officials returning to school after illness should be examined and this is particularly important in communities where the board does not permit sick leave on full or partial salary. In a summary of the studies made on the health of the teacher, the Metropolitan Life Insurance Company reports as follows: Men are absent less frequently and for shorter periods than women. This disparity is greater in the teaching profession than among other groups of employed men and women.

Great inconsistency is shown in the relation of sickness rate of age. In one city the rate increased steadily with age; in another there seemed to be no correlation between age and illness; and in another the rate declined with increase in age. The proportion of teachers absent on account of sickness in a year varies widely. No generalization can be made, except that this proportion compares favourably with absences among industrial and mercantile workers. Long, expensive illnesses are relatively rare among teachers.

A succession of minor ailments in a life comparatively free from serious risks is the way in which one report sums up the teachers' health situation. Colds and influenza are the chief causes of absences in all investigations. Yet, teachers have a lower rate in respiratory disturbances than have other indoor workers. The opportunity for contagion in the classroom makes the incidence of colds more serious among teachers than among workers in shops and offices. Tonsillitis is a common cause of absence among teachers.

Contrary to previous opinion, the rate for tuberculosis among teachers is comparatively low. Nervous disorders are a chief cause of long and expensive cases of absence. These are conspicuously more common among women than among men and absences due to nervous disorder increase with advancing years. Although we do not know the definite effect of the teachers' nervousness upon the health of children, it may be assumed that the effect of some types is serious.

If the teacher is to contribute effectively to the mental health of children she must have mental and emotional control and balance. Relatively good chances for a long life and comparatively low sickness rates are revealed in comparison with workers in other fields. This is offset by the fact that the effects upon pupils of even slight illnesses on the part of teachers is the most serious side of the teachers' health situation. The active causes of health disturbance among teachers that are related to the vocation are many. Teachers as a group reflect the hazards of a sedentary group and, although well educated, exhibit generally habitual violation of many health laws.

A relation may exist between the teacher's health and the temperature of the classroom, and fatigue may be a factor in some nervous disorders. Large classes and the strain of such situations doubtless impair the health of many teachers. Boards of education in some cities offer assistance to teachers in the correction of physical defects. Usually this takes the form of examinations and advice. While assistance of this kind is important, much more could be done by: (1) thorough and more rigid examinations for appointment; (2) improving the living conditions through adequate salaries; (3) establishing rest homes with provision for some remuneration during periods of recuperation and convalescence; (4) offering sickness insurance on a group basis; (5) providing adequate retirement allowances; and (6) furnishing some recreational facilities and encouraging outdoor recreational activities among teachers.

Salary of the School Physician—There are no standards at present. Different communities use various bases in arriving at compensation. Payment by the hour, the visit, or number of pupils is quite unsatisfactory. From the school standpoint an annual salary is the best arrangement. Efforts to secure the fulltime services of a physician and to permit no private practice are highly commendable. Rogers reports an increase in the salaries of full-time physicians in the decade 1930-40. In 1940, 32 cities of 100,000 or more population paid $4000 a year; in 1930 only 6 of this group paid as much.

The School Nurse—The school nurse is such a valuable member of the school staff that even before the health education movement spread widely through the schools, the nurse in many communities had established herself as an indispensable educational worker. The 1945 census of Public Health Nurses reports 4,321 nurses employed by local boards of education; approximately the same number give part-time to school nursing as employees of local boards of health, local voluntary health agencies, and commercial groups. While boards of education have employed more nurses in recent years, both the general education and the public health preparation have fallen below the percentage of 1941. This is probably a temporary wartime situation, and it is hoped that standards will be raised to a level even higher than the pre-war standard.

To perform satisfactorily her duties, the school nurse needs more than the nursing training given in a hospital. The latter is indispensable of course, but not adequate for school work. In addition the school nurse should be graduated from a public health nursing course that is approved by the National Organization of Public Health Nursing. The nurse should receive instruction in the teaching of health.

Duties of the School Nurse—The duties of the school nurse vary in different communities, and depend upon the organization of the work, the service of outside agencies, and the coordinated relationship of the departments of health and boards of education. The duties and functions of the school nurse have been clearly described in *The Nurse in the School,* a report of the Joint Committee on Health Problems in Education with the cooperation of the Education Committee of the School nursing section of the National Organization for Public Health Nursing.

Administrative Considerations in School Nursing—The administrator should select a staff whose qualifications are adequate for the functions to be performed. Some means of certification should be required. At present all states do offer certification for school nurses. There is great variability in this matter; the only uniform requirement in the states is registration. After selection of the nurse personnel, the position of the nurse in the school organization should be made clear. This is particularly important if the nurse is employed by the board of health and gives parttime service in the schools. Regardless of the nurse's affiliations outside the school, nursing service in the schools should be under the direction of board of education officials. This is particularly important with Red Cross nurses, tuberculosis nurses, and nurses from commercial or industrial groups.

The administrator should select a competent supervisor and arrange for all nurses to have staff instruction and professional stimulation and growth through attendance at professional meetings. The National Organization of Public Health Nursing recommends that nurses who are not making definite plans to extend their education through continuous preparation should not be selected for school positions. At five-year intervals this organization publishes "Minimum Qualifications for Those Appointed to Positions in Public Health Nursing." An organization that seeks high competence in its members should have the full cooperation of administrators.

The administrator should develop a policy regarding the nurse as a teacher. In the elementary school the problem rarely arises because of the general agreement that the teaching of health is the duty of the classroom teacher. In the high school the nurse is often called upon to teach units in home nursing, child care, growth and development of infants, care of injuries, prevention and control of communicable diseases, causes of illness, and accident prevention in home, school, and community.

At times responsibilities in teaching are placed upon the nurse for which she is not prepared. It is the function of the administrator to determine whether or not the nurse is prepared for teaching, has time to do so, and has the necessary equipment. In preparation the nurse should possess qualifications that are comparable to those held by other teachers in the school. She should be judged as are teachers by the standards of good teaching.

The time factor is difficult. When she is teaching she cannot carry on the individual conferences with pupils that are such a substantial part of her contribution. Often she is not trained for teaching and hence her efforts in this direction may be mush less productive than her services in the work for which she is prepared.

Equipment is essential or much of the technical instruction that the nurse might give. In most of the units listed above which the nurse may be prepared to teach, technical equipment is necessary. Home nursing and child care are really laboratory courses. The nurse in the high school has a range of duties somewhat more extensive than a staff nurse assigned to an examination and follow-up schedule. Generally, they fall into six fields of service.

She will:

1. Be in charge of the dispensary of infirmary, and hence will be responsible for the management of emergencies. This may involve only first-aid care or reference to home or hospital.
2. Aid in the examinations, arrange schedules, notify parents, and generally organize these services. She will actually conduct some part of the examination herself, under the direction of the physician.
3. Advice the principal regarding school hygiene, the hygiene, of instruction; advise the teachers with reference to health problems of certain students. In some schools she is selected as the health counselor, a position involving the centering of the supervision of all health activities in one person.
4. Advise the principal, when the facts warrant her comment, regarding the effect upon pupil health of school dances, examinations, pupil load, the school lunch, and other general matters.
5. Establish effective measures for the control of communicable diseases.
6. Help according to her ability in providing instruction in health but will be responsible for instruction in infant care, first aid, and care of the sick.

Salaries of School Nurses—The salary of school nurses varies according to geographical location, duties, training and experience. The usual salary ranges from $900 per year to $3500, with perhaps a fair average approximating $1800 to $2000. Supervising nurses should receive a salary comparable to other supervisors in the school system, based upon equivalent training and experience. The school nurse may be employed for the school term or calendar year, preferably the latter. The number of pupils to each school nurse varies greatly. Rogers in the 1940 survey reports means of 2,600 for cities of 100,000 or more population and means of 2,800 for cities from 30,000 to 99,999 population. This is a reduction of from three to seven hundred pupils per nurse from the means of 1930.

Transportation of the School Nurse—There is no standard procedure with respect to transportation in urban centers. In rural areas, the automobile is used nearly everywhere. Most cities do not furnish automobiles although it is common practice to allow a monthly sum for maintenance. The nurse should plan her schedule carefully by informing herself about the area to be covered in her district and the best route to follow to expedite her work.

The Uniform and Bag of the School Nurse—Obviously the nurse should wear a distinctive uniform while in school service. The traditional white uniform and hospital cap are not to be used; they suggest illness and a hospital. A white smock or a gray uniform is to be preferred. Whatever the decision may be regarding form or colour, the nurse should be consistent in the use of the type chosen. For home visiting, a smock, which can be carried in the nurse's bag, is practicable.

THE PSYCHOLOGIST AND PSYCHIATRIC SERVICE

The school psychologist is ordinarily not considered a member of the staff of the health service and yet his duties and services are often of great import to those responsible for protecting and promoting the health of children. Psychologic records should be available for this purpose. Psychiatric service in the schools is a recent development in school administration. Its purpose is often restricted to the problems of the special case in which maladjustment has occurred.

The mental hygiene programme should be regarded as more comprehensive than mere control of problem children. The school psychiatrist requires special training. The medical degree alone is not a sufficient indication of ability to diagnose disturbance and to guide youth in the perplexing problems of adjustment. This service will doubtless increase markedly in the future because of growing recognition of its usefulness in harmonizing individual adjustment problems, and because the number of children requiring psychiatric guidance will increase. The growth in mental and nervous disturbances in the adult population reflects a social condition that will eventually involve more children.

RELATIONSHIP OF SCHOOL ADMINISTRATORS TO THE HEALTH SERVICE

It is well eatablished in practice that superintendents, supervising principals, and principals are the chief administrative officers of the schools. They correspond to the line officers of an army and have similar executive functions. Staff officers comprise those who are in charge of special services—in the army, officers of the medical corps, nurses, engineers, supply and transport officials. In the schools, the staff officers are the physicians, nurses, supervisors, janitors, and others. The work of the staff is expert in the several fields, but the specialized character of expert service demands integration and coordination. This is one vital function of the school administrator. It is not his responsibility to determine the value of technical matters, but as an executive of the line to secure integration of the various lines of effort to the end that the various units of school activity shall contribute to a common educational purpose.

Those principle is well established in the school with respect to various divisions. It should be thoroughly applied in the conduct of health services. Staff officers, such as school physicians, aim therefore to give expert medical and educational aid to the solution of health problems; line officers, such as superintendents or principals, aim to coordinate the efforts of various staffs, to utilize the findings of the experts, so that the basic purposes for which schools are conducted shall be realized. To perform his functions a superintendent or principal requires competent staff officers. And likewise, the progress of the health work, for example, depends upon the executive activity of the officers of the line.

The Health room in Schools—It is desirable to place the health suite of officers, examining room, and rest rooms in proximity to the physical education unit. It is not absolutely essential but the rapid growth of the coordinated programme does bring these departments into closer relationship. If the health unit is close to the gymnasium, it will be easier to take pupils in gymnasium costume directly from physical education classes for their examinations.

In the modern school building, a room for the nurse where the health services can be cared for adequately is considered as essential as classrooms, laboratories, or gymnasiums. It should be large enough to accommodate the physician in making his examinations and at least 22 feet in length or width to provide space for tests of visual acuity. For the latter function, good lighting, preferably on the north side, is required and unless natural lighting is adequate, it should be artificially illuminated. A telephone connection is indispensable. Standard equipment of desk, filing cabinet, and chairs will be provided. In addition to these general items certain special equipment is needed.

These are:

- Snellen eye charts for testing vision or materials for the Massachusetts Vision Test. For children who do not know their letters, the Snellen E chart is desirable.
- Yarns of different colours for testing colour perception and Ishihara type colour charts.
- An audiometer for testing hearing is preferable to the use of a watch on the whispered voice. The latter two vary with the make and volume respectively.
- Scales of approved design and equipped with stadiometer for measuring the height are indispensable. The scales should be placed so that it is unnecessary to move them after they are adjusted properly. In this way the chances of faulty action are minimized.
- A full length mirror for postural corrections should be attached to the wall, although movable mirrors may be used.
- At least one cot is needed. This should be of rattan construction to serve the purposes of an examination table. If the latter is available, the cot may be of the canvas type.
- A gas or electric heater for sterilizing.

- Running hot and cold water.
- A supply cabinet of sanitary type should contain the following: scissors, forceps and tweezers; sterile gauze and sterile absorbent cotton; adhesive plaster in several sizes; gauze roller bandages of one and two inch widths; triangular bandages and splints; wooden tongue blades, wooden applicators and toothpicks; three glasscovered jars (one for tongue depressor, one for sterile gauze, and one for sterile cotton); two clinical thermometers; several glass medicine droppers; tincture of green soap, and a saturated solution of boric acid; tincture of iodine or mercuro-chrome in glassstoppered bottles; unguentine, or vaseline for burns; culture tubes and sterile swabs; lysol and 60 per cent alcohol solutions; and white enamel basins.

The Rest Room—The rest room is to be regarded as a part of the health service equipment and placed in the same suite of rooms assigned to this function in the school. Surroundings should be quiet. A north room with little light but with good ventilation is desirable. Cots equipped with blankets and mattresses, several chairs, and a table with mirror constitute the movable equipment.

7

Adolescence Education

Adolescence education is an educational response to the needs, concerns and realities of adolescents in India.

ADOLESCENCE EDUCATION: A COMEBACK TO ADOLESCENT REALITIES

It is universally accepted that the health needs, and particularly the reproductive and sexual health (ARSH) needs of adolescents, continue to be ignored and neglected. As they stand at the threshold of adulthood, they need authentic knowledge that helps them understand the process of growing up with particular reference to their reproductive and sexual health needs. By developing a critical understanding, they have to be well equipped to cope with the problems which they confront. They need guidance and independence simultaneously, education as well as opportunities to explore life for themselves in order to attain the level of maturity required to make responsible and informed decisions.

OBJECTIVES, THEMES AND SCOPE OF ADOLESCENCE EDUCATION

The thought of 'adolescence education' was preferred to terms like sex education, sexuality education, family life education, reproductive health education, puberty education, life skills education and AIDS education at the National Seminar on Adolescence Education, organised by NCERT in 1993. The National Seminar endorsed the use of the concept of adolescence education and recommended the introduction of "suitable components of adolescence education in the curricula at all stages of schooling" (NCERT, 1994). As a follow up to its recommendations, a General Framework of Adolescence Education was finalised through nationwide consultations focusing on the following three requirements:

- Incorporating all the critical concerns of adolescent reproductive and sexual health (ARSH) in the specific context of Indian socio-cultural ethos;

- Preparing the scheme of contents suitable to provide adequate coverage to ARSH concerns in consonance with the nature and scope of existing school syllabi of different stages; and
- Identifying curriculum transaction strategies focused on promoting experiential learning suited to the specific needs of this new curricular area.

Psychotherapy of school curriculum showed that some concerns were already incorporated in it. It was, therefore, thought logical for the adolescence education framework to focus on those concerns were not incorporated in the school curriculum. Content analysis of the existing curricula indicated that the three closely interrelated areas – process of growing up during adolescence, prevention of HIV/AIDS and prevention of substance (drug) abuse were not adequately covered in the school curriculum.

Although the school syllabi and textbooks contain contents on the biological aspects of the reproduction system; education in these content areas cannot be complete by providing biological information only. There is a need to focus on physiological, emotional and socio-cultural dimensions of adolescent reproductive and sexual health (ARSH) in a holistic manner. Adolescence education was thus conceptualized as an educational intervention, focusing on critical elements that would enable young people to deal effectively with the issues related to:

- Growing up healthy, including issues related to reproductive and sexual health
- Prevention of HIV/AIDS
- Prevention of substance (drug) abuse

After serious consideration, a consensus has been reached in favour of the introduction of adolescence education in schools with a view to providing authentic knowledge to students regarding the process of growing up, HIV/AIDS and substance (drug) abuse, influencing their attitudes, and developing in them the needed life skills to respond to real-life situations effectively.

The 1993–96 version of the framework was missing out the element of life skills. In operationalizing the framework, it was realised that adolescence education should lay emphasis on life skills development, so as to empower adolescents to meet the challenges and optimize opportunities that may come their way. The present revised framework not only lays specific emphasis on life skills development but also conceptualises it based on pedagogical principles.

Positive Resource of Adolescent Realities

Adolescents are a positive resource for the country. They have unlimited energy, vitality and idealism, as well as a strong urge to experiment and create a better world. Adolescence is a transition period between childhood and adulthood, usually characterized by youthful exuberance as its most endearing hallmark. During adolescence the physical, intellectual, and emotional characteristics and patterns of childhood are gradually replaced by adult ones, and girls and boys progressively evolve into a state of relative socio-economic independence (UNICEF, 1999).

The definition given by WHO defines adolescence both in terms of age (10-19 years) and in terms of a phase of life marked by special attributes. These attributes include rapid physical, psychological, cognitive and behavioural changes and developments, including, urge to experiment, attainment of sexual maturity, development of adult identity, and transition from socio-economic dependence to relative independence.

The special attributes that mark adolescence include:

- Rapid physical growth and development
- Physical, social and psychological maturity, not necessarily at the same time
- Sexual maturity and onset of sexual activity
- Urge to experiment/ try out new things
- Development of adult mental processes and adult identity
- Transition from total socio-economic dependence to relative independence

Profile of Indian Adolescents

The 2001 census tells us that 20 percent of the billion-strong population of the country would qualify as adolescents (age-group 10-19 years), *i.e.* every fifth person in this country is an adolescent. India is proud to be home to 327 million young people in the age group of 10-24 (WHO, 2007), and is also responsible for developing this vast human resource in the best possible ways. A significant aspect of adolescence is related to psychological development. It is a critical period for the development of self-identity. The process of acquiring a sense of self is linked to physiological changes, and also learning to negotiate the social and psychological demands of being young adults.

Adolescents are affected by socio-economic disparities prevailing in the country. The National Family Health Survey 3 (NFHS 3) indicates high percentage of anaemia (56% of females and 25% of males in the 15-24 age group were anaemic), which affects their physical growth, cognitive development, performance in school and at work as well as reproduction. A national-level study, 'Youth in India: Situation and Needs 2006--07' conducted by the Population Council, New Delhi and International Institute for Population Sciences, Mumbai, indicates that although most youth preferred to marry after age 18; as many as 19% of young women aged 20-24 were married before age 15, and 49% before age 18. Domestic violence is widely prevalent within marriage, with almost a quarter young (married) women reporting that they had been victims of one or other form of physical violence at some point of time within their marriage. As high as 47% of women and 16% men reported they have never received any information on sexual matters from anybody. A large proportion of young people (78% young women and 83% young men) were in favour of imparting sex education or family life education to youth. The most commonly cited preferred sources for information were parents, teacher, health care providers and other professionals and friends.

The youth study showed that only 28% of young women and 54% of young men had comprehensive knowledge about HIV/AIDS. It is noteworthy that over 35% of all reported AIDS cases in India occur among young people in the age group of 15-24 years and more than 50% of the new HIV infections occur also among young people (NACO, 2005). Substance abuse among young people is also a matter of concern. The projected number of drug abusers in India is about 3 million, and most are in the age group 16-35 (UNODC, 2003). Nearly 11% were introduced to cannabis before the age of 15 years and about 26% between the age of 16-20 years (UNODC & Ministry of Social Justice and Empowerment, 2004). Findings from NFHS-3 show that in the age group of 15-24, 40% young men and 5% young women had ever used tobacco, while 20% of young men and 1% of young women had ever consumed alcohol. Gender roles are very distinctly defined, and adolescent girls continue to face gender based discrimination.

This is evident in the declining sex ratio, incidence of domestic violence, underage pregnancy, unsafe motherhood and increasing incidence of sexual abuse, abduction and trafficking (UNFPA, 2006). The findings from NFHS3 do not indicate progressive gender role attitudes; 53% women and 56% men in the 1524 age group felt that wife beating is justified under specific circumstances. Sexual Harassment in public spaces, institutions of education, in and around home and at the workplace is a well established fact. Child abuse, bullying and ragging are also common and more so among boys.

NUTRITION EDUCATION FOR ADOLESCENT GIRLS

The Indian population has crossed the one billion mark in the new millennium, out of which about 21 per cent are adolescents (10-19 yrs). The key role of this group in enabling India to achieve its goal of population stabilization is increasingly being recognized now.

The United Nations Inter Agency Working group on population and Development has infact chosen 'adolescents' as its priority theme for the year 1999-2000. An overview of the studies available confirms the need for a special focus on the improvement in health and nutritional status of adolescents. Since majority of adolescent girls especially representing lower segments of our society are malnourished coupled with co-existence of social maladies like son preference, incidence of early marriage and high rates of maternal mortality, a strong focus on improvement in nutritional and health status of adolescents girls is warranted. Therefore a study was undertaken to assess the nutritional status of the adolescent girls and devise, carry out & measure the impact of edud~li6nal intervention on the nutrition knowledge of adolescent girls in the selected one hundred slums of twin cities under IPP-VIII, Hyderabad. The study was conducted in three stages. In the first stage, baseline data on 2500 adolescent girls (10-19 yrs) were collected using a specially designed comprehensive pretested interview schedule.

In the second stage an intensive nutrition education intervention was carried out covering all the adolescent girls living in slums for a period of 6 months mainly through IPC techniques. In the third stage, a repeat survey was conducted to find out the impact of nutrition education intervention in terms of improvement in knowledge scores. Though an effort was made to contact the same adolescent girls (follow up), only 2,326 could be covered during endline survey. The balance of 174 adolescent girls living in the same slums though covered as substitutes/replacement to make up the envisaged 2,500 sample, they were excluded for the purpose of analysis.

The mean age of the adolescent girls was 14.3 years and majority of the girls were unmarried.) The educational levels of the adolescent girls revealed that 13.2 percent of them were illiterates, around 38% of them had primary education and 44% of them had high school (7 -10 years) education. Distribution of the respondents according to religion showed that the majority of them were Hindus (69.5%) and one third of them were Muslims. Among Hindus, greater proportions were either from backward castes (32.8%) or scheduled castes (28.3%). Regarding the type of family, 82.8% of respondents belonged to nuclear family.

Majority of respondents had 6-7 members in their family comprising on an average 3 males and 4 females. Regarding the educational background of the parents, almost half of the respondents had illiterate fathers and around two third of them had illiterate mothers. The mean height of subjects is 147.1 cms and their mean weight is 38.7 kg. The heights and weights of the adolescent girls were far below the NCHS standards and the deficit increased with age. Further, the maximum increase in the height and weight was observed between 10 and 14 years of age and later it was stabilised. The malnutrition among the adolescent girls was found to be quite rampant. Only 21.9% were categorised as normal. Among those who were malnourished, 7.2% were severely malnourished, 27. 9% moderately malnourished and 43% were mildly malnourished.

The weight for height classification indicated that half of the subjects were normal. A sizeable number of them were seen to compromise on growth (1 7.8%) and a good number of them (31.8%) were also observed to be lighter as they were found to be either mildly or moderately malnourished as per the weight-for-height NCHS Standards. The prevalence of chronic energy deficiency

(BMI < 18.5) was found to be ranged between 98.7 & 51.2 percent among adolescent of 10-16 years age. However as the age increases the prevalence of chronic energy deficiency decreases and it reached to 3.7.4 percent at the age 19 years. The analysis of diet survey revealed that except the daily consumption of cereals the intakes of all other food items were found to be far below the suggested daily requirement. Regarding the nutrient intake, baring the intake of Vitamin C (51 mg), Folic Acid (137ug) and to some extent fat (20 gms), (recommended dietary allowances for adolescents as suggested by ICMR, in respect of major nutrients like proteins, energy, calcium, iron Vitamin A etc., were not met. Iron deficiency anaemia was found to be the most common nutritional problem encountered by respondents.

The data revealed that about 88% of subjects were found to be suffering from mild (49.0%), moderate (31.1 per cent) and severe (7.9%) anaemia. Only 12.0% of respondents were found to be having normal haemoglobin levels of > = 12 g/dl. The mean age at menarche observed in the study population was 12.4 years. The widely reported premenstrual symptom was headache (11.7%), white discharge (9.9%), pimples (9.5%) and a few girls reported other problems like fatigue, irritability, depression etc. Apart from pre-menstrual symptoms the girls reported menstrual problems also. The most commonly reported menstrual problem was dysmenorrhoea (pain in abdomen) (42.6%), the other problems were backache (26.5%), tiredness (23.8%) and irritability (15.3%).

Among the adolescent girls the knowledge regarding sexuality and related areas were found to be low. Majority of the girls did not know what safe sex means. The knowledge regarding STDs were found to be relatively better. The data revealed that 69.4 percent of the girls had awareness regarding STDs and 70.2 percent of the girls had awareness regarding abortion. Information about knowledge of family planning is also an important component as far as adolescent girls are concerned. Almost half of the adolescent girls were aware about the female temporary methods. Regarding the knowledge of terminal methods of family planning, all of them knew about the tubectomy and only 15.8% of them knew about vasectomy.

Out of the 40 married girls 33 girls were pregnant. Out of the total pregnant girls 48.5 percent have registered their pregnancy and all those who registered have used government services. All of them have received TT immunization and IFA tablets. The preferred place of delivery among them was government hospital (48.5%) and private hospital: was next in order of preference (42.4%). Community based IEC intervention activities were conducted for a period of six months in all the intervention areas mainly through IPC techniques. Besides regular media like Television, Radio, Newspaper and Magazines, the other IEC tools used in educational activities included Cooking Demonstrations, Posters, Informative Booklet, Innovative Games and Nutrition Melas. To inculcate the habit of taking more iron and calcium based preparations and energy and protein rich recipes in their daily meals, cooking demonstrations were held in all the intervention areas. They were held in collaboration with Food and Nutrition Extension Board, Govt. of India. Adolescent girls were taught how to prepare simple iron and calcium rich recipes. They were also exposed to nutrient values of some commonly consumed food articles, choosing the energy and protein rich food articles, right cooking methods and some tips to preserve nutrients while cooking. To infuse or build self-confidence and self-esteem among adolescent girls, some innovative games were developed. About twenty adolescent girls in each slum were exposed to participatory learning activities in the form of games. These innovative games are intended to build self confidence, knowledge and skills and to empower girls to begin to shape their own life.

The approach used in these games is called 'experimental learning'. It helps girls to participate in learning and learn from their own experiences, with facilitator-trainer as a guide. The games include 'My Daily Routine And My Meal', 'I Would Like To Introduce Myself', 'Role Model or Woman We Admire', ' My Grand Mother, Mother And Myself' and 'Good Health Practices During Menstruation'.

All the games are based on the experimental learning model. Situations and problems are presented, discussed and analyzed. Problem- solving is emphasized. All the participants learnt things through a process of experience sharing activities, reflections and discussion. A facilitator's guide was prepared to aid the field investigators to conduct the games in the community for adolescent girls.

These games are intended to motivate young girls to change undesirable behaviours and adopt new behaviours, promote participation in the learning process. It is hoped that the experience gained by the participants would be applied in similar situations being encountered by them in future. The informative booklet on' Adolescent Health and Nutrition' prepared in local language telugu are being distributed to all willing and telugu speaking adolescent girls is a ready reckoner to assess the nutritional status and nutrient requirements on their own.

The booklet also contains information on growth and development during adolescence, recommended dietary allowances, balanced diet, menstruation and some commonly asked questions/queries by adolescent girls and their clarifications. Four multicoloured posters on education, nutrition, health & hygiene and age at marriage evoked positive response among subjects.

All the respondents were given information pertaining to their heights and weights, anaemia status etc. Both moderately and severely anaemic girls were given folifer tablets through UHPs to correct anaemia. In collaboration with three NGOs *viz.*, Pratyamnaya, Sivaranjani Educational Society and CHAIN operating in the study area, seven 'Nutrition Melas' were conducted. More than 2000 adolescent girls including other than sample population participated in these one day melas.

Besides cooking demonstrations, experts have taken sessions on following areas:

1 .Adolescent growth & development,
2. Nutritional requirements & balanced diet,
3. Menstrual hygiene & Health care and
4. Women empowerment.

Poster exhibition on nutrition was also held. Services of Gynaecologist, Paediatrician, Public Health Specialist, Nutrition and Communication experts were utilized. Counselling sessions were held and many doubts with regard to nutrition, healthy cooking practices and menstruation were clarified by concerned specialists. Adolescent girls themselves presented some cultural items like songs, street play etc. All the willing adolescent girls were given TT injections by the concerned UHP staff.

Aspects like adolescent growth and development, nutritional requirements, balanced diet, desirable food habits, right cooking methods, problems during menarche, age at marriage, care during pregnancy and lactation were dealt with in detail during IEC intervention. In addition, areas like building positive personality traits, countering the normal social depiction of adolescent girls in the society, inculcating health and hygiene habits were also included in IEC campaign. Though baseline data were available, based on the suggestions given by the participating NGOs and link volunteers, sensitive aspects like sexuality, family planning methods were excluded in the IEC campaign. The following results throw a light on the impact of IEC intervention on selected aspects.

Channels/sources/methods utilized during the IEC intervention like multi-coloured posters and innovative games reached about 45% of the study population. More than 30% of the subjects were exposed to cooking demonstrations. Nearly one-quarter of the respondents received and read the pictorial booklet on adolescent nutrition. One-fifth of the sample subjects attended 'Nutrition Melas' being organized as a part of the IEC campaign. Almost all the respondents received information pertaining to their heights and weights and anaemia status.

During the pre and post education intervention period, only one third of the respondents received nutrition related information through Television, 2% of the subjects through radio and about 4% of subjects through newspaper and magazines indicating limited reach of mass media channels in the study population. The knowledge about physical changes during adolescence has improved from 7.3 percent to cent percent. In the same way 56.4 percent of the girls after intervention stressed the need of early education on menstruation as against 43.8 percent in the baseline. About 70% of the subjects specifically mention that they received information on growth and development for the first time during IEC intervention. Regarding the menstrual hygiene, almost three fourth of the girls had knowledge of right method of using the sanitary pads. That means they were cleaning and drying pads properly or they were using commercially bought pads as absorbents. After the intervention more than 85 percent of the girls reported right method of using the pads as against 75% in the pre intervention period. Further, after the educational intervention it was also observed that they were changing their pads more often than they did it previously. AII the subjects were asked to recall the foods rich in nutrients like iron, calcium, protein and energy. The result, clearly indicate that 776% could correctly identify the foods rich in iron 55.2% could recall calcium rich foods and 62% could list the energy and protein rich recipes/food articles.

The consumption of various food items based on the previous day's diet was also analyzed. It was found that more than 90 percent of the girls had consumed cereals and fats/oils on the previous day. More than 60 percent of the girls had consumed vegetables (73.6%) and pulses (63.5%). Only less than 30% of the girls had consumed milk, meat or fruits. The usage of all other food items like, millets, oil seeds, rice flakes, condiments, jaggery, sprouted and fermented foods was found to be very low (less than 10%). Further, 37.9 percent of the girls were using iodized salt for cooking in their families. The consumption of various food items also has changed after the intervention. The striking difference can be seen in the consumption of millets like ragi which is especially rich in iron and calcium.

Only 3.5 percent of the girls had consumed millets in the baseline and the figure had gone up to 97.9 percent after IEC intervention. Further, an improvement was also observed in the consumption of iodized salt. The majority of the families were (52.9%) cleaning rice in water thrice or more than that before cooking. Majority of them (83.4%) were also discarding canjee and excess water after cooking. They were also seen to sieve the flour before use (93.2%). A small proportion of the families was even discarding excess water after cooking dal/vegetables (7.7%).

The awareness regarding the nutrient loss due to discarding water was also not very high. Only 48.2% of the girls knew that there will be a loss of nutrients if they remove water. Almost all of them followed the practice of covering the vessels while cooking and 70.2% stated that they wash the vegetables before cutting. The results of post intervention suggests an improvement in the practice of right cooking methods like discarding caknjee has come down to 28.9%. The legal minimum age at marriage is not widely known in the study population. Overall only 60.6 percent of the girls reported correctly the minimum legal age at marriage for both boys and girls.

The results of the post intervention survey indicated an increase in the awareness of legal age at marriage. After the intervention, the figure increased to 83.6 percent. Data related to pregnancy, ante natal care, delivery, immunization and breast feeding were also collected from the sample population. Out of the total, 58.2 percent of the girls stated that they know what pregnancy is, and this percentage rose to 60.7% after educational intervention. Majority (68.9%) of the girls did not know when a woman should register the name for ante natal checkups. During pre educational intervention only 13.3% reported that soon after the cessation of the menstrual cycle the woman should register for antenatal checkups and this percentage rose to 24.8% after intervention. Marginal increase in the knowledge was observed with regard to the need for pregnant women to take TT immunization (36.8% - 45.8%), take adequate rest (85.4% -89.6%), avoid heavy work (11.6% -24.4%), need to protect themselves from anaemia (43.3% -51.0%) and take good food (38.9% -47.9%). Most of the girls could not identify the categories of women who fall under high risk.

Only a small proportion of the girls during pre intervention identified short stature (4.3%), young and old age pregnancy (5.1% and 3% respectively), high parity pregnancy (3.5%) etc as high risk cases. However, after intervention around 32% of adolescent girls could correctly identify all the high risk pregnant cases.

Knowledge regarding the vaccine preventable diseases, the most well known disease was Polio (72.2%) This percentage rose to 90% after educational intervention. Majority of the girls did not have a role model (806%). A comparison of data on the pre and past intervention period also did not indicate any major change regarding their role models. The pattern regarding their role model almost remained the same (77.6%) except that a few more could spell out who their role model is. Most of the girls graded themselves, a, cheerful (90 I per cent), cooperative (808%), truthful (75.9%), tidy (71.4%). However, only a very few rated themselves as courageous (27.9%) or possess self confidence (34.4). After the IEC intervention though the trend remained the same, there was slight increase in each of these categories. The mean per cent score has also increared from 66.5 to 73.9

On the whole it was felt that the adolescent girls were in agreement with the accepted social norm, For example most of the girls agreed that they are generally quiet (87.6%) emotional (80.5%) dependent (76.5%) subservient (76.7%) etc However, only some of the girls stated that they are incapable (27.2%) or unimportant (39.4%). After the intervention, the mean percent score of girls holding negative concept, regarding their social depiction came down slightly (65.3% to 58.7%). Overall the adolescent girls were found to follow good health and hygiene habits. In most of the categories the per cent distribution is above 80. A comparative analysis of pre and post intervention figures indicate that, as per the expectation, the health and hygiene habits improved (90.7%) in follow up cases.

Nearly sixty per cent of the subjects mentioned that they had attended more than one programme being organised under IEC intervention those who were exposed to IEC intervention, nearly 82% of the subject appreciated the information given under IEC intervention and 18.3% were undecided about the quality of information given to them.

LIFE SKILLS AS AN INTEGRAL PART OF ADOLESCENCE EDUCATION

In view of the above, the revised framework of Adolescence Education incorporates life skills as one of the competencies, perhaps the most critical competency developed and inculcated through education. It is generally believed that a person who is educated is equipped with all the needed abilities including life skills. But in reality this does not happen. Knowing what needs to be done or knowing what needs to be changed does not mean that the learners automatically know how to bring about behaviour changes. It is the Life skills that, if properly developed, provide the know-how and the tools to actualize behaviour change.

Life Skills in this context need to be defined as psycho-social abilities that enable individuals to translate knowledge, attitude and values regarding all the concerned issues into action. These may not be confined to only those related to health, mental health, sexual development, HIV and AIDS and Drug abuse. Life skills development empowers learners to observe the process involving "what to do, why to do, how to do and when to do". It encompasses the ability to build sound, harmonious relationships with self, others and the environment, the ability to act responsibly and safely, the ability to survive under a variety of conditions, and the ability to solve problems.

Life Skills are different from other Skills

- Other skills like mechanical skills, livelihood skills, vocational skills or language skills are technical, life skills are psycho-social (personal, social, interpersonal, cognitive, affective and universal) directed towards personal actions or actions towards others;
- Life skills are interpersonal skills empowering individuals to interact with the self as well as others and develop healthy lifestyle and responsive and responsible behaviour.; and
- Other skills are product of continued practice, while life skills are developed through interactive experiential learning.

Life Skills Development: Approach Framework

It is important to note that life skills development does not mean development of skills afresh by a set of educational interventions at a particular point of time. Life skills development is an integral part of the all-encompassing process of socialisation that continues throughout human life. School education is an integral part of this process. In fact, individuals apply the acquired life skills in different contexts differently. An individual may have acquired a life skill and she/he may also be equipped with the ability to apply that skill in a context that is fundamentally different from adolescent reproductive and sexual health.

For example, an adolescent may be applying thinking skill or communication skill very effectively while interacting with her/his teacher or even peer group during a discussion on say, globalization or environmental pollution, but she/he may not have the ability to apply those skills on an issue related to sex and sexuality or negative peer pressure. Life skills development, therefore, may be more aptly defined as a process of acquiring the ability to apply concerned skills in the specific context and not the development of that skill afresh.

Since life skills are generic by nature, an educational intervention aimed at the development of ability to apply them may be effective only when it is focused on the specific context. The intervention may have to be designed and operationalized differently for different contexts, more particularly for a culturally sensitive context like adolescent reproductive and sexual health concerns. It needs interventions to focus on acquisition of authentic knowledge, development of positive attitude, and empowerment for avoidance of risky behaviour.

The design of educational intervention has to take note of the content area and also specific life skills. Since most of the contents of adolescence education are very sensitive, interventions need to be well conceived for doing justice to the content. Contextually relevant and age appropriate contents should be focused on. It is important to exactly identify which life skills are to be focused and also the reasons for doing so. In order to organize educational interventions for life skills development effectively, it is important to identify curricular as well as co-curricular activities that have the potential for developing skill application ability. Certain specific activity will be more appropriate than others in respect of a particular life skill. For example, role play can be very appropriate in respect of negotiation skills or interpersonal skills or skills related to empathy.

One activity can be organized to attain different objectives. It is the process of organizing that activity that makes a fundamental difference by providing exact direction for attaining the desired objective. Group discussion may be able to attain knowledge, understanding and even attitude related objectives, but if it is to attain skill development related objectives, it has to be planned and conducted according to a particular process that sustains its focus throughout on skill development. Since life skills development primarily depends through the mode of experiential learning mode, the process of involving learners in the activity is very important.

ARGUMENTS FOR AND AGAINST ADOLESCENT EDUCATION

Arguments Against Earlier there were many who did not think it proper to introduce elements relating to sexual development in the school curriculum. Even now such a mindset influences the thinking of some adults.

They quite often put forth the following arguments:

- Sex and sexuality are intimately private matters which are not to be discussed in public, and that too with young children. In India individuals have been receiving information about these matters indirectly through different sources available in their respective socio-cultural settings. Therefore, there is no need to introduce such an educational programme in Indian schools.
- If schools start providing knowledge about sexual development, young children will be encouraged to experiment with the newly acquired knowledge. This will promote promiscuity and sexual permissiveness, spoiling the youth and also the school and social environment.
- • The regular discussion of sex and sexuality, which is a treasured sublime instinct of human beings, will reduce it to a mundane routine affair. The young students will be desensitised and will not be able to appreciate its sublime value in their future lives.
- Arguments for All these arguments were considered during the process of consensus building for introducing adolescence education in schools:
- It is a myth to regard the socio-cultural traditions of India as a safeguard against irresponsible sexual behaviour of individuals. There is definitely a need to make interventions to enable individuals, including young people to practice responsible behaviour and protect themselves from risky situations.
- A number of studies show that adolescents would like to get accurate information about the changes in their bodies including sexual development. However, discussion on issues related to sexuality is a taboo and there are no reliable sources of information to educate adolescents on these issues. This situation creates anxiety and confusion and generates myths and misconceptions among adolescents about various dimensions of their growing up.
- Since the average age at marriage is increasing, young people have a longer interval between their sexual maturity and marriage. In such a context, it is necessary for school curriculum to equip adolescents with authentic information on sexuality, HIV-AIDS and sexually transmitted infections (STIs). This will enable adolescents to manage their sexual development responsibly and develop a healthy attitude towards sex and sexuality.
- Sexual abuse and exploitation of young girls and boys, and even minors, is a problem in our society. These situations demand urgent educational intervention, so that young people are made aware of the need to respect the inviolability of every person, and to

safeguard themselves against abuse and exploitation.

- The impact of certain traditional values that used to influence sex-related behaviour of individuals has been waning. There is a need to reinforce those social and cultural values that may provide sustenance to responsible sexual behaviour.
- Children and adolescents are exposed to sex-related ideas and thoughts, and that too at times in a crude manner, through sources like cinema, film magazines and other periodicals, video parlours, commercial advertisements and certain television programmes. It is necessary to empower adolescents through education, so that they may appreciate and analyse such exposures in a proper perspective.
- The AIDS pandemic has added urgency to introduce adolescence education in schools. Preventive education is necessary to promote behaviour changes which can prevent the spread of HIV infection.
- Studies indicate an increasing incidence of smoking and use of tobacco, alcohol and other harmful substances by young persons. Frequently adolescents tend to see the use of these drugs as part of being grown up. It is, therefore, urgently needed to educate them on the effects of substance (drug) abuse.
- Studies indicate that education about reproductive and sexual health does not encourage students to experiment with their newly acquired knowledge. Rather, it encourages them to have positive attitude towards sex and inculcates in them responsible behaviour.
- The apprehension of teachers that teaching the elements of adolescence education will tarnish their "image" and promote indiscipline among students has been negated by experiences. Wherever teachers are responsive to the needs of adolescent students and help them cope with their problems, the teacher-pupil relation has become better and the school environment has improved.
- Although students always felt the need to get education in sex related matters, parents and teachers had serious apprehensions till very recently. But now a number of needs assessment studies conducted in different States have found that parents and teachers overwhelmingly favour the introduction of adolescence education in schools. The need to emphasise the development of life skills is being recognised on a greater scale.

CONDITION OF ADOLESCENTS INDIA AMONG THE WORST

Almost 47 per cent of girls in the age group of 11 to 19 years are underweight in India, which is the highest in the world, a UNICEF report on the 'State of the World's Children' released here today said. Also a total of 56 per cent of girls and 30 per cent of boys in the age group are anaemic which places the country along with the least developed African nations. The report says that around 25 per cent (243 million) of Indians belong to the age-group of 11-19 years.

Almost 40 per cent of the section is out of school and 43 per cent get married before the age of 18, out of whom 13 per cent become teenage mothers. School attendance in the 11-13 years age group is 86 per cent and 14-17 years is 64 per cent. On the positive front, the report shows that the number of girls who got married before the age of 18 years has decreased from 54 per cent in 1992-93 to 43 per cent in 2007-08. But the figure is the eight highest in the world and Pakistan fares much better with just 25 per cent of girls getting married before the age of 18 years.

Some 6,000 adolescent mothers die every year and there is a 50 per cent higher risk of infant deaths among mothers who are aged below 20 years. Adolescents with correct knowledge of HIV/AIDS is 35 per cent in boys and 28 per cent in girls.

The report further said that about one-third of adolescents report physical abuse and about one-third of adolescents report sexual abuse. "Certainly, now 74 per cent of adolescents are in school. Most of them are getting primary education. But there is a high-drop out rate afterwards, both in male and females. It is still an area of concern," Karin Hulshof, country representative for UNICEF said.

On child marriage, she said, there is a gradual decline in the marriage before 18 years but still the ratio is "far from satisfactory". The lack of knowledge regarding HIV/AIDS, health, abuse and unemployment are other areas where a lot of work needs to be done. Hulshof said "health and reproductive services and knowledge" must be provided to every person in the age group.

EDUCATIONAL ASPIRATIONS OF INDIAN ADOLESCENTS

Educational Aspirations refer to the early impressions of one's own academic abilities and the highest level of education an individual expects to attain has also been linked to academic achievement. Today's modern society expects everyone to be a high achiever. The key criteria to judge one's true potentialities and capabilities are perhaps scholastic/academic achievement. Academic achievement has become an index of a child's future and is the resultant of various factors like personal, social, economic and other environmental factors. For students from disadvantaged backgrounds, expectations may start out high, but may eventually be lowered as they observe the successes and failures of those around them, thus leading to social reproduction (Hanson, 1994). Children thus do not form aspirations by rational analyses, but by looking at those around them and at their own chances of mobility in a subjective manner.

Social psychological theory posits that educational aspirations strongly influence scholastic out comes and there have been many studies that cite educational aspirations are being one of the most important determinants of eventual educational attainment (Wilson and Wilson, 1992). However, several studies have showed that educational aspirations do not translate into comparable attainment among students from different racial, ethnic and gender lines (Gottfredson, 1981; Duran and Weffer, 1992; Kao, 1995; Ponec 1997; Kao and Tienda, 1998; and Trusty, 2000). Kao and Tienda (1998) and Trusty (2000) suggested that students from lower socioeconomic classes may express high educational aspirations because that reflects the dominant ideology.

They may not take suitable steps towards achieving these aspirations because the culture around them may not be able to provide them with concrete models and support. Geckova *et al.* (2010) observed that both school and the family have the potential to stimulate educational aspirations across all educational tracks. The attitude towards school and social support from the father are the most consistent predictors of educational aspirations across all three types of education.

In general, adolescent educational aspirations are found to be strongly related to their perceptions off parental support, parent's aspirations and their own early attitudes to school experience. Parental education and resources at home have an influence on aspirations, and influence adolescents educational and occupational aspirations, whether the youth come from urban, suburban, or rural areas. Wilson and Wilson (1992), Smith (1991) and Taylor (2002) stressed the importance of the home environment on adolescent educational aspirations. Buchmann and Dalton (2002) found significant influence of home environment on the educational aspirations of the adolescents in twelve countries. They found that in both developed and developing countries with relatively uniform secondary school systems, significant other such as parents and peers can play a role, whereas in countries with secondary school systems exhibiting greater diversity, such effects are lost.

Adolescents educational aspirations could, to some degree, be predicted by parental expectations and were significantly related to contributing home environment and family systems (Marjoribanks, 2003; Kirk *et al.*, 2010; Ibtesam, 2010 and Nicholas at al. 2010). Hence, it is the home which sets the pattern for the child's attitude towards people, society, aids intellectual growth in the child and supports his aspirations and achievements. Educational aspirations were found to be enhanced by bringing change in environmental and personal factors (Garg *et al.*, 2002; Grieve, 2009; Salami, 2009; and Nicholas *et al.*, 2010).

Also, students belonging to the majority/ethnic groups were found to possess higher level of aspiration, whereas the rural students or the students belonging to the poor families have lower aspirations. (Mau and Bikos, 2000; Bajema *et al.*, 2002; Khattab, 2003; Zhou, 2005; Geckova *et al.* 2010; and Strawinski, 2011). However, single parent adolescents were found to be having lower levels of aspiration (Roberts and Moss, 2007; and Park, 2008) and support of the family was found to be the significant predictor of educational aspirations among adolescents (Plunkett, 2003; Lakshmanan, 2004; Li *et al.*, 2006; and Williamson, 2007).

Adolescents' perceptions of home environment were found to show varied and conflicting results (Svedin *et al.*, 2002; Leigh and Gill, 2004 and Kaur and Jaswal, 2005). Barry *et al.* (2011) indicated that as students engage in increased alcohol use and/or truancy, educational aspirations decrease. Thus, students who indicated a desire to attend a 4-year college/university were less likely to engage in high-risk drinking behaviour and/or truancy. On the basis of the above studies conducted in the recent past, it may be summed up that adolescent development and educational aspirations in relation to home environment has remained an area of interest among researchers in education, and like the previous studies, there is a need to look into the effect of gender and home environment on educational aspirations among adolescents.

- *Objectives*:
  - To study gender differences in educational aspirations among adolescents.
  - To study educational aspirations among adolescents in relation to home environment.
- *Hypotheses*:
- There will be no significant gender differences in educational aspirations among adolescents.
- There will be a significant relationship of educational aspirations and home environment among adolescents.
- *Delimitations of the Study*:
- The present study was delimited to adolescents studying in government and private secondary schools of Patiala district only.
- The sample was delimited to 200 adolescents students studying in +1 class only.

METHOD OF ADOLESCENTS STUDYING

The population of the present study were the adolescents studying in +1 class in the schools located in Patiala city of Punjab. The total sample comprised of 200 students of +1 class taken randomly from the various government and private school of the Patiala city, giving due representation to gender and type of school. Research Tools Used: In order to collect the data for the present investigation, following tools were selected and employed by the investigator:

- Educational Aspiration Scale by Sharma and Gupta (1996) was used for measuring aspiration of pupils. It contains 45 items designed in paired comparison form. It is a self-explanatory scale and takes about 25 minutes to administer the whole scale. The total score ranges from 0 to 45.
- Home Environment Inventory by Mishra (1989) was used to measure the psycho-social climate of home as perceived by children. It provides a measure of the quality and quantity of the cognitive, emotional and social support that has been available to the child within the home. HEI contains 100 items related to ten dimensions of home environment.
- *Procedure*: The data was collected by the investigator herself after getting due permission from the school principals. The students were made aware about the purpose of the study and assured that the information will be kept strictly confidential and used only for research purposes. After data collection, the scoring was done as per the instructions given in the respective manual.

The Gender Differences in Educational Aspirations

The use of t-test was made to study the gender differences in educational aspirations among adolescents and correlation was used to study the relationship of educational aspirations with ten home environment components. Gender Differences in Educational Aspirations among Adolescents. The means and SDs along with the t-value for educational aspirations among male and female adolescents.

The mean educational aspirations score of female adolescents came out to be 27.78 with SD. of 5.22 as compared to male adolescents mean score of 28.31 with S.D. of 6.06. The t-value testing the significance of mean differences in educational aspirations among male and female adolescents came out to be 3.07 which is significant at 0.01 level. This means that there are significant gender differences in educational aspirations among adolescents. Further, Male adolescents possess significantly higher educational aspirations than their female counterparts.

Educational Aspirations in Relation to Home Environment

The coefficient of correlation of educational aspirations and ten dimensions of home environment namely control, protectiveness, punishment, conformity, social isolation, reward, deprivation of privileges, nurturance, rejection and permissiveness among adolescents. The coefficient of correlation of educational aspirations and home environment dimensions of reward (0. 17), nurturance (0.14) and permissiveness (–0.17) are significant at 0.05 level. Further, the table II shows that the coefficient of correlation of home environment dimensions namely deprivation of privileges (0.25) and rejection (–0.23) is negative and significant at 0.01 level.

It is interesting to note here that educational aspirations among adolescents are negatively and significantly correlated with the negative dimensions of home environment *viz.* deprivation of privileges, rejection and permissiveness. However, the educational aspirations among adolescents are significantly and positively correlated with positive home environment dimensions of reward and nurturance. From the above discussion, it may be concluded that home environment of adolescents in terms of its positive and negative reward mechanisms, has a very important role to play in determining the educational aspirations of adolescents.

The results are suggestive of the fact that male adolescent posses greater educational aspirations than their female counterparts. This may be attributed to the differential treatment which is given to the boys and girls in Indian society. Hence, the preferential treatment and the exposure given to the male children as compared to the female counterparts may be responsible for these results. Male children receive more independence and encouragement than females because of cultural roles assigned to both the sexes in adult life (Verma and Ghadially, 1985).

Hence, the educational needs and aspirations of the female adolescents should be identified and nurtured. The results of the present study may be seen in the context of some related research evidences. Grieve (2009) revealed high level of educational aspirations among urban African-American male adolescents. Non-significant gender differences in aspirations were found by a group of researchers (Strand and Winston, 2008; Talawar and Kumar, 2010). However, female adolescents' were found to possess higher educational aspirations (Odell, 1989; Mau and Bikos, 2000; and Singh, 2011) found that girls have higher educational aspirations than the boys. Though these findings support different hypotheses regarding gender differences, yet the studies encourage the fact that gender differences had played considerable roles in formulating the educational aspirations of the adolescents.

Home environment was also found that to be correlated with the educational aspirations of the adolescents. These results are in line with the findings of Garg et. al (2002) who found that the personal factors like home environment had a strong a direct influence on educational aspirations. Marjoribanks (2003) emphasized about family background differences among adolescents achievement, aspirations and their educational attainment. Though Leigh and Gill (2004) found substantial expansion in the educational aspirations of the adolescents student's, but their families environment and background had played no role that. Li *et al.* (2006) emphasized on creating conducive home environment conditions for student's high educational achievements and aspirations.

Further, the results of the study as reported by Roberts and Moss (2007) showed that there was a negative correlation between family environment and educational aspirations. On the contrary, Singh (2011) revealed that home environment and educational aspirations have no significant relationship with each other in a sample of school students. The results of the present study has important implications for educationists, counselors and parents. The female students should be provided counseling sessions in order to maintain a higher level of educational aspirations. Parents, teachers and counselors need to be aware of the importance of students having high and stable educational aspirations and performing academically well from as early as elementary and middle school. Counselling sessions should be provided to address school and family issues for students with low aspirations Counselors can help students understand their options, identify their goals and then get into suitable educational programmes (academic, vocational etc.) to enable them to actualize their goals.

The results of the study further emphasize upon the significant role played by home in shaping students' aspirations, no matter what the income level or background of the family is. Hence, parents need to be made aware of the various positive and negative reward mechanisms that can be helpful in enhancing educational aspirations of their wards. Parents from lower socio-economic backgrounds and who have had no college educations should be educated about the college search and choice process and financial aid at an early stage may help them to not only have higher aspirations for their children, but also help them play a more active role later on when their children are in the college search stage. It becomes foremost duty of parents to make every effort to create a conducive and healthy atmosphere in the home so as to sustain high educational aspirations in children. In nutshell, it may be said that an understanding of the dynamics of educational aspirations development among adolescents would enable educators, parents and counselors to adopt measure tailored to meet the specific needs of adolescents, thus helping enhance their career opportunities and options. It is very much desired in youth and especially in adolescents to have high educational aspirations and ambitions for social and scholastic achievement.

ADOLESCENCE EDUCATION PROGRAMME

Adolescents are most productive members of the society, due to their immense capacities. But it is sad to know that most of them are unable to utilize their potential due to lack of awareness and proper guidance. They are engaged in antisocial activities. They use Tobacco, alcohol and abuse drugs.

They indulge in sex also. Such activities result in to their "High-Risk-Behaviour", All this makes them arrogant and irresponsible. Then they create health problems for themselves and social problems for the society. Global experience has shown that educational interventions if focused on life skills development will be very effective. It will help in empowering adolescents. Then they will be able to manage their reproductive and sexual health issues and other concerns.

BACKGROUND

The Government of India has taken a decision to upscale the National School AIDS Education Programme (SAEP) and implement the Adolescence Education Programme (AEP) in all secondary and higher secondary schools. The Central Board of Secondary Education is implementing the AEP in all private schools affiliated to it.

Adolescence Education is an intervention to impart accurate and adequate knowledge about the process of growing up with a focus on reproductive and sexual health in its biological, psychological and socio-cultural dimensions, emotional health and coping with life skills. Global and Indian experiences have shown that educational interventions focused on life skills development have proven very effective in empowering adolescents to manage their ARSH issues and concerns, including avoidance of risky behaviours.

ADOLESCENCE EDUCATION PROGRAMME

The A.E.P is an intervention to impart accurate and adequate knowledge about the process of growing up with a focus on reproductive and sexual health in its Biological, Psychological and Socio-cultural dimensions. There are 13 components of the programme. The programme has a planed schedule with procedural details to educate the adolescence.

Brief Objectives

- To learn, develop and enhance life skills
- To enable the adolescents to understand developing gender sensitivity.
- To deal with gender stereotypes and prejudices
- To modify Adolescent's Behaviour for their betterment.
- To enable the adolescents to understand reproductive and sexual issues and other concerns
- To enable the adolescents to know the basic facts about,
  - Substance abuse and
  - H.I.V/Aids.

Objectives of Adolescence Education

- To ensure the integration of AE elements into the school curriculum and in teacher education courses.
- To organize activities for life skills development.
- To help students acquire authentic knowledge about Adolescent Reproductive and Sexual Health (ARSH) including HIV/AIDS and substance abuse, especially drugs.
- To inculcate in students essential life skills to develop healthy attitudes and responsible behaviour towards ARSH issues, including HIV/AIDS and substance abuse.

Training Programmes

Under AEP, the CBSE is conducting empowerment programmes for different stakeholders:

- Advocacy for Principals
- Nodal Teachers training
- Master Training for creating a pool of CBSE Resource Persons

At least two nodal teachers per school will undergo training to conduct the following school level activities:

- Advocacy activities at the school and community level.
- Using the Question Box and responding to questions raised by students.
- Conducting classroom sessions by organizing interactive student activities.
- Strengthening linkages with adolescent / youth-friendly health services.
- Peer educators will also be trained to reach the out-of-school adolescents who have either dropped out or were never enrolled.

Materials of Training Programmes

The materials for the training programmes consists of the following documents which will soon be available in each school:

- Teachers' Workbook – for Student Activities
- Reference Material-For Resource Persons, Nodal Teachers and Peer Educators
- Facilitators' Handbook for training of Resource Persons and Nodal Teachers
- Adolescence Education Programme – Flip Chart

The training programmes at three levels – Advocacy, Nodal Teacher Training and Master Training are on the web site along with dates and venues.

You may register by filling in the Pre-Registration Proforma which is available online.

AN EDUCATION PROGRAMME EMPOWERS ADOLESCENT GIRLS

Traditionally, women in such areas marry young and often give birth to children when they are not physically or emotionally ready, at great danger to their own lives. But in at least one district, things are changing. Anusaya, 14, lives in the village of Antapur in the district of Chandrapur, Maharashtra, central India. She is extremely shy but smiles easily. Until very recently, Anusaya spent her days at home cooking and cleaning, or in the fields, picking cotton under the hot sun to contribute to her family's meagre income. Today she plans to go back to school. It's a complete turnaround from a few months ago when her parents started to plan her marriage. At that point, Anusaya had already been out of school for two years.

RETURN TO SCHOOL

Rukma, 24, is a 'prerika', or volunteer facilitator, at the local Deepshikha adolescent girls' group. The Deepshikha programme works to educate and empower girls and ensure their increased participation in decision making that affects them.

Empowering Girls

Every child's right to free expression is a guiding principle of the Convention on the Rights of the Child. Now the adolescent girls in Chandrapur are becoming active members of their community and are themselves challenging discriminatory beliefs and practices. Deepshikha was launched by UNICEF in 2008 in partnership with the Government of Maharashtra and local non-governmental organizations. There are now more than 2,200 Deepshikha groups in four districts in Maharashtra, reaching more than 50,000 adolescent girls. "You can make a difference – a big difference – by capitalising on the energies of young women," says Chief of Field Office for UNICEF Maharashtra Tejinder Sandhu. "Investing in an adolescent girl also means that you are investing not just in an individual, but a whole family." Potential 'prerikas' are identified by local village committees and nominated for a 20-day training programme in which they learn about child rights, health, and sex and gender issues. After the first 10-day training session, each one goes back to her village, identifies local adolescent girls and invites them to form a Deepshikha group.

Widening Horizons

After completing 40 sessions, each Deepshikha is encouraged to form a Self-

Help Group (SHG). The SHG opens up a savings bank account, with small amounts of money added each time, to form a small-scale fund. This is accessible to group members who need to cover essential education and health care costs. The money can also be put towards small business ventures.

Reshma, 17, is bright-eyed and confident. A few years ago, her parents decided she shouldn't attend school. Reshma began learning how to sew clothes but soon realised that she wanted to do more. When the Deepshikha group started in her village, she decided she wanted to be part of it.

"The first time I attended a Deepshikha session, my parents were confused and they told me I wasn't allowed to go," says Reshma. "But then, when I told them what I'd learned about how to improve our community, they agreed to let me." Reshma's has since grown in self-confidence and her father is now a fervent support of the Deepshikha programme. "Look at the change in all these girls. They're working so hard now and they have so much courage," he says. Of his daughter, he adds: "If she can now learn something, she can become someone."

LIFE SKILLS AND A.E.P

Life Skills meaning the abilities for adaptive and positive behaviour that enable individual to deal effectively with demands and challenges every day life (WHO). It further encompasses thinking skill, social skill and negotiation skill. It also helps the young people to develop and grow into well behaved adults. Point of A.E.P, is life skills let us know about these skills And education, based on life skills. Meaning of Life Skills "The abilities for adaptive and positive behaviour that enable individual to deal effectively with demands and challenges everyday life "(WHO).

Life skills can be divided in to three categories:

1. Thinking skills,
2. Social skills and
3. Emotional skills

These skills if developed and enhanced properly help the learners to develop and grow into well balanced personality. Point of A.E.P, is life skills let us know about these skills And education, based on life skills.

Core life skills as per W.H.O. There are ten core life skills:

1. Self-awareness.
2. Interpersonal relations.
3. Communication.
4. Critical thinking.
5. Problem solving.
6. Creative thinking.
7. Dealing with emotions.

8. Coping with stress.
9. Decision making
10. Empathy.

We may add common sense and time management also. Life skills based education is a value addition programme for the youth to understand self and be able to assess their skills abilities and areas of developments. It allows the youth to get along with other people, able to adjust with their environment and making responsible decisions.

Which also incorporate to build up their values and to communicate effectively? It should include health issues concerning reproduction, family welfare and population education. Life skill education is all the more important because it is the learning of life skills. It enables learners to learn and practice skills in relation to major health and social needs *i.e.* H.I.V./ AIDS conflicts and violence. Life skills based education goes a long way to change the behaviour of the adolescents to make hem responsible and empowered.

LIFE SKILLS EDUCATION FOR OUT OF SCHOOL ADOLESCENTS

Shakti is a Hindi word, the literary meaning of which in English is Power. The objective of this project is to empower the dropouts and the under-achiever adolescents psychologically to make them well equipped in Life Skills. It is to motivate and reorient them towards a meaningful vocation, develop their personality and provide them guidance and support in vocational careers according to their aptitude and abilities.

The methodology of training is participatory and primarily activity-based. It was started in collaboration with the Municipal Corporation of Delhi (MCD). Our UVCT Chapters in Mumbai and Vishakhapatnam have also launched Shakti programmes in their centers. Started in October 1995, the project is a flag-ship programme of the Trust that provides personality development and life skills (thinking, social and negotiating skills) to school dropouts and under achievers, enabling them to become socially responsible and economically productive citizens. During the last 16 years, the Trust succeeded in assisting more than 14,000 school dropouts till May 2011, of which about 70 percent have succeeded in finding meaningful avenues, including reviving their educational pursuits. It came as a welcome note to the UVCT to get accreditation from the National Open School for its courses in Beauty Culture, Stitching & Embroidery, Typing and Word processing.

The programme has proved such a great success that the UN Inter Agencies Working Group have accepted it as a basis for their programme on *"Life Skills for Health Promotion of out-of-school adolescents"* (July 2003), and two batches were also supported by the Group on Population and Development

(UN IAWG-P&D), under the auspices of the UNFPA (United Nations Population Fund). The programme, which was initially of 30 days duration, was increased to 45 days by giving additional inputs about adolescent sexuality, reproductive child health and other population related issues. The World Health Organization (WHO) provided technical support to improve upon the then existing curriculum and train the resource-persons, with emphasis on life skills education.

By the end of May 2011, a total of 100 batches (an average of 40 participants in one Batch) in Delhi alone were trained. The Govt. of India has also adopted one of the plan scheme The programme is on-going the UN IAWG-P&D, and has since put out the programme for international circulation, under the title Life Skills for Health Promotion of Out-of- School Adolescents and graciously acknowledged the Shakti Programme of the UVCT as the basis for the same. The programme has also become a Plan Scheme of the Min. of Youth and Sports, and an international platform for mainstreaming school drop-outs and under-achievers.

The Various Skills & Values imparted during the training are:

1. *Self-Awareness*: It is one of the foremost aspects of life skills. What the disadvantaged and disabled need is a self image. The first question a participant is made to ask is: Who am I? The facilitator helps the participants, by using the Socratic Method to debate the issue of an individual's space in a family, a social group, a community and a country. The young people are made aware of their rights and duties; and their responsibilities to themselves and the society. They are made to realize the need to preserve their physical and mental health.
2. *Empathy*: The other part of self-awareness is the life skill of empathy. Awareness of the self should be counter-balanced by the awareness of others, their different thinking, feelings, desires and wishes. This requires some imagination and fellow-feeling. It is a part of the process of socialization and self-control. The Indian culture empathizes with human beings, animals and nature around us. A careful cultivation of this skill prevents aggressive stance for self-protection as well as self and group identity among the adolescents.
3. *Effective Communication*: It is like an art. It has been observed that among the wards from the less-advantaged families, communication is far from effective. Through practical experience, it can be found that a person from a middle and higher class background know both what is to be said as well as how to adjust according to the mood of the listener and the situation. The person who comes from slums or lower class background often speaks a dialect at home, which is distinct from the standard formal language used in offices,

schools and other institutes. Effective communication, thus, leads to building successful interpersonal relationships.

4. *Critical and Creative thinking*: These are the two next pair of skills. Training to inculcate thinking abilities, as such, is very rare in both formal and non-formal classrooms. As media sends out a constant stream of messages, it is important to begin with critical listening and asking right questions. Telling young people to ask for cause-effect relationship and rational thinking is very essential, if they need to withstand pressures. Creative thinking requires patience and persistence that looks for new answers to old questions. It also needs the use of intuition as well as logical thinking.
5. *Gender Sensitivity*: Gender sensitivity of a person depends upon his/her empathy, ability of critical thinking, analyzing power on his/her view of how he/she is experiencing the social system. In India gender inequality is still persisting as a curse to the society. Barring a few communities, male dominance is prevalent in every strata of the society. There is a difference between the legal and social concepts of gender equality. Contrary to the Indian Constitution's declaration on equal rights in education, sports, health facility, payment for work etc. to either gender, there's a differential and partial treatment for males and females since childhood, especially in lower and middle economic class.
6. Interpersonal Relationship: The foundation of a good Inter-Personal Relationship is based on empathy and the habit of good listening. The learning and practicing of coping with stress ad emotions also contribute in making better relations with others.
7. Decision Making: This skill is based on the understanding of who decides and how much choice there is. The participants learn how to take decisions in a day-to-day life. In areas such as education, choosing a career, daily activities and even in eating habits, one has to choose a right thing. Therefore, everyone should be conscious about the merits and demerits of all the facts he/she is facing. Decision making and Problem solving skills are inter-related. Proper decision making leads to the solution of any problem.

IMPLEMENTATION OF PROGRAMME

The method and contents will depend upon:

- Availability of human resources
- Availability of time
- Availability of audio-visual aids
- Age, educational level, sex and cultural background of the group.

Methods:

- Talks
- Group discussion
- Question box
- Question-Answer sessions
- Role play
- Drama
- Story telling
- Debates
- Showing films or slides

Though, talks is a conventially used method, the other methods, if used, could bring a variety in the programme and maintain interest of the students. Several topics could be picked up for the debates and dramas, *e.g.*, STD/AIDS, teenage pregnancy, dowry, premarital counselling, myths and misconceptions, homosexuality, child marriage, sexual abuse, gender discrimination, selection of partner.

"Question Box" approach for sex education is found to be effective. This method consists of installing a question box in a central place in the school/ college campus. By putting a notice on the Notice Board all the students are informed to write questions (without writing their name) about their health problems or questions relating to their bodies and put them in the box. Once a week the box is opened by the teachers and the questions written therein are answered.

Question box approach to sex education is found to be convenient, easy to implement, takes care of embarrassment and fulfils the needs of the adolescents. Should sex education programme be included in a regular secondary school curriculum? Though, majority of principals and teachers are in favour of including sex education in the secondary school curriculum, some have expressed their reservations for it, the reasons being

- Some topics are sensitive and may raise controversy,
- Sex education would raise unnecessary curiosity and lead to misconduct among students.
- Students are already overburdened with studies,
- Schools have no extra time to allocate for sex education.

Who Should Give Sex Education

Sexuality education should be taught by specially trained teachers or professionals or by trained peer groups. The community must be involved in the development and implementation of the programme. The programme must be carefully developed to respect the diversity of the values and beliefs represented by the community. Parents, teachers, administrators should be involved in developing a programme. In fact, briefing them about the developed programme prior to its implementation to students is quite essential. Preferably, the curriculum and the audiovisuals should be pretested.

Who Should train

Sexologists, doctors, nurses, psychologists, social workers, teachers, volunteers, NGOs, media persons, peer groups etc. They should be trained in the subjects. Since the subject of sex education is multidisciplinary, more than one resource persons may be required. Government, municipality, NGOs, can render help. Not only the knowledge of sexuality but the methodology should also be included in the training. The Trainers/Teachers should Have acquired accurate knowledge Have a good communication skill Have a good listening skill Be able to establish good rapport with students and teachers Be non judgemental Be comfortable with his/her own sexuality.

Maintain Confidentiality Selection of Teachers

It has been indicated by the adolescents in a survey that they would prefer to get such information from their teachers. Teachers are also best judges about the level of understanding of school child and they would be the best persons to screen or filter the socially unacceptable portions of such training. However, not all teachers would volunteer to participate in the project.

Teachers have their own inhibitions, misconceptions and confusions. Therefore, those teachers who volunteer for teaching sex education should be selected for training. It requires a gifted prudent and morally upright teacher to stand up before a group of young people and impress upon them that sex is precious and dignified. Therefore, not every teacher may be willing to undertake sex education and not every teacher who is willing to give sex education has the ability to do so.

Sometimes the most enthusiastic teacher may be the least suitable. The teachers should be selected only after thorough knowledge of their personality, attitudes and behaviour. Students should be encouraged to act as peer educators, and to share important information with those who don't have access to it in the way they do.

Organizational Chart

When the sex education programme is to be implemented on a large scale, the following organizational chart will be of help.

Planners: Core Committee: Govt. representatives Civic body representatives Experts in Human Sexuality Representatives from NGOs Representatives from Principals of schools/colleges Master Trainers: Sexologists Psychologists Trained social workers Doctors Key Trainers: Teachers Volunteers Beneficiaries: Students Parents Audio-visual Aids and Resource Material

- Chalk-Blackboard
- Charts/Pictures
- Models
- Slides and slide projector
- Overhead projector
- Video cassettes
- Films
- Books
- Newspaper cuttings.

At present many types of audio-visuals are not easily available. It is better to prepare one's own audio-visuals that will meet the needs of the group.

Cultural differences in customs, dress, language and behaviour becomes so important that materials judged to be suitable in one region or culture may be totally unacceptable in another. Therefore, each cultural group should develop its own appropriate teaching aids. In order to achieve the best possible outcome from any programmes, it is necessary to invest in the development of competence of people who will be involved.

Pretesting Pretesting inolves getting feedback on communication materials prior to their widespread diffusion by measuring the reaction of a group of individuals in the target audience. Pretesting is a cost effective means of avoiding a communications disaster. If materials are inappropriate, misunderstood or unappealing, they will not be worth and should be changed. Pretesting finds out whether the curriculum and the audio-visual materials are acceptable to the culture, whether the message is clearly understood and whether the materials are relevant.

Ethics in Sex Education

No body contacts No slang language No vulgar jokes No use of naked photographs/pornography No late hours No individual training Non judgemental No religious, cultural criticism No sharing of and asking for personal experiences No emotional involvement No advertisement or promotion of any commercial product. Confidentiality about the communication on sexual and personal matters. Be honest and answer truthfully all the questions posed by children.

Evaluation

It is essential to receive the feedback, evaluate and analyse and modify the programme from time to time. Evaluation helps in knowing the effectivenss and shortcomings of the programme conducted. Suitable modifications can be made in the next programme to make them more effective. The data collected can be useful for research. The evaluation form should contain personal details (name may be optional so as to hide the identity) and the comments about the contents of the programme, the speakers, the audio-visuals, the duration and other details. Evaluation can also be based on stated objectives of the course and cover attitudinal, behavioural and cognitive changes. Questionnaire or interviews in small groups intended to identify the needs of participants will determine how far these are being met. On the basis of information gained from these sources the curriculum will require continuing modification and restructuring.

Research

There are several methods of sex research. Each method has strengths and weaknesses. The selection of the method will depend upon the nature of the subject to be studied and the resources available. The methods are: Surveys, Observational research, Case studies, Clinical research, Experimental research.

Survey

Research Surveys are used for gathering information about a sample of population either by interviewing people or asking them to fill a questionnaire. Surveys are economical and permit flexibility in sampling. Surveys are affected by the accuracy of information provided by the subjects in answering questionnaires or interviewer's questions. Reliability of surveys depend upon obtaining a proper sample.

Observational Research

It involves the use of human observer or an instrument to record the events being studied. The study of sexual response done by Masters and Johnson was a landmark. The accuracy in observational research does not depend upon subject's self-reports. Volunteer bias may pose uncertainties in this method.

Case Studies

Case studies are in-depth examinations of one or more people having a particular condition. Generalization can- not be done in this method. The biases of researcher can also put limitations.

Clinical Research

It involves studies that test a type of treatment given for specific problem. The reliability will be maximum when done in comparison with a control group.

Experimental Research

It permits scientists to isolate specific variables that affect a condition or a behaviour and may allow them to draw a conclusion about cause and effect. Experimental research is expensive and difficult to perform. Volunteer bias, artificiality of situation may limit the validity of such studies. At present surveys seem to be the only possible method of research in our country. In evaluating the quality of research study it is necessary to look at such issues as the size and nature of the sample, the means by which data was collected, the type of data analysis that was done and the researcher's discussion about the limitations of the study. It is necessary to see whether the study has been replicated elsewhere. Independent verification or research is most powerful tool for confirming the validity of a study.

Planning a Curriculum

There are no published countrywide accepted national guidelines for comprehensive adolescent sexuality education. Sex educators and teachers create their own curriculum for sexuality education. Some include anatomy and physiology of sex organs, physical, emotional changes at puberty, STD and AIDS, nutrition and hygiene and family planning; while some include family life issues such as relationship between family members, gender role, socialization and child development; few provide information about cultural and social aspects of human sexuality, sexual values and attitudes, beliefs, sexual activities and functioning. Very few include information on sexual behaviour.

Every expert has been dealing with it from one's own perspective and experience. Therefore, there is a need for a comprehensive course in sexuality education. There can be no ideal curriculum that will meet the needs of every community. However, there can be a document containing guidelines on topics that may be presented to the adolescents in a developmentally appropriate manner, and to suit their needs.

These guidelines are given in the next chapter. The characteristic of local situation should determine the exact contents of the local programme. Community attitudes, developmental differences in children, local socioeconomic influence, parents' expectations, students' needs and expectations and religious and other perspectives should be paramount in designing the local sexuality education programme. The suggestions given in the agewise guidelines should also be flexible. It is important to allow as much autonomy as possible at local level to develop contents and methods which are suitable to local circumstances and preferences. In early years of life, the focus of student-interest is his own developmental adjustment with reference to sexual behaviour.

At the later stage, when he has accepted his own sexuality and established his values, he is ready to concentrate on assimilation of knowledge, especially of those aspects of sexuality that seem most relevant to his special areas of interest. Sex relationships are most sensitive of all human relationships. A programme will not be effective if there is no understanding of moral, ethical, aesthetic and religious sensibilities of the people for whom the curriculum is designed. Apart from accepting a few basic principles on which general agreement is reached, planners would be wise to adopt a flexible approach and avoid stereotypes. The programme will require modification from time to time depending upon the feedback, the need, the acceptance and the changing circumstances.

ADOLESCENCE HEALTH EDUCATION PROGRAMME (AHEP)

Reaching youngsters at an impressionable age before they become sexually active can lay the foundation for a responsible lifestyle, including healthy relationships and safe sex habits. NACO reaches out to youth through specially developed Adolescent Education Programme focused primarily on prevention through awareness building. Adolescence Health Education Programme (AHEP) is a joint initiative by the Ministry of Human Resource Development and National AIDS Control Organisation, Government of India to equip every adolescent (children between 10–19yrs) with scientific information, knowledge and life skills to protect themselves from HIV infection and manage their concerns pertaining to reproductive and sexual health.

TheAdolescence EducationProgramme (AEP) aims at:

- Co-curricular adolescence education in classes IX-XI
- Curricular adolescence education in classes IX-XI and life skills education in classes I-VIII
- Inclusion of HIV prevention education in pre-service and in-service teacher training and teacher education programmes.
- Inclusion of HIV prevention education in the programmes for out-of-school adolescents and young persons, and
- Incorporating measures to prevent stigma and discrimination against learners/students and educators and life skills education into education policy for HIV prevention.

Under the programme, teachers and peer educators are trained, who, in turn, conduct the programme amongst the student community. The programme covered 112,000 schools and trained 2,88,000 teachers.They have been provided reference material, which has been developed by NACO in collaboration with Ministry of HRD and vetted by NCERT. Adolescence Health Education Programme (AHEP) is effectively being implemented in the state by the Department of Education with technical and financial support from the Kerala State AIDS Control Society.

In Kerala Adolescence Health Education Programme (AHEP) is being implemented by General Education Department and SCERT with the technical and financial support of Kerala State AIDS Control Society. AHEP is an umbrella programme to cover all secondary and senior secondary schools. Presently it is transacting by trained nodal teachers in classes 9th and 11th for minimum of 16 hours in an academic year.

Key elements of ahep:

- Life Skills
- Process of growing up
- Health and Hygiene
- Nutrition
- Sexually transmitting diseases/HIV and AIDS/RTI
- Substance abuse
- Teacher as a councilor

Key features of the programme:

- This is a comprehensive programme covering all the areas of adolescence concerns
- There is a module for the programme prepared by the experts in the field of Adolescence Health education and it is approved by curriculum committee and appreciated by other institutions
- It is a sustainable programme as it is implementing with the support of Education department and transacting through trained teachers in the school
- The funds for the programme is getting from National AIDS Control Organization and seems to be a cost effective programme to cover maximum students in 9th and 11th classes.

ASPIRATIONS OF URBAN ADOLESCENTS

URBAN STUDENTS

Having a plan, a goal, and aspirations for the future are important aspects to living a happy and meaningful life. Having future aspirations also facilitates adjustment to life stress for students who attend urban schools; and these aspirations are an important component of the self-concept of the student (Sirin, Diemer, Jackson, Gonsalves, & Howell, 2004). A research done by Sirin *et al.* showed that the level of career and educational aspirations were equally high for both urban and suburban children. In contrast the expectations of actually achieving those aspirations were very different.

For instance the expectation of actually attaining the occupation that they wanted was quite different for White students compared with students of Colour. Urban adolescents have lower expectations than their more privileged peers. Lower expectations are a participating factor in lower graduation rates and higher drop out rates (Williams, 2005). We need to understand where these expectations stem from and we must teach students that education is the key to success. By understanding the students we can better assist them in their quest for a better future. At an early age many students who live in urban areas and attend urban schools are introduced to oppression, racism, and poverty (Sirin *et al.*, 2004). These are debilitating barriers that shape the ways in which students perceive their current self-concept and future worth. Students who are of lower socioeconomic status also have fewer opportunities to make connections with school.

In addition, with the emergence of high stakes testing these connections have become even less. Most of the students who score lower on these assessment tests are of minority and lower socioeconomic status; and these lower-scoring students are many times pushed down to special education classes or pushed aside in order to ensure higher scores for schools (Darling-Hammond, 2002). These disadvantaged students are being told by their community and their schools that they are nothing and will amount to nothing. Schools are meant to be a haven from the cruel outside world. Schools are supposed to be equal opportunity and a place in which dreams are created.

However, if these schools are pushing students out and taking away educational opportunities what can these students do, but drop out. Students at risk are faced with numerous obstacles everyday. They have to avoid violence which often times occurs in their neighborhoods and schools, they have to worry about the cost of going to college if the opportunity presents itself, and they must also worry about the societal problems they will eventually encounter. Some students are aware of what they need to avoid and what they need to do in order to succeed, but many students still do not know.

This is where the community and school systems need to intervene. Schools need to educate students and their parents on what needs to be done to achieve success. Schools need to promote school completion and students need to be informed of the problems they will eventually have if they do not graduate. They must also know that staying in school will lead to a better job and a better job will help them acquire social power they originally did not have on the basis of their socioeconomic position within the existing social order (Sirin *et al.*, 2004). Lastly, schools and communities need to keep students' dreams and aspirations alive. Future aspirations play a very important role in educational and future occupational attainment and goals of students. Once we know and understand where these students are coming from, we can better accommodate schools and curriculum in ensuring their future success.

DEVELOPMENTAL PHASE OF ADOLESCENCE

In industrialized societies, adolescence is the developmental phase during which individuals prepare for their adult lives. Schooling and mentoring opportunities are provided to adolescents by parents and other adults, who help to prepare them for their culturally ascribed adult roles. Each adolescent's perspective about their future, or future aspirations, are influenced by a number of factors that fall within the domains of individual abilities and social context.

These domains are particularly important areas to consider for urban ethnic minority adolescents, the focus of this study. [In this paper, the term "urban adolescents" refers to the participants of this study, poor and working class African American, Cape Verdean and Latino/a adolescents who resided in the inner city.] We believe that a consideration of both individual and social/ structural factors in the study of future aspirations to be particularly important, given that urban adolescents have been found to experience tension between their valuing of education and the (often) limited resources and opportunities they are afforded within their schools and communities.

Further, because of the effects of institutional racism and the limited contextual resources urban youth are afforded, we believe that future aspirations (and subsequent educational and occupational attainment) may represent a form of resistance to structural oppression. That is, urban youth who "dream and attain" resist the tracking into occupational positions that lack meaning and ascribed social power caused by structural oppression and the accompanying lack of resources. Thus, our goal in this learn was to learn about urban adolescents' future educational and vocational aspirations and to illuminate the individual and social factors that influence them.

We hoped to answer the following questions in this study:

- What do the future aspirations of urban adolescents 'look like?'
- How do these adolescents conceptualize their ability to influence expected future events, such as going to college or obtaining employment?
- What are the major factors in the social context (*e.g.*, school, family, peer group) that influence the future orientation of these adolescents?

FUTURE ASPIRATIONS OF ADOLESCENCE

Adolescence is the time when individuals are more concerned about their future than any of the other developmental phases. For adolescents, future aspirations can be conceptualized as the educational and vocational "dreams" they have for their future work lives. A large body of research indicates that adolescents' future aspirations, in the areas of career, education, and family, significantly impact their later life experiences. In an extensive review of the adolescent future orientation and planning literature, Nurmi (1989, 1991) found empirical support for the notion that the level of investment into future plans is predictive of adolescent problem behaviour, such as delinquency, problems in school and in the world of work, and drug abuse. Wyman, Cowen, Work, and Kerley (1993) found that future aspirations facilitate adjustment to life stress for students attending urban schools in the USA. They argue that, "Rather than being connected narrowly to distant goals, future expectations seem to be part of the fabric of a child's ongoing self-experience and the attitudes with which she or he engages the world" (p.658). The level of educational and career aspiration is equivalently high for both urban and suburban adolescents in the USA. In contrast, the research of Sewell and Hauser (1975) and Gorman (1998) diverge from these findings in regards to career aspirations.

Constantine *et al.* (1998) and Fouad and Bingham (1995) reported that urban ethnic minority youth generally have the same level of career aspirations as their more affluent counterparts; however, Sewell and Hauser (1975) and Gorman (1998) both found that for a predominantly White sample that career aspirations varied with social class. This discrepancy may reflect historical effects, ethnic differences, or a factor not yet identified. Regardless, future aspirations represent an important aspect of the educational and career development processes.

STRUCTURAL CONSTRAINTS OF FUTURE ASPIRATIONS

The literature suggests that a consideration of future aspirations among inner-city youth is also a consideration of external barriers to their future plans. These barriers are the product of institutional racism (Carter & Cook, 1992) and inequities in resources that are a product of social class position (Kozol, 1991; Rossides, 1990). These barriers have led to, as Wilson (1996) suggests, the "disappearance" of work from urban communities, few vocational role models, a paucity of work opportunities, and the anticipation of future work-based discrimination as the norm for urban youth.

The adult African American male participants in the qualitative study conducted by Diemer (in press) gave voice to the expectation that they were and would continue to be subjected to discrimination in their career development processes and in their labour force participation. They also perceived having fewer career development resources, such as personal networks they could utilize, compared to what they expected their White counterparts to have. Further, in a study of Mexican-American and European-American high school students, McWhirter (1997) found that Mexican-American students were more likely to perceive future barriers to their educational and career goals than their European-American counterparts.

Mexican-American participants were also more likely to feel less confident in their ability to overcome these barriers than European-American students. These results were found while socioeconomic status was being controlled for in the analyses. Relatedly, in a review of the career development literature related to Latino/a populations, Arbona (1990) argued that Latino/a adolescents have the same level of aspirations as European American adolescents, but that they are less confident in their ability to overcome these barriers. Social class also affects the likelihood of achieving more (financially and personally) rewarding work and educational and career attainment (McLoyd, 1998).

As Blustein, Juntunen and Worthington (2000) argued, "One of the key ingredients in predicting favourable [career] outcomes is access to the educational and occupational opportunity structure". In sum, the literature reviewed above suggests that, within the USA, (and, presumably, within other countries as well) social class has a strong influence upon the future aspirations and subsequent occupational attainment of adolescents, and in particular, urban adolescents.

METHOD INFORMATION OF PARTICIPANTS

Before providing information about the participants, we would like to first situate our findings in the context of the high school where we conducted our study. Several years ago, this high school lost its accreditation because the state board judged that teachers and the curriculum used in the school were failing to provide the education necessary to meet state standards. Local government then intervened and infused money into the school; one of the many changes that has been made was the introduction of a new school principal.

The new principal is an African American educator who has appeared to enjoy a close relationship with the students. Another major change that ensued at this school was the firing and hiring of more than half of the school's faculty; the current staff represent more ethnic diversity. These teachers also have participated in voluntary professional training. Finally, there has been an increase in the number of guidance teachers and librarians. Consequently, the school has regained its accreditation approximately two years before the beginning of this research.

In terms of the whole school, the ethnic status of the student population was as follows: 87.6 per cent African American, 6.9 per cent Latino/a, 3.6 per cent Asian American, and 1.7 per cent White. Participants for our study were 18 adolescents aged 14-15 years of age attending the same inner city high school. They were each bused in from different urban centers within a major city in the Northeastern USA.

During focus groups, students provided the following information about themselves: Eleven of the students were 9th graders; seven were 10th graders. There were 12 males and 6 females in the group. Their current high school had not been their first choice when they applied for school (students rank order their preferences for high school in this area). In terms of racial/ethnic background, 15 students identified themselves as African American, while the other 3 identified themselves as Cape Verdean and/or Latino/a background. One interesting point that we noted regarding the Cape Verdean participants was that there was a lack of consensus regarding the racial/ethnic self-identification that they preferred. That is, some of the Cape Verdean participants identified themselves as Black or African American, some as Latino/a, and some simply as Cape Verdean.

Finally, although some participants self-identified only one ethnic/racial group membership, it is plausible that some of the participants were members of more than one ethnic or racial group.

COLLECTED DATA FROM THE PARTICIPANTS

The school and collected data from the participants before the intervention began. The third and fourth authors supervised this project and the data collection process. The fifth author served as an auditor of the data analytic process. Our research team consisted of two international graduate students, one European American graduate student, one African American faculty member, and a Cape Verdean American faculty member who was both the parent of a student attending this school and a member of the School-Site Council at this school.

We feel that this diversity in backgrounds and perspectives among the researchers enhanced both our ability to experience the data and the rigour of our findings. However, each researcher recognized the limitations in his or her experience and background and diligently sought to privilege the participants' perspective throughout all aspects of the study. For example, we employed very open-ended questions during the focus groups to enable participants to navigate us through their worlds.

We attempted to ensure that we were really "listening" to student's words, facial expressions, and their use of material culture, without interjecting our personal views. For example, as we explained the instructions for completing goal maps and collages, we asked participants to think of examples of how to complete the exercise, rather than impose our own ideas. Any probing statements used during the focus groups were always statements derived from the student's own words (*e.g.*, rephrasing their statements to qualify the meaning of what they had stated).

These techniques, and our stance towards the research process, ensured that we remained self-reflexive and aware of our own biases in this research project. In sum, we attempted to "understand and capture the points of view of other people without predetermining those points of view ". We used a grounded theory methodology to gorund r theoretical analysis and conclusions in the data (Glaser & Strauss, 1967)..

As part of this methodological stance, we decided to collect all data from each participant before analyzing the materials so that we would not form theories from a partial data set. We also completed our literature review after we had collected the data so that we would avoid "finding" our a priori assumptions in the data set. The goal of the researchers was to understand the adolescent's experience through his or her own words. Through an inductive process, we individually looked for patterns in the data, which we then formulated into coding schema; this schema was then revised using the constant comparative method. We then met to discuss the patterns that we had found individually. Through a series of discussions (and occasional argument) we reached a conclusion about the validity and meanings of our claims.

COMMUNITY METHODS OF DATA COLLECTION

In an attempt to "give back" to the community from which we were conducting research, the data used in this study were collected before we implemented an intervention programme at this high school. The goal of the intervention was to help students to be positively engaged with school (both behaviourally and emotionally) and to develop strategies for future life transitions such as going to college or getting a job after high school.

As part of the intervention, students met together as a group with two graduate student facilitators bi-weekly over the course of an academic year. After the introductory meeting, subsequent groups took place in a classroom for approximately 60 minutes during a scheduled class period. Classroom teachers generally elected not to participate in the sessions. All of the focus group sessions were audio recorded and subsequently transcribed for analysis. Prior to the beginning to the intervention programme, the data collection process took place in four separate sessions.

To capture the perspectives of urban adolescents about their future aspirations, we used four different sources of information: an introductory focus group session, a questionnaire, goal maps and group identity collages. Researchers also kept detailed field notes during each day of data gathering, detailing their reactions to the process, analytic memos, and interesting statements participants made. The procedures that were used to gather these four sources of information are described in the following sections.

Introductory Focus Group

In the first session, the facilitators were introduced by the school principal as people interested in talking to students about their experiences in school, their communities, and what it was like being an adolescent at this school. After being introduced to students by the school principal and the two coordinators of this project, the facilitators devoted time to answering participants' questions and developing rapport with the students.

After the introductory group meeting in the classroom, facilitators held a series of focus groups (accompanied by an activity) devoted to the issue of students' future aspirations. The data from this study are derived from these four focus groups.

Questionnaire

During the next focus group, we asked students to complete a brief questionnaire that asked them to describe themselves now and five years from now and then tell us what they thought they would be doing five years into the future. More specifically, in a large classroom, the participants were asked to individually respond to the following open-ended written questions: "What kind of person are you now?"

"What kind of person will you be in five years?" and "What will you be doing in five years?" Following the questionnaire, we held a discussion with participants regarding their responses to the questionnaire. The third focus group involved creating goal maps outlining future plans for achieving specific academic or personal goals.

The goal mapping activity began with a discussion about dreams and hopes. Students were asked to think about what they hoped for in the future and to consider strategies that they could use to achieve future goals. After students described some of their aspirations, we then asked them to choose a goal that they wanted to achieve within the next 5 years. We then asked them to map out the "road" that they needed to take to get to their goals, using coloured markers and large poster-sized paper.

The following instructions were written on a chalkboard and also presented orally to participants:

- Identify where you are now.
- Identify the end point - which is the goal you chose.
- Next, identify the things you need to do to get to the end (your goal).
- Map these out as points between where you are now and your goal.
- For each point on your map, give 3-5 examples of how you will reach that point.

We then gave each student the materials, and remained present to help them or answer any questions. At the end of the activity, students presented their maps to other members of the group and discussed the meaning of their goal maps. We collected the maps and ensured that students had written their names on their completed maps.

Group Identity Collage

The participants (in groups) completed collages that represented aspects of their group identity during the fourth and final focus group session. For this activity, we asked students to make (in groups of four) a collage that would tell us about what the people making the collage were like. We suggested that students could use the ideas that they had expressed during the focus group to make a collage about how they saw themselves, the things they do, and the world in which they live. We asked students to "tell us what you and your world are like in your collage." Students were given materials, such as large poster board, magazines, scissors, glue, scotch tape, and markers. One boy chose to not participate in the activity, so he worked independently and drew a picture instead of making a collage. Before the period ended, each group explained their collage to the rest of the group.

THEORY APPROACH OF DATA ANALYSIS

We adapted a three-step grounded theory approach to analyze the data. In the first step, we delved into the data to generate a list of codes that embraced common descriptive and interpretive categories in the data. In the second step, we explored the data further to propose plausible relationships among the codes. Finally, using our findings from the first two steps, we looked for a few "conceptually dense" theories in the limited sense. Throughout the data analysis process, we extensively used the HyperResearch computer programme to code and progressively organize the data.

In the first step, we began by reviewing the data independently to identify codes that emerged from the data. Next, we began a series of constant comparisons of these codes. A large list of codes (about 35) was then developed. As the first code list was created, once again, two researchers looked back at the data and coded it separately using the HyperResearch programme. In the second step, a third researcher, the auditor who had not been to the school, joined the meetings to compare our findings and resolve discrepancies that arose. During this process, many codes were revised and refined. This recursive process enabled us to produce a number of codes that we believe represent the participants' perspectives.

The end result of this second step of our data analytic process is the results section of this paper. In the third step, we attempted to develop a conceptual framework to better understand urban adolescents' future aspirations that was grounded in our findings. Following our development of this framework, we then integrated our findings with the literature in this domain. We offer this grounded conceptual model in the discussion section of this paper.

FUTURE GOALS OF DATA COLLECTION ACTIVITIES

The data collection activities we employed were selected to illuminate patterns in the type of future goals that students were oriented to. All students envisioned attending college at some point in their future plans. However, sports played a large role in the views of college the boys held. One third of the participants, each of who were boys, indicated that playing in a "division level college sports team" was an important aspect of their future plans. Among the boys who stated that they wished to play sports, almost all of them had indicated that they planned to receive a scholarship for doing so.

The majority of participants envisioned the type of career that they aspired to beyond graduating from college. Five participants planned to be lawyers, four planned on a business career, and only one person aspired to have a career in music. One boy planned to become a police officer or security guard. Finally, only two students did not indicate a defined career path that they planned to pursue.

Structure and Process

These activities helped us to explore with participants what we have labeled the structure and process of their future plans. That is, how students perceived their future and how students went about planning their future goals. We found two patterns that were common to almost all of the students.

These patterns involved:

- The structure of their future planning and
- The processes that students had considered as they outlined the goals they hoped to achieve within the next five-year.

All participants had a basic structural plan that incorporated a beginning and an end point; this structure generally took on a narrative form. This was somewhat expected because students had been given clear instructions to include a beginning and end point and a basic structure. Only two students did not demonstrate a structure in their plans. Their plan did not progress in a logical sequence (*e.g.*, go to law school followed by graduate from high school).

The structure of student's plans was reflected by their awareness of the necessary steps to achieve one's future goals. Within the group, there was significant variability in the level of detail provided by each student's plans. For example, one participant's "goal map" involved 1) attending high school, college, and then starting a law firm.

Whereas another student's plan was more specific:

- Get a job, get money and save money
- Get through high school, avoid bad friends
- Graduate from high school, apply to colleges
- Go to New York University
- Go to law school
- Open a law firm.

There was also variability in participants' awareness of the process necessary to achieve each step of one's plan. Process was defined as participants' perception of the necessary functional requirements to fulfill the structure of one's plans. Some students' plans had a coherent structure with minimal awareness of process.

For example, the structure of one participants' plans was:

- Go to college

- Study business
- Save money.

Other participant's produced elaborate plans that described much of the process necessary to progress through the different steps of the plan.

For example, one boy described his plan in three steps:

1. High school
2. Scholarship and
3. College.

For each step, he described many details of the process such as "get good grades, try hard, no foolness, get above grade point average grades, be involved in extracurricular activities, pass the "X-test" [a 'high stakes' test students are required to take], find out what college costs, apply for college."

Overall, we observed that half of the participants were aware of both the structure and process involved in their plans, whereas the other half of students included only a basic structure to their plans, with little or no consideration of the processes necessary to progress through the structure they had created.

Self-reliance

Students consistently discussed the theme of "self-reliance." Two thirds of participants expressed the importance of exercising self-control over one's thinking, behaviour, and body to achieve success. For example, one boy said, "in order to succeed, I need to keep my act together and stay on the ball."

During the focus group session, one boy insisted that, "If Blacks work hard they will succeed in the long run, no matter what the circumstances are." He suggested that African Americans should rely on themselves to succeed despite adverse circumstances. He declared, "Racism is not over! The only way for Blacks to be chosen over Whites is to work twice as hard. ... it is all about your brain; I will make it if I work hard." However, we should note that the majority of the participants did not share this perspective.

Idea of Being Serious

The idea of becoming "more serious" in the future was prevalent among one third of the statements made by students in their goal maps and questionnaires. One third of the participants stated that in five years they wanted to "become a more serious person." This theme was mentioned in relation to one's maturity, education, and level of responsibility. A similar theme also emerged during the focus group.

Other students discussed becoming more serious as a developmental progression towards maturity. For example, one boy stated, "I am a real honest person and also a funny person. In five years, I will be a serious person," while another participant stated "I will still be a responsible person. In five years, I will be a much more serious person."

PARTICIPANTS OF TIME ORIENTATION

Participants also varied in their future orientation. A third of the participant's goal maps were focused on immediate goals. These student's plans reflected goals that involved the "here and now". For example, one student's goal map involved learning a "cross-over" dribble for playing basketball. Another student's goal was to travel to Ireland. A few students were concerned with basic survival needs and indicated that in five years, they hoped to be "still livin'" or "staying alive."

There were however, other student's who focused exclusively on details of distal plans without a consideration of immediate goals or issues involving the "here and now." For example, one participant described how he planned to go to college, start a business and make the business successful. The predominant goal of this student's map concerned "making the business grow" (*e.g.* have good credit, borrow money from a bank, get people to work with me, negotiate with other companies to work with me, and put products on sale to make a profit).

CONTEXT: RESOURCES AND BARRIERS

An awareness of resources and barriers was reflected in students' perception of their social/structural context. For example, only one third of students acknowledged environmental obstacles such as passing standardized tests, paying for the cost of college, and avoiding violence in the school. One student stated that he had to, "stay out of trouble and avoid bad friends" in order to succeed in his future goals. This boy also drew pictures of guns on his goal map between symbols of people who he indicated were "bad friends." These symbols were placed along his goal path, between his goals of completing high school and entering college. We interpreted these data to reflect students awareness of the way in which the school context and violence can serve as barriers to the realization of their future aspirations.

Other students indicated an awareness of the need to afford the cost of college. These students discussed strategies for obtaining part-time jobs to save money, having good credit to get a loan to start a business, and getting good grades so that they could obtain scholarships. Only two students in the study alluded to using resources in their context to achieve their future goals. One girl stated that she could ask for advice from adults in the environment about getting a job. Another girl mentioned that she would "ask her father for money to buy clothes." However, two thirds of the participants did not give voice to accessing contextual resources to overcome obstacles and meet their goals.

Racial and Ethnic Context

All the students in our study indicated that they were proud of their ethnic/racial heritage. The African American students underlined the fact that they felt Black and proud. For example, one boy described himself as a "Hard working African American male: Black is beautiful." Another student summarized the group's feelings concerning this issue "I am proud of being Black." This theme was also evident in many collages where pictures of African American models were put next to written descriptions such as "Beauty, style, power, fashion." Participants indicated that they believed that they had more opportunities now than previous generations of racial/ethnic minorities. One student outlined a commonly shared idea in the group session that, "There is still racism in America."

Students were eager to share some of the difficulties that they were aware ethnic minorities face in the USA. They expressed concern over the high number of African Americans in jail and out of school. They discussed how both "the bad history" and the scars of slavery within the USA were two major causes of problems that they felt they experience today. Participants also gave voice to bicultural communication skills. Some of the students in the group made the comparison between "talking Black vs. talking White." A girl described how she felt comfortable when she was around her Black friends because she could "talk Black," however; she clarified that she "knew how to talk around White folks."

CONSIDERATION OF PROCESSES ASPIRATIONS

Overall, students who appeared to have a well-structured future plan (*i.e.*, both short and long term goals in a logical order) with a consideration of processes necessary to achieve their goals, seemed to have an explicit plan to attend college. Moreover, the majority of these students not only perceived themselves as college-bound, but they also wanted to further their education and obtain a professional degree, most commonly in the law field. In sum, most of the urban adolescents in this study had future aspirations in the educational and vocational worlds.

We should note that the method of data collection seemed to highlight different loci of influence in students' perceptions of their future plans. That is, personality characteristics were highlighted when participants provided information individually, whereas in the group activities such as the collage and focus groups, elements of the social context were highlighted. Participants consistently mentioned that their personal abilities (*i.e.*, self-reliance) were highly related to what they would or could not do in the future. This finding applied to most of the goal maps and questionnaires. The analysis of collages and focus group, however, provided some insights into how students perceived their environment as an obstacle to their future goals (*e.g.* violence, racism and discrimination). When students were asked to focus on their future goals individually, they were relatively clear about what they wanted and how they could obtain what they wanted. When they were in a group, however, they were more likely to consider contextual barriers that would impede them from attaining their future goals. In sum, students mostly were fluent about the role individual factors played in their future aspirations, but also gave voice to the impact of contextual factors.

INDIVIDUAL LEVEL OF RESOURCES

Awareness of adverse social circumstances, such as racism and discrimination, did not impede most students from planning for a future involving college attendance and a meaningful career. This finding is consistent with other studies that have demonstrated equivalent levels of aspirations among urban youth and their suburban counterparts. Although students were cognizant of the social and structural barriers they faced, most students in this study indicated that they wanted to "stay on the ball." Almost all students planned to go to college, and imagined themselves to eventually secure a job that pays well. That is, despite an awareness of social and structural barriers, these youth maintained future educational and vocational aspirations.

To cope with these barriers, students suggested strategies such as "getting more serious." Students in this study perceived their social environment as a context where they have to be "tough" to combat the daily racism and discrimination that they experience. Hence, it appeared that participants felt that they needed to "get more serious" in the future so that they could cope with future contextual barriers.

Another individual-level resource for developing future aspirations was the ability to hypothesize about the structure and process of future-oriented plans. For example, one participant indicated plans to go to college, start a business (structure) and "making the business grow" through developing credit, and borrowing money (process). Although this participant incorporated both structural and functional process in his plans, other participants varied in their ability to construct the structure and process of future vocational and educational aspirations.

In summary, despite an awareness of contextual barriers, these participants still flourished at the individual level. That is, they were able to envision future educational and vocational aspirations, and gave voice to "getting serious" as a strategy for coping with barriers such as violence, poverty and discrimination.

Barriers

Another individual-level barrier to future aspirations was a present-focused time orientation. Although this time orientation may be an adaptive coping response to the (at times) violent contexts that participants lived in, this focus upon the present may have impeded the development of well-formed future aspirations. For example, the goal map of one participant involved learning a crossover dribble for playing basketball. Although this goal may have reflected a step along the way to playing collegiate or professional sports in the future, this participant reported this as a final goal on his goal map

Contextual Level

We believe that students ability to think structurally to be a valuable asset to their future aspirations. An awareness of context appeared to be a necessity for dealing with barriers to future goals and using available resources in the environment. Students who indicated an awareness of these aspects of the social context included this as a major part of the process of their goal maps. Students who indicated a well-structured future plan with a focus on the processes required to achieve their plans were more likely to consider environmental circumstances than students without a well-structured plan. In other words, it appeared that students who were more cognizant of contextual challenges were more prepared for their future.

Participants made it clear during the focus group that they wanted to differentiate themselves from stereotypical images of ethnic minorities portrayed by the media, such as people from housing projects, thugs, drug dealers, etc. One student said, "Black is not ghetto!" Similarly, another student mentioned her disrespect for some rap stars and the manner in which they speak on TV; she indicated that, "Blacks sound stupid on TV" and described how she felt that this portrayal perpetuated stereotypical images of African-Americans.

One participant indicated ways that he believed White peers are socialized in ways that perpetuate racism; "White kids are taught to hate Black people and that makes everything harder for us." Another boy in the session said, "Now we have more chances, but White people are still thinking the same way as it was in slavery." A girl summed up the majority view by stating; "White people are obstacles for our future." Despite these views and the student's perception of racism, participants still maintained a positive attitude towards other races as one boy stated, "I don't hate nobody, don't care for their race. It is not about colour." Further, the comments of one participant, "If Blacks work hard they will succeed in the long run, no matter what the circumstances are," seemed to spur other participants to more fully reflect upon the role that contextual factors played in their own lives.

Students who demonstrated the capacity for structural thinking also demonstrated a subtle nuance between structural thinking and individual-level responses. Students who had more detailed structural plans with a consideration of required processes more often indicated the importance of self-reliance to achieve their goals, compared to students who did not generate detailed structural plans. Self reliance and a value placed on cognitive abilities appeared to be a critical component of student's awareness of how to achieve future goals in concert with the ability to conceptualize structural barriers.

Barriers. Most students in this study perceived their social context as more of a barrier than a resource. However, some students gave voice to the importance of interpersonal support as a means of dealing with barriers. In the focus group, only two girls reported receiving support from others to achieve their goals. These girls were among the few participants who viewed interpersonal support as being a valuable asset to achieve their future goals. We have elected to present interpersonal support as a contextual level barrier because the vast majority of the participants (16 of the 18) did not appear to be able to use supports as a resource in the manner that these two participants did.

In the face of the myriad social and structural barriers urban youth face (cf. Kozol, 1991; Rossides, 1990; Wilson, 1996), we feel that interpersonal support may represent one (protective) factor within the control of urban youth that may help them negotiate their risk-factor laden context. However, social networks may also serve as a "conduit for social and racial oppression..." - needing social connections to secure jobs, for urban kids with limited social capital especially... As discussed in the "Individual Barriers" section, participants inability to use interpersonal resources and create alliances with institutional agents in their communities...

Gender was related to the choice of professional sports as a career. In our sample, none of the girls mentioned professional sports as a future career option. However, all the boys who aspired to be a professional in sports also indicated that they wanted to go to college. Most of these boys indicated that they would like to obtain an athletic scholarship for their efforts. Although the boys did not directly link playing sports to obtaining entrance and financial support to attend college, it was implied in many of their statements, such as in their aspirations to play "division level college sports."

We have elected to classify these findings as structural barriers because of the evidence they provide about the constraining effects of gender messages. Theory and research within the study of gender (cf. Mahalik *et al.*, 2001; Majors & Billson, 1992) indicate that societal messages about gender (such as the need for men to control the display of emotions other than anger) constrain the possibilities that men and women envision for themselves (Freedman & Combs, 1996).

In this case, we believe that the discourse surrounding "urban black male" led these urban black male adolescents to believe that their entrance to post-secondary education was dependent upon their ability to play sports. Further, this discourse likely played a role in many of these boys envisioning professional sports as the (only?) career option for themselves in the future. While it is possible that athletic ability may facilitate much-needed scholarships for some of these boys, the focus upon athletics may have closed off exploration and planning in domains other than sports. This is especially saddening, considering the very low probabilities of college athletes "making it" to professional sports leagues. Almost all of the participants reported discouraging experiences as they attempted to achieve certain goals. The participants shared their frustrations about situations when they felt they had been discriminated against or had been the object of racism. For example, one participant told us about his recent weekend trip to a downtown mall with a group of friends from his neighborhood.

He described how he and his friends were using the elevator to go upstairs while having a heated discussion with each other about their favorite music. He described the event as follows: "There were three White girls in the elevator who were trying to move away from us as much as they could. I could see it in one girl's eyes, how scared they were of us. The girls walked out of the elevator and I heard one say, "That was close!" The student further explained how it was not the intention of him or his friends to scare the girls.

Person-in-context Model

Our data led us to construct a person-in-context model, grounded in the data, that captures the influences upon urban adolescents' future aspirations. Namely, individual-level factors such as interpersonal skills, "getting serious," and self-reliance and contextual-level factors such as structural thinking about barriers and racial/ethnic and gender socialization messages emerged as influences upon urban youths' future aspirations. These factors served to either constrain or facilitate youths aspirations; as such, we labeled them either resources or barriers.

Limitations: Our exploration of urban adolescents' future aspirations was influenced by our collection of data through multiple modalities. We found that group activities and individual activities influenced the data produced by participants. While we perceived the multiple sources and methods of data to be a strength of this study, it could also be interpreted as a limitation. That is, the method of data collection may have impacted the manner that participants' reported the various influences upon their future aspirations. For instance, the individually-focused questionnaires may have led participants to give more weight to individual factors than if this study had utilized solely focus group methodology. It is unclear to what extent the methodology influenced participants constructions, however it highlights the impact that methodology can have on participant's responses.

It is difficult to know whether the findings of the present study generalize to other urban adolescents from inner city settings. Although these participants did not give voice to the impact of the school culture upon their aspirations, the unique history of the high school - and the recent efforts to improve the curriculum and the school's academic orientation - all serve to make this particular school context unique. Further, the participants in this study were also participants in the intervention programme designed to foster their school engagement and future aspirations. Although the data from this study was collected before the implementation of this intervention, the special focus of this intervention may have altered participants' willingness to share their aspirations and perspectives. This alteration may mean that these participants' responses may not be generalizable or germane to other urban adolescents. Gender appeared to influence data collection as well. The manner in which data were collected appeared to influence participants' responses. That is, there were gender differences in the themes expressed in the group identity collages and during the focus groups. Boys were very restricted in the manner that they expressed themselves. Most of the boy's collages involved few items that were generally "status" items, such as a house, a luxury car and female fashion model, or a sports hero. Girls, on the other hand, included more diverse types of pictures in their collages. Their collages frequently included family-oriented images or images that reflected interpersonal relations.

For example, pictures of brides and grooms, babies, children, mother and child, mixed groups of teenagers, and groups of girls standing together were common in the girl's collages. Girls also included more colourful and artistic items in their collages. For example, there were colourful graphic images, flowers, geographic scenes and pictures of beaches and mountain scenery. We believe that gender discourse may help to explain the manner in which the male participants restricted their self-expression during data collection, while the female participants were more expressive. Gender socialization messages, such as the "Cool Pose" (Majors & Billson, 1992), may have led these male participants to believe that it would be "wrong" to allow themselves to be expressive of themselves or their emotions during the data collection process.

Finally, the specifics regarding the neighborhood and the racial/ethnic distribution of the participant in this study may have contributed the way in which the participants reported their awareness of the contextual factors such as racism and discrimination. We observed that some of the Cape Verdean participants self-identified as "Black," and as such, reported issues such as institutional racism from the perspective of a "Black" person, rather than as a "Cape Verdean." Relatedly, although some participants were of Cape Verdean and/or Latino/a background, the issues such as bilingual education, acculturation, and immigration laws were not as salient as one would expect. It is possible that the place where the school is located may have explained this phenomenon: A historically African American community within a Northeastern city of the USA. Regardless of the reason why, it is important to note that our findings with regard to the contextual issues were mostly limited to the experiences of African Americans, and failed to capture the experiences of Cape Verdean and Latino/a adolescents' unique experiences.

Future Directions

Future researchers may consider exploring this domain, and the person-in-context model developed herein, further. For example, the relationship between self-reliance and future aspirations found in this study suggests the need for an intervention strategy that would help urban adolescents cope with the individual and structural barriers identified by participants in this study. Also, the role of gender and racial/ethnic background on the development of future aspirations has not been fully identified in this study and warrants further exploration.

Finally, the manner in which youth give structure and process to their future aspirations, and the ways in which structure and process may be more fully articulated, are also areas for future study. Regardless, future study is needed to illuminate this area of inquiry and give voice to the future aspirations of urban youth and the influences upon them. Prior research on urban adolescents' perceptions of future indicate that urban adolescents, particularly African American students, espouse positive attitudes about their educational aspirations in the abstract while they are less likely than their White peers to believe that performing well in school will provide them with future opportunities such as attending college (Mickelson, 1990; Ogbu, 1991). Mickelson (1990) called this phenomenon the "achievement-attitude paradox," and showed that while many students in urban schools value education highly, they often do not perceive education as offering them concrete help in achieving their future goals.

Drawing on Bourdieu's (1985) concept of cultural capital, it is possible to conceive of urban schools as public institutions which have the potential of generating either positive (*i.e.*, by promoting the cultural capital valued in the broader society and by supporting the welfare of urban students) or negative (*i.e.*, by reproducing the marginality of urban students) cultural capital for their students. This suggests that higher incidence of failure among urban students as reported by the current statistics may be connected to both contextual barriers as represented by failing public schools in urban cities in the USA and the pessimism about future educational opportunities experienced by adolescents in those settings.

In the present study, we only illuminated the individual and contextual factors that influence urban adolescents perception of their future, but further research is needed to provide more insight into how these factors may actually contribute to urban adolescents' current school performance, both directly and indirectly. Our perspective is that it is important for all persons to reflect upon and come to understand their place within the social order (cf. Freire, 1973; 1993).

However, for people who experience oppression, such as urban youth, we believe this understanding to be particularly important in order to resist the oppressive social order that they experience. One relatively unexplored method of resistance is, paradoxically, through achievement and attainment within the very social order that is oppressive. That is, future aspirations, and coming to understand the influences upon them, may be a means by which urban youth may resist the "tracking" of the social order into low-paying/low-status jobs through future planning and educational/occupational achievement. In light of the impact of social and structural influences upon the future aspirations of the urban youth in this study, we believe it to be important, from a moral and pedagogical standpoint, to facilitate youths understanding of individual and contextual influence and to facilitate the formation of their future aspirations.

We hope that through the presentation of the participants' perspectives, and their reflections upon their worlds, readers may more fully understand the influences upon urban youths' future aspirations and ways in which the structure and process of future aspirations may be elaborated.

8

Montessori an System of Education

INTRODUCTION TO MONTESSORI SYSTEM

Montessori education is both a philosophy of child development and an approach to quality child development activity in schools. After learning and delivering training in the areas of medicine, psychology and anthropology, Dr. Maria Montessori developed a universal philosophy of education. The approach is fully based on actual observations of children and their behaviour and teaching accordingly. This special method stresses the importance of developing a healthy self-concept. Availability of resources, level of parents and pupil, their age levels, etc. are the key determinants of developing a good Montessori approach in schools. So, it may differ from school to school. The *Montessori Certified Teacher* is an important person in assisting each child by discovering and rewarding its inner resources. Montessori schools are increasing in number and Montessori Training and Development offers quality instructions to individuals desiring to be Montessori Administrators and Teachers.

These teachers assist students in achieving life-long, positive learning experiences through a child-focused concept of physical, psychological and social development by improving their sensory and creative skills. You, as a Montessori teacher, are a trained facilitator in the classroom. You should be always ready to facilitate, assist and personally perform many jobs. These jobs may include setting vision to construction, to effective implementation of a good classroom arrangement.

Each one of you will be regarded as an important person responsible for early childhood development. Your job is to provide with effective and adequate nurturing for child development. Your purpose is to stimulate the child's enthusiasm and interest for learning and to guide it. You will not interfere with the child's natural desire to teach self and become independent. Each child works through personalized cycle of activities, and learns to truly understand according to own unique needs and capabilities. The children pass through sensitive periods of development in early life. Dr. Montessori has described the child's mind between the time of birth and six years of age as the "absorbent mind". During this stage a child has a tremendous ability to learn and assimilate from the world around it. Such learning may happen without conscious efforts. During this stage, the children are particularly receptive to certain external stimuli. A Montessori teacher recognizes and takes advantage of these highly perceptive stages through the introduction and use of several child friendly materials and activities which are specially designed to stimulate the intellect, psychic and social strengths of the children. Encouraged to focus the attention on one particular quality, the child works at its own optimum level–in an environment where beauty and orderliness are emphasized and appreciated.

A spontaneous love of "work" is revealed as the child is given the freedom to make personal choices, but requires closer observation and support in times of felt need. Since long time, Psychology has recognized that our experiences in our formative years dictate in a great deal our adult behaviour in future. The opposite to the rude, selfish adult is the loved, respected child. A system of education that devotes itself to creating a safe, positive atmosphere in which children can learn, grow, achieve, succeed, and come to respect themselves and others is truly essential in this world. Montessori system provides children with such environment.

RELEVANCE OF MONTESSORI SYSTEM

The traditional model of education was designed to provide basic literacy skills and is content-centered. It involves direct instruction from the teacher. The teacher is an authority figure. This model emphasizes mastery of factual information, book-based learning, memorization of rules and isolated content areas.

The student's role is to be a passive receiver of the knowledge. Major role of the student is to listen, read and remember the things as they are written. Assessment is done by comparing a student's progress against that of his or her peers. Instruction takes place on the whole class level. Desks are typically arranged in rows and the teacher employs methods of discipline to manage the classroom conduct. The aim is to take 'an empty brain' and fill it with things we think it should know. Most of the schools and educational institutions in Nepal still provide traditional education. Some advances may have been made towards a progressive system of education but traditional model is still largely prevalent. The Montessori system of education is a progressive model that better prepares children for a successful life in the 21st century.

Researches from all around the world have shown that Montessori children show greater social and creative outcomes compared to that of the children taught traditional education, even while reaching to upper grades. Children who leave Montessori environment and go into traditional education environment are rated as more respectful compared to other students and teachers. They are found to be able to work more independently, demonstrate greater creativity with higher level of enthusiasm for learning. Characteristics such as the ability to improvise, anticipate, create or adapt, and attributes such as leadership and teamwork, citizenship, and the ability to live and work with others are highly evidential in Montessori learnt people. These are the skills that we need for the 21st century, and here, Montessori education will surely be seen as vastly superior to traditional models of education. All these highlight the universal relevance of Montessori system of child development and education.

INTRODUCING EDIFY INTERNATIONAL

Established with a noble vision to provide support for institutional transformation, *Edify International* specializes in Social Works, Government Studies, Research and Innovation, Professional Development, Institutional Development, Human Resource Systems Support, Indigenous Promotion, and Academic Excellence. Edify vision is to lead the way to a more trusted identity as a partner organization for institutional and professional transformation in the global marketplace.

The institution intends to gain the best rating of its service relevance, real-time creation, and quality execution with lasting impact. The institutional existence at Edify International has been witnessed as the synergy effect of global service relevance, proven management and technical competence, thematically tested and customised service packages, state-of-arts institutional operating environment, market readiness for professional and institutional transformation, and finally the visionary leadership for complete transformation. The entire mission is driven by a wider spectrum of highly relevant services. Service relevance, balance of universality of services, responsiveness and accountability, collaboration and partnerships, professionalism, focus on ethical values, institutional integrity, commitment for transformation, and service with lasting impact are the working philosophies of Edify International.

- *Service relevance:* The institution specializes in the development and delivery of globally relevant services in all contexts. The orientation on service customization stands for crafting each service component more contextually relevant under every setting. The institution strives for bringing every home country the internationally proven practices to leverage timely the systems transformation.
- *Balance of universality:* The services and management approach to delivery are uniquely tailored to make them truly universal and nonaligned in respect with nationality, ethnicity, gender, profession, ideology, and other similar constructs.
- *Responsiveness and accountability*: The institution always works for

noble causes and maintains full responsibility of what it needs to do with complete accountability of the consequences or outcomes of the contribution. The institution firmly values its role and prestige to resolve any institutional problem.

- *Collaboration and partnerships*: The institution firmly believes in promoting its service reach by means of collaborations and partnerships with the various providers in a more cost-effective and quality-efficient manner.
- *Professionalism:* Every service delivery is guided by the philosophy of professionalism and commitment for the compliance with every professional values and norms as part of edification, the Nobel Service.
- *Ethical values*: The institution is always concerned on creating and imparting services that comply with socio-ethical values and norms, and respect for cross-cultural diversity and ethnicity.
- *Institutional integrity*: Edify always attempts to strive for creating harmony among various institutions by means of institutional collaborations, partnerships, and service outsourcing.
- *Commitment for transformation:* Everything it reveals its stand on institutional transformation. For this, the institution vests efforts on professional and institutional development.
- *Service with lasting impact*: The services are designed such a way that the organizations and professionals can enjoy their continued impact in long-run after delivery. It is made possible by effectively modeling each service component meeting the requirements, educating effectively the roles and responsibilities of each participant, and confirming the transfer of each skill or concept on real business.

Dr Chandra P. Rijal, an emerging management thinkers, provides overall institutional stewardship with his direct involvement in short-term and long-term planning, business development and maintaining institutional relationship. Edify International, Edify Foundation Nepal and Edify International School are the creations as a result of Dr. Rijal's vision on research and innovation, institutional and professional development. Dr. Rijal is also the single author of *Leadership Readiness: Road to TQM Implementation*–a Germany-based publication.

OBJECTIVES OF THE TRAINING PROGRAMME

GENERAL OBJECTIVES

- Develop an increased awareness of self-learning attitude towards the Montessori System.
- Understand the nature and nurture-related aspects of child development

- Learn the growth patterns and stages of child development
- Understand the learning and developmental needs of the children.
- Learn the philosophy and principles of child development formulated by Maria Montessori and other leading experts.
- Learn the areas of development and learning at Montessori system.
- Learn to develop, detail and implement Montessori system curriculum for different levels.
- Gain skills in development, presentation, and use of materials as advised by Maria Montessori.
- Understand the criteria by which self-teaching is evaluated.
- Learn to set and implement criteria for the measurement of the development and learning performance of Montessori children at different levels.
- Learn to prepare teaching manuals appropriate for different levels.
- Make a vision of classroom management and transform it in to reality.
- Learn about behavioural and psychological counseling of the teachers, parents and children.
- Learn to facilitate parenting education.
- Demonstrate proficiency in all aspects of the Montessori approach to education and life.

PARTICIPANT SPECIFIC OBJECTIVES

- *Montessori Administrators*: Develop leadership and management skills that enable themselves to actively and successfully administer Montessori institutions/schools.
- *Montessori Trainers*: Deepen the understanding of the ideas and principles of Dr. Maria Montessori and develop necessary skills to pass the knowledge gained to future generations of Montessori teachers.
- *Montessori Teacher*: Develop knowledge, skills and expertise that enable them to create a well-prepared environment and an atmosphere of learning and inquisitiveness.
- *Public Schools*: Incorporate Montessori system of learning and curriculum into the ECD education that has been implemented in pre-primary schooling in Nepal.
- *Private Schools/Montessori Centers*: Incorporate Montessori system of learning and curriculum into their pre-primary and/or Kindergarten curriculum.

EDIFY APPROACH OF TRAINING ON MONTESSORI SYSTEM

The training programme will include seminars, workshops, case studies, simulations, fun games, practical demonstrations, project works with simplified language and participant involvement. On top of it, as suggested, harmonize your learning through imparting on you a self-learning concept on bring in the philosophies of customer focus, total participation, system standardization, continuous improvement, leadership commitment and gaining macro and micro systems support in the mission to implement Montessori approach-based institution development, teaching learning and system audit.

CURRICULUM OF EDIFY MONTESSORI SYSTEM TRAINING PROGRAMME

- Learn the Foundations of Montessori System:
  - Learn the stages of child development
  - Explore the nature and nurturing aspects of child development
  - Understand the child psychology and process of its development
  - Learn the relevance of Montessori philosophy, principles and practices in action
  - Develop in self the basic qualities required as a Montessori Teacher
  - Develop skill competence of learning through enquiry, real-life contexts and exploration
  - Develop positive attitude towards people, environment and learning
  - Learn and apply basic behavioural and psychological counseling to facilitate Montessori system implementation
  - Learn and practice emerging approaches in early childhood development and education
- Learn the Montessori System Teaching Learning Areas, Development and Implementation of Child Development and Learning Approaches and Materials at Different Levels:
  - Practical life skills
  - Sensorial skills
  - Mathematical skills
  - Language skills
  - Science and construction skills
  - Socio-cultural skills
  - Creative art and craft work skills
  - Outdoor activities
- Manage the Classroom and Learning Areas in Montessori System:
  - Make a vision of the classroom and develop a blueprint of it
  - Perform situational analysis

  - Conduct classroom and center resource audit
  - Develop a layout of the room and its redesign
  - Organize the areas for specific subjects sensorial, socio-cultural, mathematics, language, practical life, science, art and craftwork; creating an inspiring classroom on a budget
  - Take into consideration the child health, hygiene and other quality measures of classroom arrangements
  - Inspire and motivate pupil to learn by making classroom more appealing and visible
  - Take into account the management of work plans
  - Initiate positive change in classroom arrangements as an ongoing process
- Sett Monitoring, Evaluation and Performance Measurement Criteria at Montessori System:
  - Establish and promote a collective monitoring system
  - Set criteria to measure the development and learning performance of the children
  - Set a descriptive summary of child's daily interactions
  - Set observation and recording mechanism on child performance at individual and group level
  - Develop and implement the portfolio of child's individual and group creations
  - Perform individual assessment of the child through observation
- Provide Parenting Education for Montessori Parents:
  - Establish the areas of parents involvement in child development and learning
  - Provide orientation and demonstration sessions to the parents
  - Perform routine counseling and development of the parents

Acceptance into the Montessori Training and Development programme is based on evaluation of the application packet, previous academic record and a personal interview. The educational standard for the course is an intermediate degree in any field.

Exceptions are considered on an individual basis. Successful candidates should demonstrate

- Pleasing, fair and peaceful personality
- Possessing good health and hygiene practices
- Clear oral and written communication skills
- Child-loving nature
- Academic skills for effective comprehension
- Passionate for rigorous creative and craftworks involvement
- Positive attitude on socialization and child entertainment

- Well-organized, punctual, honest and committed for child development
- Effective team management and peer work skills
- Able to manage time and resources more effectively
- Commitment to undertake this training as an alternative education
- Full of desire to support human development in positive and life-affirming directions

CONCEPT OF NURSERY EDUCATION

Preschool education or Infant education is the provision of education for children before the commencement of statutory and obligatory education, usually between the ages of zero and three or five, depending on the jurisdiction. In British English, nursery school or simply "nursery" or playgroup is the usual term for preschool education, although the term preschool is also commonly used. In the United States preschool and Pre-K are used, while "nursery school" is an older term. Preschool work is organized within a framework that professional educators create. The framework includes structural, process and alignment components that are associated with each individual unique child that has both social and academic outcomes. At each age band, an appropriate curriculum should be followed. For example, it would be normal to teach a child how to count to 10 after the age of four. Arguably the first pre-school institution was opened in 1816 by Robert Owen in New Lanark, Scotland. The Hungarian countess Theresa Brunszvik followed in 1828. In 1837, Friedrich Fröbel opened one in Germany, coining the term "kindergarten".

DEVELOPMENTAL AREAS

The areas of development which preschool education covers varies from country to country. However,

The following main themes are represented in the majority of systems.

- Personal, social, economical, and emotional development
- Communication, including sign language, talking and listening
- Knowledge and understanding of the world
- Creative and aesthetic development
- Educational software
- Mathematical awareness and development
- Physical development
- Physical health
- Playing
- Teamwork
- Self-help skills
- Social skills
- Scientific thinking
- Creative arts
- Literacy

Allowing preschool aged children to discover and explore freely within each of these areas of development is the foundation for developmental learning. While the National Association for the Education of Young Children and the National Association of Child Care Professionals have made tremendous strides in publicizing and promoting the idea of developmentally appropriate practice, there is still much work to be done.

It is widely recognized that although many preschool educators are aware of the guidelines for developmentally appropriate practice, putting this practice to work effectively in the classroom is more challenging. The NAEYC published that although 80 per cent of Kindergarten classrooms claim to be developmentally appropriate, only 20 per cent actually are.

AGE AND IMPORTANCE

It is well established that the most important years of learning are begun at birth. A child's brain at this age is making connections that will last the rest of their life. During these early years, a human being is capable of absorbing more information at a time than they will ever be able to again. The environment of the young child influences the development of cognitive skills and emotional skills due to the rapid brain growth that occurs in the early years.

Studies have shown that high quality/ or any high rated preschools have a long term effect in improving the outcomes of a child, especially a disadvantaged child.

However, some more recent studies dispute the accuracy of the earlier results which cited benefits to preschool education, and actually point at preschool being detrimental to a child's cognitive and social development. A study by UC Berkeley and Stanford University on 14,000 Kindergarteners revealed that while there is a temporary cognitive boost in pre-reading and math, preschool holds detrimental effects on social development and cooperation. The Universal Preschool movement is an international effort to make access to preschool available to families in a similar way to compulsory primary education.

Various jurisdictions and advocates have differing priorities for access, availability and funding sources. There has been a shift from preschools that operated primarily as controlled play groups to educational settings in which children learn specific, if basic, skills. It examines several different perspectives on teaching in kindergarten, including those of the developmentally appropriate practice, the academic approach, the child-centered approach, and the Montessori approach to the curriculum.

GRATUITY

The gratuity of infant education has been established in some countries, as Spain, beginning in the second cycle but extending to the first cycle.

FUNDING FOR PRESCHOOL PROGRAMMES

While a majority of American preschool programmes remain tuition-based, support for some public funding of early childhood education has grown over the years. As of 2008, 38 states and the District of Columbia invested in at least some pre-kindergarten programmes, and many school districts were providing preschool services on their own, using local and federal funds.

The benefits and challenges of a public preschool are closely tied to the amount of funding provided. Funding for a public preschool can come in a variety of sources. According to Levin and Schwartz funding can range from federal, state, local public allocations, private sources, and parental fees. The problem of funding a public preschool occurs not only from limited sources but from the cost per child. The average cost across the 48 states is $6,582. There are four categories that determine the costs of public preschools: personnel ratios, personnel qualifications, facilities and transportation, and health and nutrition services.

According to Levin and Schwartz these structural elements depend heavily on the cost and quality of services provided. The main personnel factor related to cost is the qualifications each preschool require for a teacher. Another determinate of cost is the length of a preschool day. The longer the session, the more increase in cost. Therefore, the quality of programme accounts presumably for a major component of cost. Collaboration has been a solution for funding issues in several districts. Wilma Kaplan, principal, turned to collaborating with the area Head Start and other private preschool to fund a public preschool in her district.

"We're very pleased with the interaction. It's really added a dimension to our programme that's been very positive". The National Head Start Bureau has been looking for more opportunities to partner with public schools. Torn Schultz of the National Head Start Bureau states, "We're turning to partnership as much as possible, either in funds or facilities to make sure children get everything necessary to be ready for school". The goal for funding is to develop a variety of sources that provide for all children to benefit from early learning within a public preschool.

SPECIAL EDUCATION IN PRESCHOOL

In the United States, students who may benefit from special education receive services in preschools. Since the inception of the Individuals with Disabilities Education Act Public Law 101-476 in 1975 and its amendments, PL 102-119 and PL 105-17 in 1997, the educational system has moved away from self-contained classrooms and progressed to inclusion.

As a result, there has been a need for special education teachers to practice in various settings in order to assist children with special needs, particularly by working with regular classroom teachers when possible to strengthen the inclusion of children with special needs. As with other stages in the life of a child with special needs, the Individualized Education Plan or an Individual Family Service Plan is an important way for special education teachers, regular classroom teachers, administrators and parents to set guidelines for a partnership to help the child succeed in preschool.

9

Frocbelian System of Education

CONCEPT OF KINDERGARTEN

Kindergarten (German, literally meaning "garden for children" or "childer-garden"), is the word created by Friedrich Fröbel for the Play and Activity institute that he created in 1837 in Bad Blankenburg as a social experience for children for their transition from home to school. Kindergarten is used around the world to describe a range of different experiences that have been developed for children at this developmental stage. Many of the activities developed by Friedrich Fröbel are also used around the world under other names.

Singing and growing plants have become an integral part of life long learning. Activity, experience and social interaction are now widely accepted as essential aspects of developing skills and knowledge. In most countries, kindergarten is part of the preschool system of early childhood education. Children usually attend kindergarten any time between the ages of two and seven years, depending on the local custom. In the United States and anglophone Canada, as well as in parts of Australia, such as New South Wales, Tasmania and the Australian Capital Territory, *kindergarten* is the word often restricted in use to describe the first year of education in a primary or elementary school.

In some of these countries, it is compulsory; that is, parents must send children to their kindergarten year. In the United States, many states widely offer a free kindergarten year to children of five to six years of age, but do not make it compulsory, while other states require all five-year-olds to enroll. The terms preschool or less often, "Pre-K", are used to refer to a school for children who are not old enough to attend kindergarten.

Also, some U.S. school districts provide a half day or full day kindergarten at the parents' election. In British English, nursery or playgroup is the usual term for preschool education, and *kindergarten* is rarely used, except in the context of special approaches to education, such as Steiner-Waldorf education.

PURPOSE

Children attend kindergarten to learn to communicate, play, and interact with others appropriately. A teacher provides various materials and activities to motivate these children to learn the language and vocabulary of reading, mathematics, and science, as well as that of music, art, and social behaviours. For children who previously have spent most of their time at home, kindergarten may serve the purpose of helping them adjust to being apart from their parents without anxiety.

It may be their first opportunity to play and interact with a consistent group of children on a regular basis. Kindergarten may also allow mothers, fathers, or other caregivers to go back to part-time or full-time employment.

HISTORY

In an age when school was restricted to children who had learned to read and write at home, there were many attempts to make school accessible to the children of women who worked in factories. In Scotland in 1816, Robert Owen, a philosopher and pedagogue, opened an infant school in New Lanark. Another was opened by Samuel Wilderspin in London in 1819. Countess Theresa Brunszvik was influenced by this example to open an *Angyalkert* on May 27, 1828 in her residence in the city of Buda. This concept became popular among the nobility and the middle class and was copied throughout the Hungarian kingdom.

Friedrich Fröbel opened a *Play and Activity* institute in 1837 in the village of Bad Blankenburg in principality of Schwarzburg-Rudolstadt, Thuringia, which he renamed Kindergarten on June 28, 1840 to mark the four-hundredth anniversary of Gutenberg's invention of movable type.

The women trained by Fröbel opened Kindergartens throughout Europe and around the World. The first kindergarten in the United States founded in Watertown, Wisconsin, by Margarethe Meyer-Schurz in 1856 was conduted in German.

Her sister had founded the first kindergarten in London, England. In 1860, Elizabeth Peabody founded the first English-language kindergarten in America in Boston, after visiting Watertown and travelling to Europe. The first free kindergarten in America was founded in 1870 by Conrad Poppenhusen, a German industrialist and philanthropist who settled in College Point, NY, where he established the Poppenhusen Institute, still in existence today. The first publicly financed kindergarten in the United States was established in St. Louis in 1873 by Susan Blow.

Elizabeth Harrison wrote extensively on the theory of early childhood education and worked to enhance educational standards for kindergarten teachers by establishing what became the National College of Education in 1886. Montisori, Steiner and most recently the Reggio Emilia approach are part of the rich an evolving tradition of child centered, activity based learning that has been nurtured around the world though the kindergarten movement.

AIMS AND CONTENT IN KINDERGARTEN SYSTEM

AFGHANISTAN

In Afghanistan, the equivalent term to kindergarten is pronounced as *kudakistan* and is not part of the actual school system. Children between the age of 3 and 6 attend kindergartens, which are often run by the government. According to law, every government office must have a kindergarten area within it.

Early Childhood Education in Afghanistan

Early childhood development programmes address the needs and development of young children from birth to 6 years of age, their families, and their communities. They are multidimensional and designed to support children's health, nutritional, cognitive, social, and emotional abilities, enabling them to survive and thrive in later years. Reflecting cultural values, they must be deeply rooted within families and communities, blending what are known about environments that enhance optimal child development with an understanding of traditional child-rearing practices that support and/or curtail a child's development.

The goal of the ECD strategy is to help families ensure that their children reach school age, not only healthy and well nourished, but intellectually curious, socially confident, and equipped with a solid foundation for lifelong learning. Develop and implement programmes to provide better start in lives to younger age children before their schools as well as to support school-age children who are out of school and missed their schooling by providing them Non-formal Education and vocational training.

Background

ECD programmes have a relatively short history in Afghanistan. They were first introduced during the Soviet occupation with the establishment in 1980 of 27 urban preschools, or kodakistan. The number of preschools grew steadily during the 1980s, reaching a high of more than 270 by 1990, with 2,300 teachers caring for more than 21,000 children.

These facilities were an urban phenomenon, mostly in Kabul, and were attached to schools, government offices, or factories. Based on the Soviet model, they provided nursery care, preschool, and kindergarten for children from 3 months to 6 years of age under the direction of the Department of Labour and Social Welfare. The vast majority of Afghan families were never exposed to this system, and most of those who were never fully accepted it because it diminished the central role of the family and inculcated children with Soviet values. With the onset of civil war after the Soviet withdrawal, the number of kindergartens dropped rapidly. By 1995, only 88 functioning facilities serving 2,110 children survived, and the Taliban restrictions on female employment eliminated all of the remaining centers in areas under their control. At present, no programmes of any size exist, facilities have been destroyed, and trained personnel are lacking. In 2007, there are about 260 Kindergarten offering early year's stimulation to over 25000 children.

It is estimated that 2.5 million Afghan children are less than 6 years of age. A range of both biological and environmental risk factors act synergistically to exert a powerful negative influence on the growth and development of the Afghan child. A mix of religious and tribal customs and beliefs permeates Afghan society, with kinship substituting for government in most areas. Communities are traditionally closely knit with a strong emphasis on the extended family. Roles are clearly defined and central to the social order. Decades of war, massive displacement, and changing power structures caused the collapse of community-support networks and the erosion of the extended family—one of the most basic traditional coping mechanisms. Large numbers of women are widowed and have had to assume unaccustomed and nontraditional roles as family breadwinners.

One quarter of all children die before the age of 5 as a result of birth trauma, neonatal tetanus diarrhea, pneumonia, and vaccine-preventable diseases. Iron-deficiency anemia is widespread, affecting half to two thirds of children under 5 years of age. Large numbers of children are chronically malnourished; 45–59 per cent show high levels of stunting. Malnutrition half of all girls marry before the age of 18, and many soon after adolescence. Confronted with these interlocking threats to development, children arrive at school unable to take advantage of learning opportunities. It is not surprising that dropout rates are high. Figures from 1999 show that one in four children dropped out of school in grade 2 and almost one in two in grades 3 and 4. In addition to the child's physical and health status, other factors contributing to high dropout rates are family issues and competing priorities for the child's time, irregular teacher attendance, subject irrelevance, and poor quality of teaching.

At present, no policies deal with early childhood and no institutions have either the responsibility or the capacity to provide such services. In the past, the Ministry of Labour and Social Affairs was accountable for kindergartens, nurseries, and crèches, while orphanages fell within the purview of MOE. At present, the Ministries of Education, Labour and Social Affairs, and Women's Affairs have expressed an interest in overseeing the early childhood sector. As the Government continues to define and restructure ministerial responsibilities, the strengths and limitations of various options, including an inter-ministerial coordination agency, should be carefully considered. While formal structures do not exist, it is not clear whether any informal childcare arrangements exist at the community level other than those provided by family members. As women enter the work force, it is likely that a market for private preschool services will emerge in urban areas.

AUSTRALIA AND NEW ZEALAND

In each state of Australia, *kindergarten* means something slightly different. In Tasmania, New South Wales and the Australian Capital Territory, it is the first year of primary school. In Victoria, kindergarten is a form of preschool and may be referred to interchangeably as preschool or kindergarten. In Victoria the phrase for the first year of primary school is called *Prep*, although in Tasmania 'Prep' refers to the year after kindergarten and before grade 1. In Queensland, kindergarten is usually an institution for children around the age of 4 and thus it is the precursor to preschool and primary education. The year preceding the first year of primary school education in Western Australia, South Australia or the Northern Territory is referred to respectively as *pre-primary, reception* or *transition*. In New Zealand, kindergarten refers to the 2 years preceding primary school, from age 3 to 4. Primary Education starts at age 5.

CANADA

In Ontario there are two grades of kindergarten: junior kindergarten and senior kindergarten. Junior kindergarten begins for children in the calendar year in which they turn four years old. Both kindergarten grades are typically run on a half-day or every-other-day schedule though full day Monday to Friday kindergarten is being introduced. In Ontario, both the senior and junior kindergarten programmes, also called the "Early Years", are optional programmes. Mandatory schooling begins in Grade One.

Within the province of Quebec, junior kindergarten is called *prématernelle* is attended by 4 years olds, and senior kindergarten is called *maternelle,* mandatory by the age of 5, this class is integrated into primary schools. Within the French school system in the province of Ontario, junior kindergarten and senior kindergarten are called *maternelle* and senior kindergarten is sometimes called *jardin d'enfants,* which is a calque of the German word *Kindergarten*. In Western Canada and in Newfoundland and Labrador, there is only one year of kindergarten. After that year, the child begins grade one. The province of Nova Scotia refers to Kindergarten as Primary.

CHINA

In China, the equivalent term to kindergarten is *yòu ér yuán*. The children start attending kindergarten at the age of 2 until they are at least 6 years old. The kindergartens in China generally have the following grades: 1. Nursery/ Playgroup: 2–3 years old children 2. Lower Kindergarten/ LKG: 3–4 years old children 3. Upper Kindergarten/ UKG: 4–5 years old children 4. Preschool: 5–6 years old children. Some kindergartens may not have preschool.

DENMARK

Kindergarten is a day-care service offered to children from age three until the child starts attending school. Kindergarten classes are voluntary and are offered by primary schools before a child enters 1st grade. Two-thirds of established day-care institutions in Denmark are municipal day-care centres while the other third are privately owned and are run by associations of parents or businesses in agreement with local authorities. In terms of both finances and subject-matter, municipal and private institutions function according to the same principles. Denmark is credited with pioneering forest kindergartens, in which children spend most of every day outside in a natural environment.

FRANCE

In France, pre-school is known as *école maternelle*. Municipality-run, free *maternelle* schools are available throughout the country, welcoming children aged from 2 to 5. The ages are divided into *Grande part, Moyenne part, Petite part* and *Toute petite part*. It is not compulsory, yet almost 100 per cent of children aged 3 to 5 attend. It is regulated by the municipalities.

GERMANY

The German preschool is known as a *Kindergarten* or *Kita,* short for *Kindertagesstätte*. Children between the ages of 3 and 6 attend *Kindergärten,* which are not part of the school system. They are often run by city or town administrations, churches, or registered societies, many of which follow a certain educational approach as represented, *e.g.,* by Montessori or Reggio Emilia or "Berliner Bildungsprogramm", etc. Forest kindergartens are well established. Attending a *Kindergarten* is neither mandatory nor free of charge, but can be partly or wholly funded, depending on the local authority and the income of the parents. All caretakers in Kita or Kindergarten must have a three year qualified education, or are under special supervision during training.

Kindergärten can be open from 7 a.m. to 5 p.m. or longer and may also house a *Kinderkrippe,* meaning crèche, for children between the ages of eight weeks and three years, and possibly an afternoon *Hort* for school-age children aged 6 to 10 who spend the time after their lessons there. Alongside nurseries, there are day-care nurses working independently from any pre-school institution in individual homes and looking after only three to five children typically up to three years of age. These nurses are supported and supervised by local authorities. The term *Vorschule,* meaning 'pre-school', is used both for educational efforts in *Kindergärten* and for a mandatory class that is usually connected to a primary school. Both systems are handled differently in each German state. The *Schulkindergarten* is a type of Vorschule.

INDIA

In India, pre-school is divided into three stages - Playgroup, Junior Kindergarten (Jr. KG) or Lower Kindergarten (LKG) and Senior Kindergarten (Sr. KG) or Upper Kindergarten (UKG). Typically, a Playgroup consists of children of age group from one and half to two and half years. Jr. KG class would comprise children three and half to four and half years of age, and the Sr. KG class would comprise children four and half to five and half years of age.

The kindergarten is a place where young children learn as they play with materials and cope up to live with other children and teachers. It is also a place where adults can learn; they observe children and participate with them. It can serve as a laboratory for the study of human relations. The value of Kindergarten as a laboratory for studying about people will depend, in part, on the opportunities children may have there for play and for relationships with others.

The main objectives of kindergarten school are:

- To develop a good physique, adequate muscular co-ordination and basic motor skill in the child.
- To develop good health habits and to build up basic skills necessary for personal adjustments such as dressing themselves, toilet and eating habits.
- To develop emotional maturity by guiding the child to express, understand, accept and control his feelings and emotions.
- To develop good desirable social attitudes, manners and to encourage healthy group participation.
- To encourage aesthetic appreciation
- To stimulate the child's beginning of intellectual curiosities concerning his immediate environment.
- To encourage the child's independence and creativity by providing him with sufficient opportunities.

"The school is an opportunity for progress of the student. Each one is having the freedom to develop freely." In most cases the pre-school is run as a private school. Younger children may also be put into a special toddler/ nursery group at the age of 2. It is run as part of the kindergarten. After finishing Senior kindergarten, a child enters Class 1 or Standard 1 of primary school. Often kindergarten is an integral part of regular schools, though sometimes they are independent units and are often part of a larger chain.

ISRAEL

In Israel, there are 2 streams, private commercial and state funded.

Attendance in kindergarten is compulsory from the age of 5 years. Private kindergartens are supervised by the Ministry of Education and cater for children from 3 months to 5 years. State kindergartens are run by qualified kindergarten teachers who undergo a 4 year training. They cater for children from 3 to 6 years in three age groups; ages 3–4, 4-5, 5-6. At the conclusion of the Hova year the child will either begin primary school or will repeat the Hova year, if not deemed psychologically and cognitively ready for primary school.

JAPAN

Early childhood education begins at home, and there are numerous books and television shows aimed at helping mothers and fathers of preschool children to educate their children and to parent more effectively. Much of the home training is devoted to teaching manners, proper social behaviour, and structured play, although verbal and number skills are also popular themes. Parents are strongly committed to early education and frequently enroll their children in preschools.

Kindergartens, predominantly staffed by young female junior college graduates, are supervised by the Ministry of Education, but are not part of the official education system. The 58 per cent of kindergartens that are private accounted for 77 per cent of all children enrolled. In addition to kindergartens there exists a well-developed system of government-supervised day-care centers, supervised by the Ministry of Labour. Whereas kindergartens follow educational aims, preschools are predominately concerned with providing care for infants and toddlers.

Just as there are public and private kindergartens, there are both public and privately run preschools. Together, these two kinds of institutions enroll well over 90 per cent of all preschool-age children prior to their entrance into the formal system at first grade. The Ministry of Education's 1990 Course of Study for Preschools, which applies to both kinds of institutions, covers such areas as human relationships, health, environment, words and expression. Starting from March 2008 the new revision of curriculum guidelines for kindergartens as well as for preschools came into effect.

SOUTH KOREA

In South Korea, children normally attend kindergarten between the ages of three or four and six or seven in the Western age system. The school year begins in March. It is followed by primary school. Normally the kindergartens are graded on a three-tier basis. They are called "Yuchi won" Korean kindergartens are private schools. Costs per month vary. Korean parents often send their children to English kindergartens to give them a head start in English. Such specialized kindergartens can be mostly taught in Korean with some English lessons, mostly taught in English with some Korean lessons, or completely taught in English. Almost all middle-class parents send their children to kindergarten. Kindergarten programmes in South Korea attempt to incorporate much academic instruction alongside more playful activities. Korean kindergarteners learn to read, write and do simple arithmetic. Classes are conducted in a traditional classroom setting, with the children focused on the teacher and one lesson or activity at a time. The goal of the teacher is to overcome weak points in each child's knowledge or skills.

Because the education system in Korea is very competitive, kindergartens are becoming more intensely academic nowadays. Children are pushed to read and write at a very young age. They also become accustomed to regular and considerable amounts of homework. These very young children may also attend other specialized afternoon schools, taking lessons in art, piano or violin, taekwondo, ballet, soccer or mathematics. In North Korea, children attend kindergarten between the ages of four and five. Kindergartens are divided among the upper class and lower class, where upper-class kindergartens are completely educational, and lower class have little education.

MEXICO

In Mexico, kindergarten is called "kindergarden" or "kínder," with the last year sometimes referred to as "preprimaria". It consists of three years of pre-school education, which are mandatory before elementary school. Previous nursery is optional, and may be offered in either private schools or public schools.

At private schools, kinders usually consist of three grades, and a fourth one may be added for nursery. The fourth one is called maternal. It goes before the other three years and is not obligatory. While the first grade is a playgroup, the other two are of classroom education. The kindergarten system in Mexico was developed by professor Rosaura Zapata, who received the country's highest honour for that contribution.

In 2002, the Congress of the Union approved the *Law of Obligatory Pre-schooling,* which already made pre-school education for three to six-year-olds obligatory, and placed it under the auspices of the federal and state ministries of education.

NEPAL

In Nepal, kindergarten is simply known as "kindergarten". Kindergarten is run as a private education institution and all the privately run educational instituitions are in English medium. So, kindergarten education is also in English medium in Nepal. The children start attending kindergarten at the age of 2 until they are at least 5 years old. The kindergartens in Nepal have following grades: 1. Nursery/ Playgroup: 2–3 years old children 2. Lower Kindergarten/ LKG: 3–4 years old children 3. Upper Kindergarten/ UKG: 4–5 years old children The kindergarten education in Nepal is almost similar to that of Hong Kong and India. All the books in private education institution are in English except one compulsory Nepali. Children are trained perfectly in Nepalese kindergartens.

NETHERLANDS

In The Netherlands, the equivalent term to kindergarten is *kleuterschool.* From the mid-19th century to the mid-20th century the term *Fröbelschool* was also common, after Friedrich Fröbel. However this term gradually faded in use as the verb *Fröbelen* gained a slight derogatory meaning in everyday language. Until 1985, it used to be a separate non-compulsory form of education after which children attended the primary school. After 1985, both forms were integrated into one, called *basisonderwijs*. The country also offers both private and subsidized daycares, which are non compulsory, but nevertheless very popular.

PHILIPPINES

In the Philippines, education officially starts at the Elementary level and placing children into early childhood education through kindergarten is optional to parents. *Early Childhood Education in the Philippines are classified into:*

- Center-based programmes, such as the Barangay day care service, public and private pre-schools, kindergarten or school-based programmes, community or church-based early childhood education programmes initiated by nongovernment organizations or people's organizations, workplace-related child care and education programmes, child-minding centers, health centers and stations; and
- Home-based programmes, such as the neighbourhood-based play groups, family day care programmes, parent education and home visiting programmes.

Early childhood education is strengthened through the creation of Republic Act No. 8980 or the Early Childhood Care and Development Act of 2000.

ROMANIA

In Romania, *grădiniþă,* which means "little garden" is the favoured form of education for preschool children. The children are divided in "little group", "medium group" and "big group". In the last few years, private kindergartens have become popular, supplementing the state preschool education system.

UNITED KINGDOM

The term kindergarten is rarely used in Britain to describe pre-school education; pre-schools are usually known as nursery schools or playgroups. However, the word "kindergarten" is used for more specialist organisations such as forest kindergartens, and is sometimes used in the naming of private nurseries that provide full-day child care for working parents. In the UK children have the option of attending nursery at the ages of three or four years, before compulsory education begins. Before that, less structured childcare is available privately.

Some nurseries are attached to state infant or primary schools, but many are provided by the private sector. The government provides funding so that all children from the age of three until they start compulsory school, can receive five sessions per week of two and a half hours each, either in state-run or private nurseries. Working parents can also spend £55 per week free of income taxes, which is typically enough to pay for one or two days per week. The Scottish Government defines its requirements of nursery schools in the Early Years Framework and the Curriculum for Excellence. Each school interprets these with more or less independence but must satisfy the Care Commission in order to retain their licence to operate.

The curriculum aims to develop:

- Successful Learners
- Confident Individuals
- Responsible Citizens
- Effective Contributors

Nursery forms part of the Foundation Stage of education. In the 1980s England and Wales officially adopted the Northern Irish system whereby children start school either in the term or year in which they will become five depending on the policy of the Local Education Authority. In Scotland, schooling becomes compulsory between the ages of 4½ and 5½ years, depending on their birthday. The first year of compulsory schooling is known as Reception in England, *Dosbarth Derbyn* in Welsh and Primary One in Scotland and Northern Ireland.

10

Fundamentals' Right to Education in India

INTRODUCTION

India is a signatory to three key international instruments that guarantee the right to elementary education – Universal Declaration of Human Rights, 1948, the International Covenant on Economic, Social and Cultural Rights, 1966 and the Convention on the Rights of the Child, 1989. The Indian State was also proud to join, albeit after 52 years of independence, the host of countries that provide for a constitutional guarantee to free and compulsory education. Historically, there has been a demand for a law on FCE in India and there have been several aborted Central-level legislative attempts towards this end.

The last of such aborted attempts came in 2005–2006, *i.e.,* the draft prepared by the Central Advisory Board of Education namely the Right to Education Bill, 2005. The chief opposition to this Bill came from private unaided schools that lobbied against a provision in the Bill that required a 25 per cent reservation for poor children in private unaided schools. The opposition was so virulent that the Bill was modified to drop this provision. Subsequently, this altered version was circulated to all the States as a Model Bill for them to follow.

The provision for reservation in private unaided schools is certainly laudatory and plays a crucial role in bridging the gap between private and public schools. However, one should also acknowledge that in order to strengthen the campaign against inequitable schooling, the first step is to prioritise and strengthen government schools across the country. The problem of education today is largely attributable to a complete loss of faith in the quality of existing government schools.

Therefore, purely with a view to achieving a strategic interim victory in people's struggle for the implementation of the right to FCE, the crisis of public schools and the problem of 'public versus private schools' may have to be temporarily separated. This would ensure that the private schools' lobby does not derail the entire process of legislating. To this end, legislations for FCE should be divided into two stages. First, any legislation for FCE should be limited to addressing issues pertaining to public schools, *i.e.*, government schools. At a later stage, the first law should be supplemented by another that addresses private schools and the problems of inequality created by 'public versus private' schools.

Therefore, all issues raised in this study should be first debated and threshed out in the context of public schools in order to build a very strong, clear policy regarding public schools across India. However, it should be noted that these issues are also relevant in the context of private schools. In the context of elementary education, the phrase 'rights-based' is bandied about by policymakers and civil society alike with very little enquiry into its meaning, content and the implication of using it.

What does a rights-based model of elementary education entail? Why is there a demand or need for Central-level legislation for education? Can such a need be justified using the law? How do existing State-level legislations on elementary education fare in a 'rights-based' assessment? This document explores these issues and presents a concrete legal case for a Central level skeletal umbrella legislation giving effect to the Constitutional guarantee of FCE.

In exploring the issues, the reader is cautioned that this study does not seek to provide an exhaustive rights-based framework. Instead, it is an effort to raise issues for a national debate on a rights-based model of elementary education and does not seek to provide conclusive answers to all the problems faced by the current system of elementary education. While the writers acknowledge that a strong budgetary commitment is important to realise the right to education, the study itself does not examine budgetary allocations required for universalisation of elementary education.

It is once again reiterated that this study merely seeks to identify some core non-negotiable minimum norms and provisions that form the backbone of a rights-based approach to education. In attempting to discuss these aspects, the document does not provide a descriptive narrative or critique of all policies and schemes of the Central and State Governments.

EN ROUTE TO A FUNDAMENTAL RIGHT TO EDUCATION IN INDIA

THE DEMAND FOR FREE AND COMPULSORY EDUCATION IN THE PRE-CONSTITUTION ERA

There is disagreement amongst scholars regarding the origin and nature of the education system in ancient India. Some of them hold the view that it is difficult to speak of ancient Indian education with certainty, as our information is based on the documents of 'unequal value and unequal date.' Nevertheless, it may be stated that education in India has been notorious for not being socially inclusive. Till the 19th century, it was largely considered a privilege restricted to persons at the higher end of the caste or class system. History is replete with examples of caste, class and gender-based discrimination in imparting education. Education was the sole privilege of the priestly castes primarily because of the religious basis for the content of education, coupled with the elitist medium of instruction that was chose to impart the knowledge. Admission to Gurukulas or Ashramas was not open to all. People from lower castes, and so-called 'shudras', in particular, were barred from receiving education. Buddhism and Jainism overthrew the dominance of classical Vedic education by the end of the eighth century A.D, forcing education beyond the confines of hermitages. Thereafter, several learned Brahmins started Pathasalas in important towns where they received patronage.

The Muslim rulers of the Indian sub-continent also did not consider education as a function of the State. It was perceived as a branch of religion and therefore entrusted to learned theologians called 'Ulemas'. Therefore, in ancient and medieval India, education was intertwined with religion. From the location of Gurukulas to excluding sections of the society from accessing education, the system of education was clearly not accessible to all persons. The discovery of the sea route to India, in 1498, influenced the course of development of education in the Indian sub-continent. Although many scholars have commended the British policy of introducing modern education, it was not a spontaneous benevolent act.

The progress in education was facilitated with a view to serving their vested interests, *i.e.*, to train Indians as clerks, managers and other subordinate workers to staff their vast politicoadministrative machinery. However, education of the 'Indian masses' was largely neglected, and by the beginning of nineteenth century, it was in shambles. For instance, while reporting about the situation of education in Bellary (presently in the State of Karnataka) in the early nineteenth century, Campbell, the then District Collector observed that 'it cannot have escaped the government that of nearly a million of souls in this district, not 7000 are now at school ... In many villages where formerly there were schools, there are now none.'

In support of this, a missionary notice of 1856 stated that in all other parts of the country 'a school, either government or missionary is as rare as a lighthouse on our coast ... three or four schools existing among three or four million of people.' The neglect of education by the British was also acknowledged by the Wood's Despatch. In this context, the demand for FCE in India can be traced back to the early stages of the freedom struggle in British India. It subsequently became an integral part of the freedom struggle. The Indian National Congress fought valiantly for the expansion of elementary education and literacy, in general, and in rural India, in particular. In the evidence placed before the Education Commission (Hunter Commission) appointed in 1882, Dadabhai Naoroji and Jyothiba Phule from Bombay demanded State-sponsored free education for at least four years. This demand was indirectly acknowledged in the Commission's recommendations on primary education. The Commission also recommended that schools should be open to all castes and classes.

The first law on compulsory education was introduced by the State of Baroda in 1906. This law provided for compulsory education for boys and girls in the age groups of 7–12 years and 7–10 years respectively. The first documented use of the word right in the context of elementary education appears in a letter written by Rabindranath Tagore to the International League for the Rational Education of Children in 1908. In 1911, Gopal Krishna Gokhale moved a Bill for compulsory education in the Imperial Legislative Council, albeit unsuccessfully.

The Legislative Council of Bombay was the first amongst the Provinces to adopt a law on compulsory education. Gradually, other Provinces followed suit as control over elementary education was transferred to Indian Ministers under the Government of India Act, 1919. However, even though Provincial Legislatures had greater control and autonomy in enacting laws, progress in universalising education was poor due to lack of control over resources. In 1937, at the All India National Conference on Education held at Wardha, Gandhi mooted the idea of self-supporting 'basic education' for a period of seven years through vocational and manual training.

This concept of self-support was floated in order to counter the Government's constant excuse of lack of resources. The plan was to not only educate children through vocational training/manual training by choosing a particular handicraft, but also to simultaneously use the income generated from the sale of such handicrafts to partly finance basic education. Furthermore, education was supposed to be in the mother tongue of the pupils with Hindustani as a compulsory subject.

Two other interesting features of the Wardha Scheme are as follows:First, within the 'basic education course', there were two divisions, the 'lower basic' or 'primary' corresponded to classes I–V. The 'upper basic' or 'post-primary' corresponded to classes VI–VII. The division between primary and postprimary was created with a view to giving pupils the option of shifting to another form of education if they so desired after the first five years of 'basic education'.

Second, a minimum wage for teachers was stipulated under the Wardha Scheme. Based on these ideas, the Wardha Scheme of Education was formulated for rural areas. The next landmark development in the history of FCE in India was the Post War Plan of Education Development of 1944, also called the Sargent Plan, which recommended FCE for eight years (6–14 years' age group). Despite the consistent demand for FCE during the freedom struggle, at the time of drafting the Constitution, there was no unanimous view that the citizens of India should have a right to education, let alone a fundamental right. The Constitution Assembly Debates reveal that an amendment was moved to alter the draft Article relating to FCE, by removing the term entitled to ensure that it was merely a non-justiciable policy directive in the Constitution.

DEMAND FOR A FUNDAMENTAL RIGHT TO EDUCATION

The period spanning between 1950 to the judgement in Unnikrishnan's Case in 1993 saw several legal developments. The Indian Education Commission (Kothari Commission) 1964–1968, reviewed the status of education in India and made recommendations. Most important amongst these is its recommendation of a common school system with a view to eliminating inequality in access to education. Immediately thereafter, the National Policy on Education, 1968 was formed. The 1968 Policy was the first official document evidencing the Indian Government's commitment towards elementary education.

The Policy dealt with issues of equalisation of educational opportunity and required the common school system to be adopted in order to promote social cohesion. However, it was not supported by legal tools that could enforce such policy mandates. Interestingly, it even required that special schools should provide a proportion of free-studentships to prevent social segregation in schools. A second round of studies was conducted by the Ministry of Education in conjunction with the National Institute of Educational Planning and Administration, and this process contributed to the formation of the National Policy on Education, 1986. This policy, while re-affirming the goal of universalisation of elementary education, did not recognise the 'right to education'. The 1986 Policy is also severely criticised for having introduced non-formal education in India.

The 1986 Policy was reviewed by the Acharya Ramamurti Committee in 1990, and this review process contributed to the revised National Policy on Education of 1992. The Acharya Ramamurti Committee recommended that the right to education should be included as a fundamental right in Part III of the Constitution. However, this recommendation was not implemented immediately.

A great legal breakthrough was achieved in 1992 when the Supreme Court of India held in Mohini Jain v State of Karnataka, that the"'right to education' is concomitant to fundamental rights enshrined under Part III of the Constitution" and that 'every citizen has a right to education under the Constitution'. The Supreme Court subsequently reconsidered the judgement in the case of Unnikrishnan, J P v State of Andhra Pradesh. The Court (majority judgement) held that 'though right to education is not stated expressly as a fundamental right, it is implicit in and flows from the right to life guaranteed under Article 21... (and) must be construed in the light of the Directive Principles of the Constitution. Thus, 'right to education, understood in the context of Article 45 and 41 means: (a) every child/citizen of this country has a right to free education until he completes the age of fourteen years and (b) after a child/citizen completes 14 years, his right to education is circumscribed by the limits of the economic capacity of the State and its development'. In the meanwhile, major policy level changes were made under the dictates of the IMF-World Bank Structural Adjustment Programme and the World Bank-funded District Primary Education Programme (DPEP) was introduced in 1994. Under DPEP, the national commitment towards FCE up to 14 years was reduced and primary education for the first five years was introduced. Further, the concept of multi-grade teaching and para-teachers was also introduced. While policy level changes had diluted the quality of FCE, the Unnikrishnan Judgement empowered people with a legal claim to FCE. Several public interest litigation petitions were filed in different High Courts to enforce the Unnikrishnan Judgement and acquire admission into schools. This created tremendous pressure on the Parliament and thereafter a proposal for a Constitutional amendment to include the right to education as a fundamental right was made in 1996.

The Constitution (Eighty-Third) Amendment Bill was introduced in the Rajya Sabha in July 1997. The 83rd Amendment proposed that Article 21-A be introduced (fundamental right to education for 6–14 years), former Article 45 be deleted (the then existing directive principle on FCE) and Article 51-A(k) (fundamental duty on parents) be introduced. Between 1997 and 2001, due to change in Governments, the political will that was required to bring about the amendment was absent. In November 2001 however, the Bill was re-numbered as the 93rd Bill and the 83rd Bill was withdrawn. The 93rd Bill proposed that former Article 45 be amended to provide for early childhood care and education instead of being deleted altogether. This Bill was passed in 2002 as the 86th Constitutional Amendment Act. Currently, under Article 21-A of the Constitution, every child between the ages of 6–14 has a fundamental right to education, which the State shall provide 'in such manner as the State may, by law, determine'. Early childhood care and education (for children in the age group of 0–6 years) is provided for as a directive principle of State Policy under Article 45 of the Constitution.

DETERMINING THE CONTENT OF LAW

COERCIVE AND NON-COERCIVE RULES WITHIN A RIGHTS FRAMEWORK

It is evident that there is a fundamental right to FCE in India. However, apart from a mere mention of the age group for which such a right is guaranteed, Article 21-A does not throw any light on its content. The content of the right is left to be regulated by law. In order to implement the fundamental right to education through a rights-based model of legislation, one needs to determine the features of such a model. However, before examining the elements of a rights-based model of legislation, it may be apt to briefly discuss Amartya Sen's caveat with respect to legislating for the implementation of a human right.

He points out that legislations, which go a long way towards ensuring enforceability of specific minimum entitlements, may also have the negative effect of giving restrictive or limited interpretations of the content of the concerned human right. Legislations may also give rise to policy inaction on the ground that specific legal rules have been complied with. For example, if a law lays down that the duty of the State is to ensure x, y, z, then the State will restrict its activities to ensuring x, y, z without looking beyond that framework. Therefore, while legislation is certainly a welcome development, it should not be treated as the only vehicle of implementing human rights. The legislation should also be supplemented by other noncoercive rules for effective implementation of the human right.

This caveat needs to be taken into account during legislative processes and adequate safeguards need to be built into the law. While there cannot be a fool-proof mechanism of countering negative outcomes of law, the identifiable negative outcomes may be mitigated. For instance, governmental inaction could be countered through institutionalised periodic review of policy as well as law to ensure that progressive changes are made to both from time to time. In addition to such periodic review of policies, there should also be an institutionalised periodic review of the implementation of not only the policy but also the law. Furthermore, the quality of elementary education also depends on the quality of teaching staff, non-teaching staff, sensitivity and awareness of administrative staff in the various government departments Therefore, training and developing the capacities of such personnel is a critical component of elementary education.

In particular, this caveat assumes great importance in the context of education in India because the fundamental right to education as enshrined in the Constitution is limited to the age group of 6–14 years. This not only excludes early childhood care and education but also excludes higher education. Internationally, the human right to education includes the right to education at all stages that are fundamental and basic, including the right to early childhood care and education. The right to education has been recognised in several international instruments, of which the three key international instruments are the Universal Declaration of Human Rights, 1948 (UDHR), the International Covenant on Economic, Social and Cultural Rights, 1966 (ICESCR) and the Convention on the Rights of the Child (CRC). While some instruments uphold the right to 'elementary education', others use the phrase 'primary education'. Article 26 of UDHR lays down that free education should be provided at least in the 'element ary and fundamental stages' and is compulsory. Article 13 of ICESCR and Article 28 of CRC provide inter alia that 'primary education' shall be free and compulsory. In its General Comment No. 13, the Committee on Economic, Social and Cultural Rights (the Committee) has tried to clarify and expand on the meaning of the phrase 'primary education'.

The Committee has stated that primary education is that which caters to the 'basic learning needs of the children'. Ideally, any law implementing the fundamental right to education should off-set this exclusion. However, in the event that the law does not provide for a right to early childhood care and education, then the State should draw up concrete schemes (non-coercive rules) to ensure that early childhood care and education is provided. Currently, in India, the Integrated Child Development Scheme provides for early childhood care and education.

However, the nature of pre-school education, the quality of the services, as well as its linkage with formal school education need to be examined in great detail.

CONCEPTUALISING A RIGHTS-BASED MODEL

Having discussed the importance of the supplementary role of non-coercive rules, this part will now examine the building blocks of a rights-based model. Broadly, it may be stated that such an approach includes four essential elements.

- It should evaluate claims of rights–holders and corresponding obligations of duty bearers. In the context of education, there exists a relationship between the (State – child), (child – parent), (State – parent) and (State – community – child/parent). The law should be very clear on how each of these relationships will be regulated. The nature of the legally enforceable claim that a child would have against the State (officials, teachers, managerial staff and so on) should be outlined unambiguously, *i.e.,* the minimum entitlements should clearly be specified in law. Minimum entitlements may be broadly categorised into quantitative and qualitative entitlements. There is no fixed and clear demarcation between quantitative and qualitative entitlements and the two categories may be said to be over-lapping. Entitlements such as period of compulsory education, meaning of free education and whether it entails freedom from payment of money, number of schools, distance from residence, quantification of education facilities, number of teachers, infrastructure requirements for school, minimum content of education, curriculum, pedagogy, guarantee against violence and exploitation in schools, and guarantee of safe school environment should be legally guaranteed as enforceable minimum norms.

- A rights-based model should develop capacity-building strategies for not only rightsholders' to claim their rights but also for duty bearers to fulfill their obligations. Capacitybuilding of rights-holders involves two fundamental elements
  - Being aware of the right
  - Creating an enabling environment to access such a right Therefore, awareness and dissemination of information to the public regarding their rights is an inherent part of a rights-model of elementary education. Capacity of duty bearers through human rights education and requisite professional training (for teaching staff, non-teaching staff, district education officials, officers in the ministry of education and so on) is also part of such a model.
- There should be room for monitoring and evaluating outcomes and processes using human rights principles and standards. For example, in the context of elementary education, the three non-negotiable principles that need to be adhered to are the principles of nondiscrimination, equality and child participation. These principles should also be used in evaluating the performance of the State in implementing the right to FCE. Further, the law should clearly lay down methods of locating accountability for failures in the system which can be used as a method of grievance redressal in case of rights violations. In locating accountability, the duty-bearers should be clearly identified. A special grievance redressal mechanism should be in place to expedite disposal of grievances and ensure that children are admitted into schools in the shortest possible time. For example, the Karnataka Grama Panchayat's (School Development and Monitoring Committees [SDMC] Model) Bye-Laws, 2006 has a separate time-bound grievance redressal mechanism for a range of complaints such as employing children as child labour, physical and sexual abuse, sexual harassment, other forms of indignity, negligence, dereliction of duties, misdemeanor and misconduct, mismanagement, misappropriation of funds and so on by teaching, non-teaching staff as well as SDMC members.
- A rights-based model should incorporate the recommendations of international human rights bodies to inform each step of the process. For example, under international law, the right to basic education also includes the right to early childhood care and education. Another useful aide in developing a rights-based model of legislation is Asbjoern Eide's three-level typology of States' duties, which was developed in the context of right to food. This typology is now widely accepted and used as a framework for examining States' human rights obligations generally. Eide, human rights impose a three-fold duty on the State.

- The duty to respect implies the duty to refrain from interference and the duty to ensure that measures that prevent access are not introduced by the State. This would necessitate the creation of an enabling framework of law that removes barriers (atleast those that can be identified) to education. For example, in the context of school education, demand of documentary proof of residence, birth certificate and so on, which operate as huge barriers against admission into schools should be eliminated/mitigated.
- The duty to protect requires the State to ensure that the State/ enterprises/individuals do not deprive children of their right. For example, the dereservation of plots reserved for government schools would be an act of depriving right to education. Similarly, engaging children as labour would deprive them of their right to remain in full-time regular schools.
- The duty of the State to facilitate and fulfill human rights implies that the State should pro-actively engage to facilitate and provide for the implementation of FCE. It is the duty of the State to strengthen people's access to and utilisation of resources. Further, whenever an individual or group is unable to enjoy the right to FCE, for reasons beyond their control, States have the obligation to fulfill (provide) that right directly. This third element is extremely crucial as it creates a positive duty on the State as opposed to a negative duty. It also distinguishes the traditional truancy model of legislation from a rights-based model. Compulsory education laws have traditionally revolved around monitoring of attendance and penalty for truants/parents. Historically, police officers worked part-time as truant officers. Therefore, truant officers' primary function was akin to that of the police; and many of the attendance order boxes were also placed in police stations. The policing model of education and crime is theoretically opposed to a right sapproach because it is not enabling. It is premised on a fundamentally flawed assumption about human behaviour that poor parents are unwilling or reluctant to send their children to school. Based on this assumption, the law draws up an elaborate framework of monitoring and penalising defaulting parents and children instead of strengthening access and resource-utilisation of poor parents and their children. For example, consider a situation where a poor parent is unable to send her child to school because of the need for an additional source of income or additional help for household chores. Under the truancy model, a parent who does not send her child to school is automatically denounced as an unwilling parent who does not appreciate the benefits of formal school education. This unwilling parent is penalised under the truancy model. This policing model does very little to

change the underlying causes of truancy. In complete contrast to this, in a rights-based model, the State should take measures to strengthen the access right of the child by creating an environment which is conducive to formal schooling. In this context, it is pertinent to mention MV Foundation's experiments with re-allocating time and household chores of mothers to ensure that girl children are allowed to go to school, *i.e.,* a simple time-management technique solved truancy as opposed to imposition of penalty. Alternatively, it has been shown that where crèches are provided at the worksite, the attendance of girl children dramatically improved. Such examples prove that policing attendance is a completely futile method of enforcing attendance. A rights-based model does not have any room for punishing poor parents and their children for absenteeism. It is the duty of the State to create an enabling framework of law as part of its duty to fulfill the right.

EQUALITY AND NON-DISCRIMINATION IN SCHOOL EDUCATION

In addition to being enabling, the law should also guarantee equality and non-discrimination in education. The first component of equality is equality of resources and the problem of economically generated inequalities in education. In education, economic inequality leads to inequality in access, participation and outcomes in education. Scholars have identified processes within education systems that contribute to such inequality. For example, studies have repeatedly shown that selection or admission procedures, grouping procedures used to locate students in different streams in higher education, systems of curriculum, syllabus design and assessment contribute to inequality in the education system.

Most Indian schools have entrance examinations, collect capitation fees, have strenuous interview procedures and so on at the stage of admission; several schools also adopt a system of classifying 'toppers' in one section and failures in another. Tackling such inequality is a very complicated process and requires intervention that may fall outside the purview of education laws. Nevertheless, one solution that has been presented is that admission, selection procedures, and grouping should be made 'transparent and open to democratic scrutiny and public challenge'.

Therefore, a rights-based law which adopts the principle of equality should adopt a two-pronged approach of banning identifiable discriminatory processes as well as ensuring that all other processes in schools are documented and made public in order to facilitate public scrutiny and challenge, if required. Another facet of equality in education to be addressed is the equality of respect and recognition in education, *i.e.,* status-related inequalities based on class, caste, race, religion, language, gender and sexuality, profession of parents, disability and so on. In order to solve problems that arise out of status-discrimination, two approaches have been suggested – a policy of inclusion coupled with information dissemination on status-inequality, *i.e.,* equality education and human rights education. It is also important to look at 'human rights education' from the point of view of minimum entitlement in school curriculum.

Equality of power also forms an important element of equality in education. Power may be said to operate from the macro to the micro level. At the micro-level or school-level, equality of power may be facilitated through democratic decision-making on issues concerning the school, where children as well as parents are allowed to participate in the decision-making processes. For example, the Government of Karnataka has introduced school-level democratic decision-making to some extent through the Karnataka Grama Panchayat's (School Development and Monitoring Committees [SDMC]) (Model) Bye-Laws, 2006.

The bye-laws provide that an SDMC, which includes parents and children, should be formed in every government/government-aided school. All decisions regarding the school are required to be taken by this body; and all members are given equal decision-making power during meetings. At the macro-level, democratising education would imply that all actors in education have the opportunity to engage in education planning.

An ideal rights-based law may also need to acknowledge and provide for methods of participatory education planning at the Centre and State levels. We conclude that in a rights-model of legislation for elementary education, all the facets of equality should be included and methods of facilitating such equality should be made part of the legal entitlements of a child.

QUANTITATIVE MINIMUM ENTITLEMENTS

Entitlements may be divided into two categories – quantitative and qualitative. It should be noted that this categorisation is not intended to be in the nature of water-tight compartments. One important aspect of quantitative entitlements is the concept of 'free' education. The meaning of 'free' in the international context is at variance with the manner in which 'free' is conceptualised in the Indian context. While the Committee is against direct costs such as imposition of fees, donations, capitation fees, etc., there seems to be some ambiguity with respect to 'indirect costs'. The Committee has laid down that indirect costs, though generally not permissible, may be allowed on a case-to-case basis. There is no uniform international State practice on this issue.

While assessing a demand that text books should also be provided free of cost as part of 'free education', the Constitutional Court of the Czech Republic has held that free does not imply that the State has to bear all costs. The Court has stated that 'free' in primary education means that the State would bear the costs of establishing schools, their maintenance and operation. However, tuition and teaching materials need not be free. Reportedly provided free of charge in Austria, Bulgaria, Denmark, Finland, Germany, Iceland, Italy, Japan, Sri Lanka and Sweden. In some others, like Nepal and Russia, subsidies are provided for text books.

Loan arrangements are also made in countries like Armenia where textbooks are reportedly loaned to pupils against payment of an annual fee and/or the parents have to contribute to the cost of textbooks. The UN Special Rapporteur has recommended that 'free' would imply that all direct and indirect costs of education should be the responsibility of the Government. A similar approach is taken by the Committee on the Rights of the Child. The meaning of the term 'free' may also be inferred from the Observations of the Committee on the Rights of the Child (ComRC).

For example, in its 27th Session, the ComRC observed as follows: 'In addition, the Committee is concerned that in practice primary education is not free and that many parents have to pay school fees as well as related costs such as for uniforms and equipment, which remain too expensive for most families.' Despite the international variance in the meaning of this term, if costs, both direct and indirect, are viewed as a 'barrier' to education, then automatically, in a rights-approach, there can be no room for direct or indirect costs of education.

Experiences at the field show that the notion of free education cannot be limited to a tuition fee waiver or a few incentives such as mid-day meal scheme. For example, a majority of children from scheduled castes and scheduled tribes require residential schools to receive meaningful school education. Despite all existing incentives, the economic and social conditions of such parents compel them to withdraw their children from schools due to their inability to provide them with the bare minimum requirements at home which would facilitate learning after school hours.

The concept of free education must take into account such factors as well. Other important aspects of minimum quantitative entitlements are related to minimum schooling years, infrastructure requirements, number of schooling hours, ratio of students to teacher, qualification of teachers, number of neighbourhood schools and so on. Another crucial component of minimum entitlement is closely connected with the issue of bridge/transition course. In order to ensure that the right to formal schooling ultimately reaches children who have been marginalised due to socio-economic conditions, the law should also provide for a right to be integrated into mainstream schools after imposing an outer limit on the number of years in a bridge course and the options available to the child after the completion of the bridge course.

QUALITATIVE MINIMUM ENTITLEMENTS

Under the category of qualitative entitlements, one of the most complex aspects is the curriculum of education. In this context, it is apt to mention that the UN Special Rapporteur has stated that the right to education in international human rights law includes not only the right to 'human rights in education' but also includes the 'right to human rights education.' Curriculum is not only important from the point of view of entitlements but is also important in the context of compulsion and the nature of relationship between the State and the parent regarding the child's education.

Since 'compulsion' involves State coercion, it has on several occasions been diametrically opposed to parental religious, moral and philosophical convictions.

Therefore, any law on FCE should clarify the following aspects of compulsion:

- Compulsion of attendance and consequences of non-attendance
- Compulsion in curriculum.

COMPULSORY ATTENDANCE WITHIN A RIGHTS-BASED FRAMEWORK

Compulsory attendance backed by punitive measures is the central attribute of the truancy model of legislation. In contradistinction to the truancy model, a rights approach should necessarily be enabling. This implies that a rights-based law should aim to provide solutions to problems/barriers. In any event, a rights-approach does not permit the imposition of punishment on persons who are unable to send their children to school due to socio-economic or cultural barriers.

It should be reiterated at this point that the nature of the punitive measure is immaterial, *i.e.,* even community service (punitive measure) as provided for under the Right to Education Bill, 2005 goes against the basic tenor of a rights-approach to education.

The imposition of punitive measures is a classic illustration of Amartya Sen's argument that in the overzealous attempt to create a law enforcing a human right, the human right itself may be detrimentally affected. In their zeal to ensure school attendance, officials restrict their activity to strict enforcement of the law and refuse to address policy issues that fall outside the purview of law. The entire State machinery is more concerned with policing attendance rather than creating environments which are conducive to compulsory education by addressing complex problems arising out of child labour, child marriage, lack of housing, malnutrition, migration and so on. The other aspect of compulsory attendance is the creation of legal exceptions to compulsion.

The truancy model coupled with the exceptions to compulsion is a method of negating 'social accountability.' A study of Statelaws reveals that the clause on exceptions to compulsion is often used as a method of completely negating State's accountability. For example, several State laws make 'absence of a neighbourhood school' an exception to compulsion.

Instead of imposing a duty on the State to provide neighbourhood schools, the benevolent State exempts parents from penalty where there are no neighbourhood schools. Such an approach is completely opposed to a rights-based model. In a right sapproach, a neighbourhood school would arguably be a minimum quantitative entitlement which is justiciable.

COMPULSORY EDUCATION VS. FREEDOM OF RELIGION

On the issue of compulsion and legal exceptions, one needs to examine the conflict between compulsory education and right to freedom of religion. At the very outset it is important to clarify that all human rights instruments re-affirm parental choice with respect to education in accordance with their religious and moral conviction. Article 25 of the Constitution guarantees freedom of religion. However, this is subject to the other provisions in Part III of the Constitution, which deals with fundamental rights. This would imply that the fundamental right to freedom of religion [Article 25] is subject to the fundamental right to FCE [Article 21-A].

Three types of conflicts may arise between education and religion:

1. Direct conflict where parents may want to provide purely religious education to their children. For example, where a child is inducted into the monastic order of a particular religion at the age of six and thereafter is being given religious instruction; the obvious question is whether such a practice should be exempted as a religious/cultural right or whether it may be viewed as violation of a child's fundamental right to primary education. In cases of such direct conflict, it may be argued that since Article 25 of the Constitution, is subject to Article 21-A, no parent would be in a position to choose religious education to the exclusion of free and compulsory formal secular education.
2. Conflict, which has plagued many countries in recent times, revolves around the limits of religious expression in schools. For example, bans on wearing hijabs, schools displaying pictures of gods and goddesses of a particular faith, prayers conducted in a particular faith and so on. In such cases, there may be conflicts between a student's right to education, right to religion and the secular nature of the State especially in public schools.
3. Conflict occurs where religious beliefs are opposed to the curriculum of education in government schools. The following case illustrates the need for clarity on the right to content of education, as part of the guarantee to FCE. The issue of parental choice and content regulation was dealt with by the European Court of Human Rights in the case of Kjeldsen, Busk Madsen and Pedersen v. Denmark. The applicants were parents of children who were going to State

primary schools in Denmark. As per the Danish Constitution, all children have the right to FCE in State primary schools. The State had introduced compulsory sex education in State primary schools as part of the curriculum. This change in the curriculum was introduced by a Bill passed by the Parliament. There were guidelines and safeguards against a) showing pornography, b) teachers giving sex education to pupils when they were alone, c) giving information on methods of sexual intercourse and d) using vulgar language while imparting sex education. The applicants, who were parents of school going children, gave several petitions to have their children exempted from sex education in the concerned State schools. However, these requests were not met and all of them withdrew their children from the said schools.

The applicants argued that the Denmark Government had violated Article 2 of Protocol No. 1 to the European Convention on Human Rights which states "No person shall be denied the right to education. In the exercise of any functions which it assumes in relation to education and to teaching, the State shall respect the right of parents to ensure such education and teaching in conformity with their own religions and philosophical convictions." The State argued that Article 2 would cover only religious instruction and not all forms of instruction.

The Court rejected this argument and held that any teaching should respect parental' religious and moral convictions. However, the Court also held that article 2 would be violated only if while imparting sex education, the teachers advocated sex at a particular age or particular type of sexual behaviour. Moreover, the parents still had the freedom to educate their children at home to instill their own religious convictions and beliefs and therefore, imparting sex education *per se* was not a violation of the Article 2.

The Danish Case assumes importance in the Indian context because there have been several controversies regarding curriculum in schools in the context of religion. For instance, the saffronisation of education by the Bharatiya Janata Party and Indian government's policy of 'modernisation of Madrasas (religious schools of Muslims)' pose serious questions of curricular entitlements and safeguards.

While these two examples raise several complex questions regarding curriculum, it also has a common thread – that of a right to secular education of all children, irrespective of their religion. The saffronisation of education combines content regulation with the need for social accountability of the Government. A combination of a positive and a negative right to curriculum may adequately guard against problems such as saffronisation. Every child should have a right to a core non-negotiable content in education that is coupled with a duty of the State to refrain from arbitrarily interfering with such content. In defining the core minimum content of curriculum, it is advisable to prescribe the non-negotiable minimum in terms of competencies that need to be achieved at the end of each grade. The advantage of defining the core minimum in terms of competencies is that it gives States and teachers the freedom to contextualise learning within a specific local setting by creating localised syllabus. As regards the negative right, given the nature and increasing evidence of polarisation based on religion in India, it may be stated that right to education should at least include certain safeguards against propaganda-driven curriculum or syllabus.

Therefore, guarding against arbitrary alteration or revision of existing curriculum would necessitate the creation of a systematic process and procedures for developing and revising syllabus at all levels – Centre, State, District and so on. Therefore, the negative right is procedural right against arbitrary State intervention, whereas the positive right is a substantive right to minimum competencies. The case of madrasas raises the crucial question of balancing the interests of religious minority institutions and the right of the child to secular education.

Madrasas are largely autonomous and therefore decide upon their curriculum, hours of study, duration of study and so on. The Central Government's policy of modernising madrasas by introducing subjects such as mathematics and science has been criticised as being violative of not only Madrasas' autonomy but also doing injustice to children's right to secular education and free and compulsory full-time formal education. Without getting into the merits and demerits of modernising madrasas, it may be argued that while minority groups have the right to manage their own educational institutions, the same cannot be considered as having fulfilled the requirement of Article 21-A unless:

- Certain core minimum in terms of competencies is adhered to
- There are procedural safeguards against arbitrary alteration of syllabus

COMPULSION AND MEDIUM OF INSTRUCTION

Another controversial issue in the Indian context would be medium of instruction and right to education. For example, while defining the nature of the relationship between the parent and the State and also defining the scope of compulsion, the law should address whether a child should be compelled to attend a government school where the medium of instruction is completely alien to the child. Alternatively, the law should examine whether the right to education includes the right to be educated in a manner that is not alien to the child, *i.e.,* where language is not a barrier to education.

This issue has been examined by the European Court of Human Rights in the Belgian Linguistic Case. The applicants were French-speaking Belgian nationals who were aggrieved that the Belgian Government had not set up any government school in their District whose language of instruction was

French. It is important to note that there were other French-medium schools, which were not within the same District. The Court held that the State was under no obligation to respect the linguistic preferences of parents. This is because Article 2 of Protocol No. 2 to the European Convention on Human Rights states that the State "...shall respect the right of parents to ensure such education and teaching in conformity with their own religious and philosophical convictions."

The Court held that the phrase 'religious and philosophical convictions' does not include linguistic preferences. The Court further held that non-provision of education in a particular language of instruction does not amount to discrimination based on language. Even though it may be argued that lack of schools in a particular medium of instruction does not amount to discrimination, given the extent of migration and diversity in language in the Indian context, the latter may be a genuine barrier to school education. For example, in Manipur, several Naga children are being educated in a language and curriculum that is completely alien to them.

As a result of this, the Naga underground movement has issued threats to the Manipuri schools demanding that the Naga population in these schools be taught in a manner that is acceptable to the Nagas. This is illustrative of the fact that in order to make elementary education an effective right, the law should necessarily address the language issue in such a manner that it enables all children to attend schools.

ROLE OF THE COMMUNITY WITHIN A RIGHTS FRAMEWORK

The law would also need to lay down the kind of relationship the State should create with respect to 'State–communities–children' in the context of education. For example, how would the law respond to employers who engage children in labour; how would the law respond to the government's slum demolition drives which completely ruin a school-going child's ability to attend schools? These two examples are classic cases of third party intervention that hinders a child's right to education. The State's duty to protect the right would imply that the State should protect a child's right to education from any form of interference or hindrance.

Another aspect of the 'State–communities–children' relationship is the empowerment of communities, *i.e.,* communities should be empowered with a right of participation in school education. The Karnataka example of community participatory methods of school management is a case in point. Using such creative legal tools, the law could create avenues for legal claims to be made by children viz-a-viz such imperfect obligations. It has also provided a brief insight into some very controversial issues that need to be debated and discussed in order to arrive at a rights-based model of elementary education.

ASSESSMENT OF STATE LEVEL LEGISLATIONS FROM THE 'RIGHTS' PERSPECTIVE

Clarity regarding the phrase 'rights-based' alone is not sufficient for realising the fundamental right to education. In order to effectively ensure that every child is guaranteed the core non-negotiable minimum, the model of legislation becomes crucial. For example, how can a child in Sikkim and a child in Kerala be guaranteed this core non-negotiable minimum right to education? If, for example, a child in Sikkim receives only five years of compulsory education and a child in Kerala receives eight years of compulsory education, then this would definitely be violative of 'equitable' education.

Prima face, there exists a case for the creation of uniform standards across India for ensuring that children are entitled to the same guarantees and core non-negotiable minima. This prima facie case for uniformity is further strengthened by our analysis of the existing State-level laws on elementary education. The following States' laws have been examined – Jammu and Kashmir, Maharashtra, West Bengal, Himachal Pradesh, Karnataka, Tamil Nadu, Kerala, Rajasthan, Delhi, Sikkim, Punjab, Andhra Pradesh, Madhya Pradesh and Meghalaya. The Meghalaya law does not even pay lip service to the concept of compulsory elementary education.

All the State laws penalise poor parents for their children's poor attendance in schools and are in no way enabling. Many of them even criminalise non-attendance and make the offence punishable with a fine. Clearly these laws are based on the truancy model of education. In addition, most of the State laws do not guarantee compulsory education to all children. On the contrary, to quote Weiner, "...compulsory education laws in India do not make education compulsory: they merely establish the conditions under which state governments may make education compulsory in specified areas [emphasis provided by authors], *i.e.*, they merely make compulsory education permissive.

It is entirely up to the discretion of the local authority concerned to draw up a scheme for compulsion under such laws. Therefore, where compulsory education is merely permissive, the question of a justiciable right to education does not arise at all, unless a particular area is brought under a scheme of compulsory education. The West Bengal Primary Education Act, 1973; the Bombay Primary Education Act, 1947; the Tamil Nadu Compulsory Primary Education Act, 1994; the Karnataka Education Act, 1983; the Rajasthan Primary Education Act, 1964; Delhi Primary Education Act, 1960; the Kerala Education Act, 1958; the Assam Elementary Education Act, 1974; Sikkim Primary Education Act, 2000; Punjab Primary Education Act, 1960; and the Andhra Pradesh Education Act 1982 fall under this category. Surprisingly, even post – Article 21-A, most states continue to maintain on document that compulsory education for all children is merely permissive, and this is clearly unconstitutional. The extent of State inaction is evidenced by the very fact that even after four years of the Constitutional amendment in 2002, they continue to be governed by obsolete laws which are clearly violative of the Constitutional mandate.

Out of the remaining laws that we analysed, the Jammu and Kashmir School Education Act, 2002; the Himachal Pradesh Compulsory Primary Education Act, 1997; and the Madhya Pradesh Jan Shiksha Adhiniyam, 2002 make primary education compulsory. However, out of these three, the Himachal Pradesh Act again seems to directly contravene the mandate of the Constitution as it defines a child as a person between the age of 6 and 11. This leaves us with the Jammu and Kashmir law and the Madhya Pradesh law. Apart from defining a child as aged between 6 and 14, the Jammu and Kashmir law does not specify any other details or minimum entitlements. It does not affirm any principle of human rights law. It fails to provide for a grievance redressal mechanism or monitoring method. The Madhya Pradesh law makes compulsory education mandatory for all children from the age of 6–14 years. It also refers to the principle of non-discrimination. It defines 'free' as a tuition fee waiver. However, it provides that where the Parent Teacher Association of a particular school consents to imposing a school development fee, then such a fee may be imposed. Arguably, this too would directly violate the constitutional mandate of free education for all children between the age of six and fourteen. Therefore, the current position regarding State laws on compulsory education is that none of them has been amended to bring it in line with the basic guarantees provided by the Constitution. In addition, all of them fall squarely within the truancy model of legislation.

This analysis clearly demonstrates:

- There is no uniformity amongst State level laws
- None of the State laws uses a rights-based approach to elementary education.

11

Early Childhood Care and Education

Early childhood care and education (ECCE) refers to a wide range of programmes, all aimed at the physical, cognitive and social development of children before they enter primary school – theoretically from birth to about age 7 or 8. The benefits of ECCE programmes, which extend into adulthood, are well documented.

They contribute to good child development outcomes that set the foundation for lifelong learning and help in the monitoring of health and nutrition status during this critical period of development. The provision of ECCE programmes can free members of the household from childcare responsibilities, allowing a parent to work or an older sibling to attend school. Of course, early childhood care also takes place in the context of families. Parenting practices have strong effects on learning and development.

MONITORING EARLY CHILDHOOD CARE AND EDUCATION

To monitor progress towards the goal stated in the Dakar Framework as 'expanding and improving comprehensive early childhood care and education, especially for the most vulnerable and disadvantaged children', it is important to distinguish between care and education and to identify the typical age groups that programmes serve and the extent to which statistical reporting covers formal and non-formal programmes. The International Standard Classification of Education (ISCED) defines pre-primary education, or ISCED level 0, as comprising programmes that offer structured, purposeful learning activities in a school or a centre (as opposed to the home) to children aged at least 3 years.

Such programmes are normally held to include organized learning activities that occupy on average the equivalent of at least two hours per day and 100 days per year. These criteria may not reflect the full extent of participation in ECCE programmes, as they exclude care and education provided below age 3. Moreover, data collection systems that focus largely on state or state-regulated providers may not cover non-formal care and educational activities administered by other state authorities or private entities for children aged 3 and up. Assessing quality in ECCE provision is difficult, both conceptually and empirically, and has been insufficiently addressed at the global level.

There is a real lack of information about inputs and about how they are used to achieve good outcomes in programmes for young children. The use of standards is increasingly the norm in more developed countries, as is the use of assessment instruments to measure outcomes. But learning achievement alone is an inadequate basis on which to judge programme quality, especially in developing countries, where the focus is on ensuring a wider range of child development outcomes. An important part of assessing ECCE provision is determining how well programmes reach the most vulnerable and disadvantaged children.

This has become more feasible with the greater availability of household survey results that allow the disaggregation of participation data by gender, household wealth and rural or urban residence. At the same time, however, these results may underestimate the extent of the differences, as national surveys are not typically used to collect information about the most marginalized populations.

PARTICIPATION IN ECCE PROGRAMMES

National ECCE systems vary considerably in terms of age group served, number of years provided and content. The intended age group for pre-primary programmes varies widely. However, in most countries, participation is not obligatory and children may start programmes at any age. In some cases, programmes can be taken for only one year, as in Sri Lanka and the Philippines. In other cases, they can be taken for up to four years, as in many Central and Eastern European countries, or even five years, as in Mongolia. The most common duration is three years, typically serving ages 3 to 5 or, less frequently, 4 to 6. In a few countries, the year before the official entrance age for primary education is compulsory.

The annual statutory number of hours of preprimary schooling in developing countries in 1999 ranged from 195 hours in Iraq to more than 1,250 hours in Colombia, Cuba and Saint Kitts and Nevis – a ratio of 1:8 between minimum and maximum. Programmes in about half the countries for which data are available fell in the range of 700 to 999 hours per year. Programmes of longer duration are not necessarily of better quality – their impact on child outcomes also depends on support provided in the home and on the quality of the activities provided. Gross and net enrolment ratios (GER and NER) – explained in the section below on school participation – are typically used to measure levels of participation in ECCE programmes.

The GER should be interpreted within the context of the official age groups for pre-primary education. Most countries in the EFA regions of sub-

Saharan Africa, the Arab States, Central Asia and South and West Asia have low enrolment levels, while those in the Latin America and the Caribbean region and the North America and Western Europe region have generally higher levels. The considerable difference between the GER and the NER in several countries indicates that a large proportion of those enrolled are outside the intended age group. In the most common pattern, participation rates increase with age, and peak in the year before entry into primary school. In Poland, the peak covers practically all 6-year-olds, because the last year of pre-primary is compulsory. One year of compulsory pre-primary education has become the norm for most European countries. While almost all children in Poland enter primary school at age 7, in Colombia and Ghana there is a greater mix of pre-primary and primary school participation among children of the same age, even at the official entry age for primary school. By contrast, in Côte d'Ivoire, as in many other sub-Saharan African countries, pre-primary participation levels are extremely low at all ages.

Levels of participation in primary school are also relatively low. Pre-primary school life expectancy summarizes these diverse participation patterns into the average number of years of pre-primary education that a child could expect to receive if current participation rates remain constant. It indicates that the highest levels of pre-primary school life expectancy are found in North America and Western Europe (2.2 years), followed by Central and Eastern Europe (1.8 years) and Latin America and the Caribbean (1.6 years). The high rates in Central and Eastern Europe partly reflect the legacy of heavily subsidized preprimary programmes accompanying high female labour force participation.

In the best-performing countries of sub-Saharan Africa a child could be expected to attend almost two years of pre-primary programmes, but the numbers drop off sharply and the regional average is only about 0.3 years. Despite high values in Lebanon and Kuwait, the Arab States' regional average closely follows sub-Saharan Africa's. Pre-school life expectancy is a measure of the quantity of programme provision and does not necessarily reflect programme quality, but extremely low participation levels indicate that ECCE in the countries concerned may bring few benefits to society. Progress towards wider access to pre-primary programmes since 1998 has been slow.

Gross enrolment ratios have increased by more than 10 per cent in fourteen countries of sub-Saharan Africa, although they started from very low levels. The GER rose by 133 per cent in Congo (from 1.8 per cent to 4.2 per cent), due to recovery after the disruption caused by conflict. Increases above 50 per cent were reported in Algeria, Burundi, the Libyan Arab Jamahiriya and the Islamic Republic of Iran. The decline experienced in countries of Eastern Europe and Central Asia during the 1990s has stabilized and the situation has started to improve in most countries. The biggest gains were in countries with an established base to build on (GER between 20 per cent and

30 per cent): Azerbaijan, India, the Islamic Republic of Iran, Tonga and Tunisia. However, in other countries in the same group, such as China and Lesotho, levels were stable or declined. Most sub-Saharan African and other 'least-developed' countries showed low participation levels (often below 10 per cent) and, in some cases, declines. Most of these countries belong to the 'heavily indebted poor countries' group and are generally affected by the HIV/AIDS pandemic and high levels of poverty. They face the greatest challenge when it comes to achieving the good care, health, education and development of young children. The difficulty of expanding access to ECCE programmes in the least developed countries is the focus of a recent World Bank study. Almost half of the 133 developing countries considered in the study would not achieve a pre-primary GER of even 25 per cent by 2015, based on current trends.

The study suggests that one of the main ways for poor countries to increase ECCE is by expanding the role of the private sector via community-based provision. One danger of such a strategy, however, is greater inequality, since generally only the better-off communities and households are able to invest in ECCE programmes. Achieving gender equality in access and provision is especially important during this critical period of child development. The countries for which data are available are divided almost evenly between those where gender disparities in preprimary education, as measured by the gender parity index (GPI), favour boys and those where they favour girls. The disparities in favour of boys are generally less striking than those for primary education in South and West Asia, sub-Saharan Africa and certain Arab States. One possible explanation is the degree of civil society participation in ECCE provision. Many non-governmental organizations (NGOs) and other associations are concerned with the interests of women and young children and seek to ensure that girls participate at least as much as boys.

Nevertheless, in some countries, such as Morocco and Pakistan, the GER for girls is still no more than three-quarters of the ratio for boys. In the British Virgin Islands, Nepal, Oman, Tajikistan and the Turks and Caicos Islands, girls' participation remains 12 per cent–15 per cent below that of boys. The UNICEF Multiple Indicator Cluster Surveys (MICS), conducted in or around 2000, collected data on the percentage of children aged 3 and 4 who attended organized learning or early childhood education programmes, along with the average number of hours attended in the week before the survey.

The number of hours attended ranged from ten or fewer in sub-Saharan African countries such as Burundi, Chad, Guinea-Bissau and Sierra Leone to more than thirty in Azerbaijan, Mongolia and Tajikistan. Countries whose attendance rates and hours attended were both relatively high included the Dominican Republic, the Republic of Moldova, Suriname, Trinidad and Tobago and Viet Nam. By contrast, in Burundi, Chad, the Central African Republic, the Democratic Republic of the Congo, Guinea-Bissau and the Niger, only a small proportion of 3- and 4-year-olds attended and for only a few hours per week.

WHO BENEFITS FROM ECCE PROGRAMMES?

While countries providing GERs are evenly divided between those favouring boys and those favouring girls, disparity in net attendance rates among 3- and 4-year-olds in the surveyed countries is more often in favour of girls. In almost two thirds of the surveyed countries, they attend ECCE programmes more than boys. Furthermore, disparities in favour of either sex are more pronounced for attendance rates than for GERs. The disparity in favour of girls is highest in the Lao People's Democratic Republic, the Philippines and Botswana; the disparity in favour of boys is highest in Chad, the Niger and Tajikistan.

Attendance rates in pre-primary programmes are considerably higher for urban children than for those living in rural areas and higher for children from better-off households than poor ones. Countries with higher-than-average attendance rates that have minimized differences in urban versus rural attendance include Equatorial Guinea and Suriname. The greatest differences in attendance between rich and poor were found in the Dominican Republic, Viet Nam and the Republic of Moldova. Research has shown that children from the poorest backgrounds benefit the most from ECCE provision in terms of care, health and education, yet UNICEF MICS and other studies show that they are also more likely to be excluded from it.

ASSESSING THE QUALITY AND COST OF ECCE

It is difficult to assess the quality of ECCE provision, as outcomes are hard to measure, although projects using increasingly refined instruments are being carried out. Most such studies measure the impact of ECCE participation on the progression of pupils through the primary school grades and on their overall achievement. Indicators that can assist in assessing the quality of early childhood programmes cover such aspects as physical environments, staff training and qualification levels and numbers of children per class and per caregiver.

The characteristics of how provision is organized and managed, the clarity of curricular goals and the quality of the education process are also keys to good child development outcomes. But data for these indicators are often difficult to collect and interpret in a comparative framework. Pupil/teacher ratios (PTRs) vary greatly in preprimary education. The PTR is the ratio of the total number of pupils to the total number of teachers at a given level. PTRs are highest in sub-Saharan Africa, where 40 per cent of the countries for which data are available have between twenty-five and thirty-four children per teacher, and lowest in Central and Eastern Europe and Central Asia, where the ratio is below 15:1 in seven out of ten countries. In general, PTRs tend to be higher in primary than in pre-primary education, as younger children need more individual care and attention. For instance, in sub-Saharan Africa, over three-quarters of the countries have PTRs over 35:1 in primary education, while only one in ten does at the preprimary level. In Central and Eastern Europe and Central Asia, over 70 per cent of the countries have fewer than fifteen pupils per teacher in preprimary but fifteen to twenty-four in primary. This pattern is less clear-cut in the Arab States and in North America and Western Europe. These averages represent only rough indications of the quality of processes and outcomes.

A recent study, covering mostly industrialized countries, reports that ten out of twenty-one countries had child/staff ratios that differed according to children's age, socioeconomic background, home location, staff qualifications and location of institution. These ratios varied from an average of 25–30:1 for 5- and 6-yearolds to 15:1 for 3- and 4-year-olds. Crèches, catering to 0- to 2-year-olds, generally had fewer than eight children per adult. For 4- to 6-year-olds, the average ratio was as low as 15:1 in programmes targeting the socially and economically disadvantaged. According to another source, national standards for child/staff ratios in OECD countries for 0- to 3-year-olds range from 3:1 in Denmark to 10:1 in Portugal, and for 3- to 6-year-olds from 6:1 in Denmark and Sweden to 20–28:1 in Italy. The quality of ECCE programmes is limited in some countries by low staff qualifications. Many teachers are employed on a contract basis, receive low salaries and have limited or no professional training. Among sixty-nine countries providing data, 20 per cent report that all ECCE teachers have received training, while in another 20 per cent fewer than half are trained. Trained personnel make up less than one quarter of teaching staff in Trinidad and Tobago, Cape Verde and Ghana. In three quarters of these sixty-nine countries, the proportion of untrained teachers at pre-primary level is higher, and sometimes much higher, than at primary level. In OECD countries, pre-primary staff are generally well qualified.

In most Western European countries and Japan, staff need university qualification, while in the United States lower qualification is sufficient. A review of staff qualifications in nineteen developed countries conveys a picture of preprimary programmes delivered by highly qualified staff. Recent changes to qualification requirements pointed to increasing professionalization. Staff dealing with 4-year-olds in all but two of the countries had qualifications similar to those of primary school teachers – usually at least three years of university training. Among middle-income countries for which data are available, teacher qualification standards and salary levels (entry level with minimum qualification) do not differ greatly between preprimary and primary levels. In lower-income developing countries, qualifications and salaries are lower at pre-primary than at primary level. Minimum salaries at both levels are reported to be similar in, for instance, India, Indonesia, Malaysia, Paraguay and the Philippines, but the number of hours of instruction is lower in preprimary than in primary school, which results in higher pre-primary unit costs. Pre-primary expenditure per child is also higher where preprimary PTRs are lower than in primary school, *e.g.* in Brazil, Chile, Indonesia, the Philippines and Tunisia.

Pre-primary unit costs are also substantially higher than primary costs in the Czech Republic, Slovakia and the United Kingdom. While in Slovakia pupil/teacher ratios may explain the cost level, this explanation may not hold true in the United Kingdom, which has PTRs of 24:1 in pre-primary and 17:1 in primary school. Nevertheless, it can be seen that unit costs are lower at pre-primary level than at primary level in almost two thirds of the countries providing data.

SCHOOL PARTICIPATION

This section focuses on pupil participation at primary level and briefly discusses participation at secondary and tertiary levels. Universal primary education (UPE) means that all children of primary-school age participate in the school system and complete primary school. This requires initial enrolment at the officially prescribed age, regular attendance and the progression of most pupils from one grade to another at the appropriate time, so that everyone completes the curriculum. Such results are possible only if the school system has the capacity to accommodate entire cohorts of children and deliver decent-quality teaching.

Timely completion of primary schooling with a reasonable degree of mastery of the curriculum – notably basic cognitive skills such as literacy and numeracy – appears to be necessary for primary education to yield the expected benefits over the long run, and is obviously a condition for successful participation in post-primary education. As far as UPE is concerned, quantitative and qualitative objectives are inseparable. For example, improving school quality is one way to increase demand for education and improve school participation. The returns accruing to children from a given amount of schooling will also be crucially affected by its quality.

HOW CLOSE IS THE WORLD TO UNIVERSAL PRIMARY EDUCATION

Enrolment

Enrolment is the most basic element of school participation. It is also the most easily measurable indicator of progress towards UPE. As noted earlier, two enrolment ratios are usually distinguished. The gross enrolment ratio (GER) is the ratio of the number of children enrolled at a given level (*e.g.* in primary school), whatever their age, to the number in the age range officially corresponding to that level (*e.g.* ages 6 to 12). The GER is expressed as a percentage. It can exceed 100 per cent, because of early or, more frequently, delayed enrolment, as well as grade repetition – which result in children other than those of the official age(s) being enrolled at a given level.

GERs measure the overall capacity of school systems in purely quantitative terms, though wide differences in levels of resources per pupil often make broad comparisons difficult. The net enrolment ratio (NER) only takes into account enrolled children who belong to the official age range (*e.g.* 6- to 12-year-olds enrolled in primary school), regardless of whether younger or older children are also enrolled; thus it cannot exceed 100 per cent. As a measure of the coverage of children in the age range officially associated with a given level of education, the NER comes closer to being an indicator of school quality. UPE implies a NER at or near 100 per cent.

A high GER is not necessarily a sign of progress towards UPE if the NER is much lower. More than one-third of the countries for which data are available still have GERs below 100 per cent, although those with NERs above 90 per cent may have sufficient capacity for UPE. In the more than forty countries with GERs below 100 per cent and NERs below 90 per cent, capacity will need to increase strongly for UPE to be reached. This shows that lack of coverage and inefficiency in primary education tend to occur together. Striking regional patterns emerge.

The greatest concentration of educational deprivation (and poverty in general) is found in Africa and South Asia. In sub-Saharan Africa, only a handful of small countries both reach GERs of 100 per cent or more and have NERs above 90 per cent. Some larger countries combine GERs below 100 per cent with NERs below 70 per cent or even below 50 per cent. The only other countries reporting NERs below 70 per cent are a few Arab States and Pakistan. Just six countries, all in Africa, have primary education NERs below 50 per cent. Dealing with these data at the country level, however, masks the extent of educational deprivation in South and West Asia.

There, despite somewhat higher national GERs and NERs, highly populated regions within countries have lower enrolment levels than do many African states. Most of the world's countries, however, have attained NERs of at least 70 per cent, and in North America and Western Europe, Latin America and the Caribbean and East Asia and the Pacific, most countries combine GERs above 100 per cent with NERs above 90 per cent. In Central and Eastern Europe, however, the situation is problematic: more than half the countries in the region have GERs below 100 per cent, and some have NERs between 70 per cent and 90 per cent. Unsatisfactory as the current situation may be, there was much progress in enrolment during the 1990s, both over the whole decade and its last third. By 2001, NERs had increased in nearly all countries that started the decade below 70 per cent, leading to some convergence at the global level – NERs in primary education ranged from 16 per cent to 100 per cent in 1990, but from 34 per cent to 100 per cent in 2001. In twenty countries NERs increased beyond 90 per cent and several countries that still had not reached 90 per cent in 2001 nevertheless showed dramatic progress since 1998, with increases of over 10 percentage points (Burundi, Ethiopia, Guinea, Lesotho, Morocco, Mozambique and Sao Tome and Principe). On the other hand, in about one fifth of all countries providing data, NERs declined more than two percentage points between 1990 and 2001.

In many cases these were Central and Eastern European or Central Asian countries that had had relatively high NERs at the beginning of the period. Others were developing countries, especially in sub-Saharan Africa, that experienced prolonged economic crisis during the decade. In Nepal, the Republic of Moldova and Zambia, whose NERs were already below 90 per cent in 1990, enrolment had dropped by more than 10 percentage points by 2001. Similar changes occurred between 1998 and 2001, although on a smaller scale. As things stand, the world appears divided between a large group of countries with high and stable NERs and a smaller (but still relatively large) group of countries with low NERs, only some of which are making quick progress towards joining the first group.

This is definitely a cause for concern, as is the fact that significant fractions of the population remain excluded from primary school in countries with higher NERs, especially in disadvantaged areas or communities. By definition, achieving UPE entails achieving gender parity in enrolment. When initial enrolment is low, its growth is often genderimbalanced, with enrolment ratios for males increasing much earlier than those for females. A GPI between 0.97 and 1.03 is considered as reflecting gender parity. In 2001, there were seventy-one such countries, or about 40 per cent of the countries for which data are available. Gender disparity in enrolment is characteristic of many of the countries with low overall enrolment.

All but three of the countries with a GPI below 0.90 are in sub-Saharan Africa (notably West Africa), the Arab States, and South and West Asia. Progress towards gender parity was notable since 1990 and the trend has continued in 1998–2001. Thus, quick progress in gender parity can be achieved even in poor countries with low enrolment ratios. Nevertheless, the GPI fell recently in several countries.

Out-of-school Children

Despite the progress in enrolment made throughout the 1990s in a majority of developing countries, large numbers of children of primaryschool age are still not participating. The most easily available estimate of the number of these 'out-of-school children' is calculated from the NER, although, since some children of primary age are enrolled in pre-primary schooling and, occasionally, at secondary level, this method slightly overestimates the actual number of children who are out of the school system. Worldwide, there were about 103 million of them in 2001, after a slow decline since 1998 (106.9 million) and 2000 (104.1 million).

Clearly, enrolment ratios are not increasing quickly enough for universal enrolment to be achieved in the short or even medium term. At the world level, the NER rose from 81.7 per cent in 1990 to 84 per cent in 2001. Should this trend continue, the NER would reach 85 per cent in 2005 and 87 per cent in 2015. The regional distribution of out-of-school children naturally reflects NER and population figures. Some 96 per cent of out-of-school children live in developing countries. Sub-Saharan Africa and South and West Asia together account for almost three quarters of unenrolled children. About 57 per cent of such children are girls. The proportion is 60 per cent or higher in the Arab States and South and West Asia.

PUPIL PROGRESSION: WHERE QUANTITY AND QUALITY MEET

Reaching universal enrolment in primary schools is necessary for UPE, though not in itself sufficient. UPE also requires universal (or, more realistically, near-universal) completion of the primary curriculum, which can be achieved only if schools are of sufficient quality. Assessing the progression of pupils through primary schooling provides information on further quantitative aspects of the school system, as well as a first approach to assessing quality.

Late Enrolment

One initial issue is the age at which children are enrolled for the first time. While primary education is officially meant to start at age 5 or 6 in most countries, late enrolment is common throughout the developing world, for a variety of reasons, *e.g.* children's participation in family economic activities and the difficulty of walking to distant schools. Late enrolment means children would be completing their primary education at an age when constraints on school participation become stronger than during early childhood: more opportunities or pressure to work or get married and more limitations on girls' mobility, may reduce the probability of completing primary school. Moreover, late mastery of basic cognitive skills provides weaker foundations for further learning.

Intake rates can be used to assess the extent of late versus timely enrolment. The gross intake rate (GIR) is the number of new entrants to the first grade of primary school, regardless of age, as a percentage of the number of children at the official primary-school entrance age. The net intake rate (NIR) takes into account only those new entrants who are of the official entrance age. Like the NER, the NIR cannot exceed 100 per cent, while the GIR can, where early or late enrolment is common. It is remarkably complex.

All Western European and North American countries have GIRs close to 100 per cent, indicating school systems with the capacity to enrol all children and where the official age for initial enrolment is enforced.

To some extent, the same situation prevails in Central and Eastern Europe and Central Asia, although with somewhat higher GIRs. Countries of East Asia and the Pacific and of Latin America and the Caribbean have generally higher GIRs – with a median above 105 per cent and hardly any country having a GIR below 95 per cent – indicating either that insufficient access to pre-primary schooling leads to early enrolment, or that many children enrol late, or both. The situation is similar in South and West Asia, although with lower rates. The Arab States and, especially, sub-Saharan Africa include some countries with very high GIRs and some with very low ones.

Many school systems in these two regions have probably not yet reached the capacity to enrol all children in the first grade, while others are overloaded with late enrollers. Low GIRs are, by and large, specific to these two regions; out of the 107 countries for which data are available, the only ones outside these regions with GIRs below 90 per cent are Azerbaijan, the Islamic Republic of Iran, Latvia and the Netherlands Antilles. The rate falls below 65 per cent in eight countries: Burkina Faso, the Central African Republic, Congo, Eritrea, Mali and the Niger in sub-Saharan Africa and Djibouti and Sudan in the Arab States.

More direct evidence on late enrolment can be gained by examining NIRs. Slovakia's profile is typical of most high- and middleincome countries: 90 per cent of the children enrolled in the first grade are the official age or one year older. Against this benchmark, the extent of late enrolment in sub-Saharan African countries appears clearly: children two or more years older than the official age represent about 20 per cent to 40 per cent of first-grade pupils.

Retention

Once children are enrolled, it is crucial to ensure that they remain at school long enough to complete the curriculum and acquire basic skills. For a variety of school- or family-related reasons, large numbers of children drop out of school, or more accurately, are 'pushed out' (*e.g.* by the costs of schooling or by a child-unfriendly environment in the classroom) or 'drawn out' (to participate in household economic activities) before completing the fifth grade. These children are likely to be those who found it most difficult to cope with school and whose achievement levels are especially low.

The returns they will have from a couple of unsuccessful years of school attendance may be insignificant, compared with those that completion of primary schooling would bring. Reducing dropout rates is thus crucial. Covering ninety-one countries, shows that the survival rate to grade 5 (the proportion of children enrolled in grade 1 who eventually reach grade 5) varies considerably and is especially low in sub-Saharan Africa. The survival rate is below 75 per cent in thirty countries and below 66 per cent in half of the sub-Saharan African countries for which data are available. There is much more variation in countries with high survival rates, however. Survival rates tend to be higher for girls than for boys, in all regions.

This fact is not inconsistent with the typical gender gap in enrolment; in countries where parental preference for sons is strong and/or the school system and society discriminate against girls, families that manage to send their daughters to school tend to be more advantaged than those who send only their sons. Thus, on average, female pupils have more favourable family backgrounds than male pupils. Survival rates increased in many countries during the 1990s. For example, between 1998 and 2001, the increase was about 10 percentage points in Cambodia, Djibouti, the Lao People's Democratic Republic, Malawi, Mozambique, Namibia and Samoa. At the same time, however, substantial declines were registered in Chad, Colombia, Eritrea, Ghana, Madagascar, Mauritania, Rwanda and South Africa.

Grade Repetition

Grade repetition is another indicator of pupils' progress, although it can be difficult to interpret, because it depends on policy: some countries systematically promote pupils to the next grade while others apply stringent achievement criteria. Where grade repetition is possible, however, its incidence is a measure of the proportion of children who do not master the curriculum (*e.g.* because school quality was insufficient). A high level of grade repetition is a sign of a dysfunctional school system often exacerbating dropout and resulting in overcrowded schools.

In Senegal, where 14 per cent of primary school pupils repeat grades, a cohort study of some 2,000 pupils in nearly 100 schools found that repeating a grade at an early stage increased the risk of dropping out the following year by 11 per cent. Relatively few countries are affected by very high levels of grade repetition: two-thirds of the countries displayed have rates below 10 per cent. There is much diversity among the remaining countries, however, and in those where more than a quarter of pupils are repeating grades (such as Chad, Comoros, Gabon, Madagascar and Rwanda), repetition is equivalent to an additional year of participation per child. Finally, the condition of a primary education system is best judged by the proportion of children of each age cohort who complete the cycle and the level and distribution of their learning achievement.

MEETING LEARNING NEEDS BEYOND PRIMARY EDUCATION

Education for All extends well beyond primary education. Secondary education has been the standard minimum level of education for many years in most high-income countries and is increasingly required in developing countries for access to most jobs. Developing good-quality secondary school systems is thus an important policy objective, especially for countries that, by and large, have achieved UPE. At least some secondary education is compulsory in 144 of the 183 countries for which data are available (most of the exceptions are countries of sub-Saharan Africa and South and West Asia). However, the rules are not enforced in many countries and international standards are less explicit for secondary than for primary education.

For example, the 1950 Constitution of India (a country that is still far from having reached UPE) mandates free and compulsory education up to age 14. A recent constitutional amendment made education for ages 6 to 14 a 'fundamental right'. In most developing countries, a large proportion of primary-school graduates do not make the transition to post-primary education. Among countries in which lower-secondary education is supposed to be compulsory, only one-third have secondary-level GERs higher than 80 per cent.

Unfortunately, data on secondary and higher education are less available than those pertaining to primary education. The following discussion focuses on enrolment. Most countries in the world had reached primary GERs of 80 per cent or more by 2001, with exceptions in sub-Saharan Africa, South and West Asia and the Arab States. By contrast, the median secondary GER for developing countries in 2001 (57 per cent) was about half that for developed countries (106 per cent), and the only developing countries with GERs above the developed-country median were Brazil and Seychelles. The industrialized countries of Western Europe and North America have almost reached universal secondary education, with GERs often above 100 per cent and NERs above 90 per cent.

Secondary education is also well advanced in Central and Eastern Europe, where most GERs range from 80 per cent to 100 per cent. These levels are also reached by a few countries of East Asia and the Pacific, Latin America and the Caribbean and the Arab States, but those regions also include many countries with GERs around or even below 60 per cent. Meanwhile, there is extreme diversity within sub-Saharan Africa, which, like South and West Asia, some Arab States and a few countries of East Asia and the Pacific, has a concentration of countries with GERs below 40 per cent. With the notable exception of South Africa, sub- Saharan African countries with high secondary GERs have small populations.

The vast majority of the sub-continent's youth thus have little access to secondary education. Much the same is true for South and West Asia, where the countries with larger populations, such as Bangladesh, India and Pakistan, have secondary GERs between 24 per cent and 50 per cent. Here the gap between developed and developing countries is even more pronounced: the median GER is 55 per cent among the former, 11 per cent among the latter. With a few exceptions, countries in Western Europe and North America achieve ratios of 40 per cent or more, as do some countries in Central and

Eastern Europe and a handful of developed countries in East Asia and the Pacific. Elsewhere, higher education systems are far less developed. China's and India's tertiary GERs are substantially below 15 per cent. In more than a third of all developing countries for which data are available, GERs are below 5 per cent. This is the case in most sub-Saharan African countries. By and large, widespread access to higher education remains a privilege of high-income-country residents.

On the other hand, participation in secondary and tertiary education is growing, in many countries. Between 1998 and 2001, GERs rose by more than 2 percentage points in 80 out of 131 countries at the secondary level and 56 out of 95 countries at the tertiary level.

Gender Disparities in Secondary and Higher Education

Disparities between the sexes are even more prevalent in secondary and higher education than in primary education. Among the eighty-three developing countries for which data are available for all three levels, about 50 per cent have achieved gender parity (*i.e.* GPIs falling between 0.97 and 1.03) in gross enrolment in primary education. The share drops, however, to less than 20 per cent in secondary education and barely 5 per cent in higher education. Of the thirty-seven developed countries with data, some 95 per cent (all except Estonia and Portugal) have achieved gender parity in primary education, around 66 per cent have achieved it in secondary education and about 60 per cent in higher education.

Finally, of the ten countries in transition for which data are available, all except Tajikistan have achieved parity at both primary and secondary levels, and half have done so in tertiary education. A large group has low enrolment combined with gender imbalance (in favour of men) of widely differing magnitude – there is little association between enrolment and the *depth* of gender disparity at low levels of enrolment. Of the forty-six countries with secondary-level GERs below 50 per cent, forty-two show gender disparity favouring men. On the other hand, a large group of countries has a gender imbalance in favour of women, associated in most cases with high overall enrolment: most of the fifty-three countries with GERs above 90 per cent show gender disparity in favour of women.

School Life Expectancy

A good synthetic measure of enrolment patterns can be obtained by combining enrolment ratios by age at the different levels of the education system. The resulting indicator, school life expectancy (SLE), represents the average number of years of schooling that individuals can expect to receive. Caution is required when using SLE, however; like GER, it is sensitive to the extent of grade repetition. In at least twenty countries, repetition contributes more than one year to school life expectancy – and up to two years in Algeria,

Brazil, Gabon, Rwanda and Togo. Regional SLE averages and the countries with the highest and lowest values, both for primary and secondary education and for post-secondary education.

Regional patterns are consistent with those discussed earlier: a child in sub-Saharan Africa can expect to attend an average of five to six fewer years of primary and secondary schooling than a child in Western Europe or the Americas. Dramatic subregional disparities are found in sub-Saharan Africa and the Arab States, the difference between the countries with the highest and lowest SLEs being up to fivefold.

The world average is 10.3 years – 9.2 years of primary plus secondary and 1.1 of postsecondary education, which also presents the change in SLE between 1990 and 2001 and between 1998 and 2001. Globally, the world's children gained a year of school life expectancy during the 1990s. Progress was quickest in regions with already high SLEs, such as Latin America and the Caribbean (where grade repetition is very common) and North America and Western Europe. Less progress was registered in sub-Saharan Africa, and South and West Asia. Unsurprisingly, most of the progress took place in primary and secondary education in developing countries and in higher education in developed countries.

TEACHERS, FINANCE AND QUALITY

The relatively high primary-school enrolment ratios around the world today are the result of rapid expansion of school supply over the twentieth century, especially in the second half. There is much debate about the relationship between, on the one hand, the rapid increases in enrolment and in the quantity of education provided (in terms of years of school completed), and, on the other, the quality of that education, whether in terms of a school system's characteristics or of the achievement of its pupils. The view that emphasis on access to education has led to inadequate attention being paid to quality, and that improving the quality of existing schools should now be a policy priority, is gaining ground.

But even if some trade-off exists between the coverage and the level of perpupil funding of a school system, this does not necessarily imply that developing countries have to choose between further expanding access to primary schooling and improving its quality. When expressed as a percentage of GDP, the increase in education expenditure required to improve both coverage and per-pupil funding is not insurmountable when seen in light of total government expenditure. The real issue is the political economy of allocating public expenditure among sectors, rather than constraints on education budgets *per se.*

Moreover, there is much scope for reducing inefficiency in existing school systems. In particular, developing ECCE programmes while improving the functioning of primary schools is likely to result in more timely entry into the school system and less grade repetition, thus allowing additional enrolment. And while per-pupil funding may not increase as quickly as enrolment when, for instance, major school construction programmes are under way, some countries may have both higher enrolment ratios and better schools than others, as a result of policies giving priority to education.

Increased concern for education quality has been reflected in growing pressure to collect data on, and develop adequate indicators of, school quality. Some of this pressure results from global initiatives such as Education for All. Change is also taking place at the national level, where policy-makers need better understanding of the factors that are most effective in improving learning outcomes. It should be clear that no single or simple set of indicators will enable policy-makers to assess progress towards improved quality. Instead, a range of indicators is needed to capture the complex, multi-level nature of the concept.

Moreover, some aspects of a broadened vision of education quality are difficult to quantify in internationally comparable ways. This section looks at indicators related to quality that are readily available and internationally comparable. It thus tends to focus on inputs, such as numbers and characteristics of teachers, and the level and allocation of education funding. Many other aspects, such as teaching practices and teacher incentives, are known to matter just as much but data on them are insufficient. Resources, however, are a necessary albeit insufficient condition for learning, and the inadequate resource levels found in many developing countries imply that school reform should include additional funding, alongside attention to more complex considerations.

Considerable evidence indicates not only that children from poor families have less access to education than those who are better off, but also that those who do participate receive a lowerquality education. Even countries that have achieved some degree of equity in terms of overall access still tend to favour certain population groups or areas in the allocation of education resources.

MONITORING THE QUALITY OF TEACHERS AND TEACHING

Teacher and teaching quality, broadly defined, have often been identified as the most important organizational factors associated with student achievement. Unfortunately, they are difficult to measure and monitor. How teachers are prepared for teaching is a critical indicator of education quality. Preparing teachers for the challenges of a changing world means equipping them with subject-specific expertise, effective teaching practices, an understanding of technology and the ability to work collaboratively with other teachers, members of the community and parents.

Teacher Qualifications, Training and Content Knowledge in Primary Education

Available data suggest that large proportions of primary-school teachers lack adequate academic qualifications, training and content knowledge, especially in developing countries. This suggests that much pre-service training may be ineffective. Pre-service training usually combines theoretical and content knowledge with teaching practice in schools but there are wide variations in the relative weight given to these two elements and in their modes of delivery.

In some countries, where there is a pressure to recruit new teachers quickly, the length of college-based training is shortening and the sequencing of practical and academic training changing. The level of education (classified according to ISCED levels) required by national qualification standards for entering primary school teaching and the proportion of the teaching force that meets this requirement, in twenty-six sub-Saharan African countries. National standards vary considerably, from lower secondary (equivalent to nine or ten grades of basic schooling plus one or two years of training) to a tertiary degree (in South Africa).

The average number of years of academic study and teacher training required to become a primary school teacher ranges from just over twelve years among countries where the standard is lower secondary to seventeen years where it is higher education. How well countries meet their own standards can also vary considerably. Less than 10 per cent of the teaching force meets even the low minimum standard of lower secondary in Benin or Burkina Faso, and many other countries fall short of standards set at the upper secondary level, notably Angola, Chad and Namibia. In Botswana, Côte d'Ivoire, Kenya and Zambia, however, almost the entire teaching force reaches the upper secondary standard.

Furthermore, while the growing supply of educated youth in most countries may be thought to imply that newly recruited teachers will have higher qualification levels, the proportion of new primary-school teachers meeting national standards has actually been falling in several countries. For example, only 30 per cent of teachers in their first year of experience met the standards (post-secondary non-tertiary) in the Gambia. The proportions were even lower in Botswana (10 per cent), Lesotho (11 per cent) and Chad (19 per cent), where the standard was an upper-secondary qualification, and in Togo (2 per cent), Guinea-Bissau (15 per cent) and Cameroon (15 per cent), where it was lower-secondary.

This phenomenon may reflect the increasingly common practice of recruiting teachers without the necessary qualifications in response to pressures caused by expanding levels of enrolment. Further evidence comes from primary-school surveys conducted in 1995 in fourteen of the world's poorest countries – in sub-Saharan Africa and South and West Asia.

Interestingly, in most of them a majority of teachers had received at least some training even though they had very low academic qualifications (an extreme case is Benin, where 92 per cent of primary-school teachers had less than ten years of education but 99 per cent had received training). Ethiopia and Uganda stand out, the former owing to above average and the latter to below average proportions of educated and trained teachers.

As it covers seventy-two countries with data on teacher training for 2001. Although the coverage is insufficient for general patterns to emerge (*e.g.* no data are available for OECD countries or most large countries of Latin America and the Caribbean), large disparities between countries can be seen; a minority of countries provide training to almost all their teachers. Several countries, notably in sub-Saharan Africa, feature large gender gaps, though sometimes it is women who are favoured (this is the case to some extent in one-third of the sample). Having low average levels of teacher qualification and training leaves much scope for unequal distribution within countries.

High levels of adult illiteracy are a good indicator of socio-economic and educational deprivation, for they reflect the history of local school systems as well as what families invest in children's education. Most trained teachers tend to be in the parts of the country that need them least. In the states with, at worst, 12 per cent illiteracy, 60 per cent or more of the teachers meet the national training standards, but elsewhere the situation is extremely variable.

The six states of the Nordeste region, generally the most disadvantaged area of Brazil, have among the lowest proportions of trained teachers. Teachers' formal qualifications however may not reflect teacher quality as adequately as the ability to make the best use of learning materials, students' work and their own subject knowledge.

These skills are even more salient in especially difficult situations, such as countries in conflict. Teacher subject knowledge is crucial and has been shown to be a good predictor of student achievement. In many developing countries, levels of subject knowledge are a problem. A recent study in seven southern African countries finds that some primary-school mathematics teachers possess only basic numeracy, actually scoring less in tests than students. Provision of training and other forms of support based on relevant quality indicators can help build the confidence of undertrained teachers and enable them to become more competent.

Teacher Absenteeism

Teacher absenteeism, a persistent problem in many countries, reduces the quality of education and results in a waste of resources. In 2003, investigators for a World Bank study who made random visits to 200 primary schools in India found no teaching activity in half of them. Up to 45 per cent of teachers in Ethiopia had been absent at least one day in the week before a visit – 10 per cent of them for three days or more, and in Uganda and Zambia the shares of teachers who had been absent in the previous week were 26 per cent and 17 per cent, respectively. This continues to confirm the findings of school surveys conducted in fourteen low-income countries in 1995, which showed high rates of absenteeism, especially in sub-Saharan African countries, *e.g.* the United Republic of Tanzania (38 per cent), Uganda (30 per cent) and Zambia (25 per cent), and in South and West Asia, *e.g.* Bhutan (14 per cent), Nepal (11 per cent) and Bangladesh (8 per cent).

High levels of teacher absenteeism generally indicate severe dysfunctions in the school system, but they may have many different direct causes. Lax professional standards and lack of support and control by education authorities are major issues in many countries. Education policy deficiencies can also play a role, for instance where teachers are reassigned to other classrooms or schools must travel to obtain their monthly pay or need to take a second job to supplement insufficient salaries. Appropriate support and better incentive structures may help reduce levels of teacher absenteeism. The high level of prevalence of HIV/AIDS in a growing number of developing countries, especially in sub-Saharan Africa, is a major factor influencing teacher absenteeism and lack of effectiveness, sometimes leading to high teaching-staff attrition rates.

The impact on efforts to extend or improve the national school system can be dramatic. For example, it is estimated that 815 primary-school teachers in Zambia died from AIDS in 2000 – the equivalent of 45 per cent of the teachers trained that year. The disease's impact on school systems is a major reason that HIV/AIDS has wide-ranging effects over the long run. With epidemics developing in many countries of South and West Asia, East Asia and the Pacific, Central Asia, and Central and Eastern Europe, HIV/AIDS is a major global constraint on the provision of good-quality education.

TEACHER DEPLOYMENT AND EDUCATION OUTCOMES

Besides qualifications and training, the number and distribution of teachers are important policy parameters helping to determine the quality of education pupils and students receive. At the school level, the most visible element of teacher deployment is class size, or the number of pupils a teacher has to teach. While the impact of class size on educational outcomes remains a matter of debate and depends on the pedagogy used, the very large class sizes observed in primary schools in many developing countries are clearly not conducive to adequate learning.

Children in areas not yet covered by primary-school systems probably need smaller class sizes than the average because they are often first-generation learners from underprivileged social groups and are more likely to belong to a minority whose language is not used as a medium of instruction. Furthermore, curricula are usually divided into grades, requiring one teacher per grade for effective teaching or requiring special training in the case of multigrade teaching. While data on class sizes and the number of teachers per grade in each school are not widely available, teacher deployment policies can be approached through the pupil/teacher ratio. High PTRs may signify an overstretched teaching staff, while low ratios may mean there is additional capacity.

However, the PTR measured at the national level can mask disparities among regions and schools. For instance, the national primary PTR in Mauritania is 35:1, but some schools may have one teacher for every ten pupils while others have one for every sixty pupils. Moreover, the ratio depends on an accurate count of teachers who have classroom responsibilities, and should be adjusted, as far as possible, to account for part-time teaching, teaching in shifts and multigrade classes. Keeping in mind these caveats, The ratios are low in regions where enrolment ratios are high – in particular North America and Western Europe, Central and Eastern Europe, and Central Asia – and high in regions where enrolments are low, notably South and West Asia and sub-Saharan Africa, with median values of 40:1 and 44:1, respectively.

This implies that teacher numbers are a problem in the very countries that most need more teachers in order to increase significantly the coverage of their primary school systems. In the Arab States, East Asia and the Pacific and in Latin America and the Caribbean, most countries have fifteen to thirty-four pupils per teacher.

Unacceptably high PTRs exist in many schools and districts of individual countries, of course, but this is more a matter of the distribution of teachers than of their total number. The evolution of the median PTR by region from 1990 to 1998 and 2001, for countries with data available for all three years, makes these regional patterns even clearer. It shows PTRs that are relatively low and have been declining or fairly stable in all regions except sub-Saharan Africa, where the median rose from 40:1 in 1990 to 47:1 in 2001. The situation in this region may be explained by demography: high population growth translates into larger cohorts of potential primary-school pupils and increasing enrolment – with which the school system cannot keep pace. In three sub-Saharan countries that saw an especially steep rise in PTRs between 1998 and 2001 – Ethiopia (23 per cent), Nigeria (28 per cent) and the United Republic of Tanzania (22 per cent) – efforts to widen access to primary education partly explain the rise. Indeed, the PTR increased in almost every country where the net enrolment ratio increased, *e.g.* in Ethiopia from 46:1 to 57:1 and the United Republic of Tanzania from 38:1 to 46:1. More generally, in sub-Saharan African countries whose PTR grew over the decade, that growth slightly accelerated after 1998.

The PTR also increased between 1998 and 2001 in East Asia and the Pacific, reversing the trend of the early and mid-1990s. Once again, while countries with a strong political commitment towards education have both high enrolment and low PTRs, those starting with low enrolment ratios may face severe quantity/quality trade-offs, in the short run. These can be avoided only if countries can mobilize substantially more resources for education or recruit additional teachers at lower salaries without compromising teaching quality. The latter course has been tried in many countries, but more evidence as to its effectiveness is needed than is yet available.

Indeed, expansion of educational opportunity and the concomitant demand for teachers tend to put quality at risk if entry requirements for teachers are relaxed and/or the workload of the current teaching force increases. In countries where PTRs are already very high, further demands on teachers could be detrimental to teacher capacity and morale and result in diminished learning outcomes among students. In general, low PTRs are associated with high survival rates to the last grade of primary school. However, the dispersion in the survival rate is higher within the group of countries with high PTRs than within that with low PTRs.

Thus, the negative relationship appears to be between these two groups rather than within them. The PTR here should be interpreted more as a general indicator of the state of the school system than as a cause of low survival rates, as countries with comparable PTRs achieve dramatically different survival rates. Many other factors enter the picture. On the other hand, it is difficult to believe that high PTRs are not an issue in countries such as Chad, where the PTR exceeds 70:1 and where only one in three pupils starting school reaches the final grade.

WHEN MONEY MATTERS: INVESTING IN EDUCATION

While teachers are the most important resource in education, it is worth looking at other resources available to schools that have an important impact on prospects for high-quality teaching. Detailed data on factors such as school buildings and equipment or teaching/learning materials may not be available for a large sample of countries, nor would they be very informative on their own. Aggregate expenditure on education, however, is a good indicator of policy-makers' commitment to education quality. This indicator of policy preferences may not have the same significance everywhere.

Differences in relative prices of education inputs, allocation of funding between teacher salaries and other inputs, and demographic structure mean different countries may have to spend at different levels to achieve comparable quality. For example, Germany and India spend comparable proportions of their GDP on education (slightly more than 4 per cent) but Germany's wealthy, ageing population has access to a completely different education system than India's poor, young and still quickly growing population. Regional patterns are consistent with those observed for enrolment ratios and teacher deployment: the highest median is that of North America and Western Europe and the lowest that of sub-Saharan Africa. Given differences in GDP levels and the proportions of school-age children in the population, this implies dramatic differences in per-pupil resources between the two regions. Several large countries of South and West Asia and of East Asia and the Pacific are also notable for low levels of expenditure. The high levels found in a few island states can be explained by specific factors. For example, the GDP of the countries may be small, or they do not benefit from economies of scale because their schoolage population is small, or students have to leave the country for higher education, implying substantial costs if this is subsidized by the state.

While most countries have predominantly public education systems, government expenditure is not total expenditure. A different picture would emerge if data on private expenditure on education were available. Countries have different mixes of public and private schooling, and a shift of emphasis from what *governments* invest in education to what *societies* invest is needed to take this into account.

Household expenditure on education, for instance, is generally substantial even in many countries where at least primary schooling is officially provided free by the state. The share of private expenditure in primary and secondary education has been estimated at 42 per cent in Jamaica, 33 per cent in the Philippines, 30 per cent in Chile, 24 per cent in Indonesia and 21 per cent in Colombia, to take but a few examples. During the late 1990s, showing changes in real expenditure in the relatively few countries that provided data for both 1998 and 2001. Spending levels were generally stable in North America and Western Europe but quite a few developing countries increased spending considerably, notably in East Asia and the Pacific, and Latin America and the Caribbean.

A few large countries reduced expenditure significantly, however, *e.g.* the Philippines (–24 per cent) and Indonesia (–8 per cent). Public and private expenditures on education are often intertwined and complementary, notably where governments provide partial funding to private institutions. For instance, in Zimbabwe, 80 per cent of primary-school pupils attend government-dependent private schools whose teachers are paid by the government, while other costs are borne by local communities. Such public/private partnerships are being promoted increasingly as a way to mitigate the impact of uncertainties and insufficiencies in public expenditure.

They raise quality and equity issues, however, since communities differ in their ability to attract government expenditure as well as raise private funds. The allocation of education expenditure matters a great deal in translating funds into education outcomes. Teachers' salaries tend to account for by far the greatest item of expenditure, especially in developing countries. Debates have been raging about differences in salary costs among countries and whether high salaries impede efforts to expand and improve school systems so as to achieve EFA goals. Data on the share of primary teachers' salaries in total public current expenditure for primary education are available for fifty-one countries; among these, the shares exceed 90 per cent in eleven countries.

By comparison, figures for the share of textbooks and other teaching materials in public current expenditure for primary education, among the twenty countries providing such data, range from 0.8 per cent in Belize to 12 per cent in the Republic of Moldova.

Clearly, teachers' salaries are a central issue in the political economy of education. More generally, it has been suggested that teacherrelated inputs receive a disproportionate share of expenditure. Designing adequate salary and nonsalary incentives to motivate teachers appears to be a priority, as the need to save resources for other inputs has to be balanced against the need to pay teachers well enough to attract and retain qualified individuals. While the degree of causal relationship between education expenditure and outcomes has proved difficult to estimate, the two are clearly related. The relationship is most evident for the few developing countries participating in the study, countries of Central and Eastern Europe and countries of Western Europe with relatively low expenditure levels, such as Greece and Ireland.

Among other countries of Western Europe, variation in literacy scores is limited even as expenditure doubles from about PPP US$40,000 to about PPP US$80,000. This suggests that resources can have a strong impact on outcomes when initial spending is low, but that the impact levels off as spending increases: additional resources might be wasted or devoted to other purposes than improving the kind of performance measured by literacy tests.

As the graph does not take into account factors such as the efficiency of resource allocation and use or family background, large differences in literacy scores may be observed between countries with similar spending levels, *e.g.* Poland and Chile or Argentina. Note also, that Mexico, Chile and Argentina reach similar average scores, even though Mexico spends only PPP US$12,189 per student, compared with PPP US$17,820 in Chile and PPP $18,893 in Argentina.

The graph is also silent about whether there is a causal relationship or just a correlation between expenditure and performance. What matters is rather the consistency of regional patterns regarding the variables analysed in this chapter. Some countries have high achievement levels coupled with high enrolment ratios and high expenditure; others combine low enrolment with low expenditure and low achievement. Thus, while it is true that increasing resources remains fundamental in many countries, it is unlikely to improve performance significantly if other factors behind the differences are not addressed.

QUALITY AND EQUALITY OF LEARNING

School systems are meant to produce a multitude of outputs, from equipping students with knowledge and cognitive skills to cultivating creative minds and fostering civic and moral values. Assessing their success in doing so is difficult, for two reasons. First, different stakeholders assign their own values to different objectives, and maximizing one kind of output may not be consistent with maximizing others: *e.g.* creative thinking may conflict with values emphasized by authoritarian curricula. Comparing school systems on the basis of one type of output may not do justice to those who emphasize other types. Second, some outputs are easier to measure and compare than others. It is relatively straightforward to measure mastery of simple skills through standardized testing, but more difficult to do the same for critical thinking and creativity. Although knowledge and cognitive skills have not necessarily been the only priority of many government school systems, they have received the lion's share of attention in assessment exercises that have provided internationally comparable data.

While each country has its own system of classroom-based assessment and public examinations, national and international assessments of student learning through standardized tests are increasingly used to monitor and evaluate the overall quality of education systems, to diagnose their relative strengths and weaknesses and to shed light on policy options that could enable good-quality learning for all. This section focuses on the evidence emerging from such assessments. It should be noted that although cognitive skills can be measured, defining which achievement levels can be deemed satisfactory is a complex issue.

NATIONALAND INTERNATIONAL ASSESSMENTS OF COGNITIVE SKILLS

In Nicaragua in 2002, 70 per cent of students reached only the 'basic' level in language and more than 80 per cent did so in mathematics. In Uruguay in 1999, the performance of 40 per cent of sixth-graders was considered 'unsatisfactory' or 'highly unsatisfactory' in language and the share was 60 per cent in mathematics. In El Salvador in 1999, 40 per cent of sixth-graders reached only the 'basic' level in language, mathematics, science and social studies. In Honduras in 2002, 90 per cent of sixthgraders performed at 'low' or 'insufficient' level in language and mathematics. Thus, whatever the relevance of the criteria used, all four countries consider the overall performance of their school system unsatisfactory.

The SACMEQ study showed poor performance among primary school students in reading literacy, according to standards established by national reading experts and sixth-grade teachers. In four out of seven countries, fewer than half of sixth-graders achieved the minimum level in reading. Only 1 per cent of sixth-graders tested in Malawi and 37 per cent in Zimbabwe achieved the desirable level in reading. Thus, no country in this study met the target suggested in 1990 at Jomtien for 2000 with respect to reading skills. Although average achievement is much higher in developed than in developing countries, low achievement is an issue in many middle-income countries and affects significant minorities of the population in high-income countries.

The PIRLS results indicate that large numbers of fourthgraders in several of the thirty-five countries participating in the study have limited reading skills. More than half the students failed to reach the bottom quartile (the international benchmark) in Argentina, Belize, Colombia, the Islamic Republic of Iran and Morocco, among the middle-income countries, and in Kuwait, among the high-income countries – which typically have a less-than-20 per cent share of low achievers. 18 per cent of 15-year-old students in the OECD as a whole (mostly high-income countries and a few middle-income ones) performed at or below level 1, indicating very low reading ability. Among students in middle- and low-income countries, 40 per cent or more performed at or below level 1 – for example, more than 60 per cent in Albania, Indonesia and the former Yugoslav Republic of Macedonia, and as high as 80 per cent in Peru.

DISPARITIES IN ACHIEVEMENT WITHIN COUNTRIES

The data presented consistently suggest that low achievement is widespread and that it most seriously affects countries whose school systems are weak in terms of enrolment and resources. The distribution of achievement levels within countries is another cause for concern, as low-achieving pupils never represent a random sample of the population. Although the specific determinants of low achievement are best examined in a national context, results from national and international assessments suggest that pupils from rural areas and from socioeconomically disadvantaged backgrounds are particularly vulnerable.

Learning disparities associated with socioeconomic status begin in the early grades and continue through all levels of education. Children with low academic achievement may be more vulnerable to grade repetition and dropout. Since most school subjects build on fundamentals introduced in early grades, low-achieving primary school pupils may also face difficulties in later grades. Indeed, poor learning outcomes in early school years are often a good predictor of educational, social and economic disadvantages in adulthood.

The relationship between academic performance and socio-economic status varies by country as much as average achievement itself. The relationship is sometimes termed a 'socio-economic gradient' or 'learning bar'. In the graph illustrating the LLECE results, the learning bars show the relationship between reading achievement of third and fourth graders and the years of schooling completed by their parents. The PISA graph shows the relationship between reading performance and a statistical composite indicating socio-economic status (SES), made up of the parents' level of education and occupation and indices of the family's material, educational and cultural possessions. Socio-economic gradients vary considerably among countries. In the LLECE study, Cuba had the highest level of student achievement and the smallest variation in parents' educational attainment.

Detailed analyses of the LLECE data revealed several factors in Cuba's success, including universal day care, more prevalence of home educational activities, smaller class sizes, higher levels of school and classroom material resources, better-trained teachers, greater parental involvement in school, a strong classroom disciplinary climate and relatively few multigrade or ability-grouped classes. In several large countries, such as Indonesia, on average, students from the most favourable backgrounds perform worse than OECD students from the least favourable backgrounds, clearly suggesting unsatisfactory performance of the school system itself.

ASSURING QUALITY WHILE EXPANDING ACCESS: A DUAL CHALLENGE

Achieving good-quality learning for all requires that all school-age children have access to learning opportunities and that all students receive good-quality schooling. In reality, countries achieve various mixes of attainment and achievement. Four scenarios may be distinguished: some school systems combine quantity and quality, others fail either on quantity or on quality and others combine low quantity with unsatisfactory quality. Policy priorities may vary accordingly, from mere adjustments to further improvement of already high-quality schooling to complete reshaping of the system. The standard notion of a quantityquality trade-off is often thought of as implying that countries cannot combine high quantity and high quality, but the concept is probably more relevant in a short-term, dynamic perspective.

Thus within a country, quickly expanding the school system without reducing its quality, or immediately achieving high quality in new schools, may be difficult. Indeed, no trade-off appears on any of the panels. There is no clear pattern for SACMEQ and PASEC, and PIRLS countries achieve widely variable quality for comparably high enrolment ratios. There is more variation in the PISA sample, in which it appears clearly, once again, that countries with stronger school systems combine better quality and quantity than others. The key question for achieving EFA, then, is not whether existing school systems should be expanded, given that this may put quality at risk, but rather how countries that combine high quantity and quality have arrived at this satisfactory situation.

LITERACY AND SKILLS DEVELOPMENT

The spread of basic cognitive skills such as literacy and numeracy is key to individual and societal development. Universalizing quality education implies that the children who benefit from it will become literate adults, though, of course, elementary education should include more than the mere mastery of basic cognitive skills. But much can also be done outside the formal school system to help youth and adults who have never been enrolled or have not completed enough schooling to become literate. Whether the immediate benefits of adult literacy programmes are of the same magnitude as the future benefits of formal schooling is a difficult question, but opportunities to reduce the proportion of the adult population that is illiterate should not be neglected, as this is an important complement to EFA in the child population. The spread of literacy is a major societal change, but its nature is bound to be country-specific, given the history of each written language and the individual and collective uses of literacy that will arise.

Literacy thus depends not only on efforts by governments, international organizations and NGOs to provide primary schooling and literacy education, but also on individuals' family and socio-cultural context and their attitudes towards written matter. A related process is the teaching of life skills, which are meant to help individuals function effectively in society.

DEFINING AND MEASURING LITERACY

Measuring EFA and other international goals concerning literacy requires agreement on operational definitions of the literacy status of an individual. This is a difficult exercise and several indicators are in use. Data typically originate in censuses or, more rarely, household surveys. As a general principle, these indicators are predicated on the traditional UNESCO definition of literacy, *i.e.* 'the ability to read and write, with understanding, a short simple sentence about one's everyday life'. Other definitions are also used.. A recent shift in the discourse of international organizations, from a dichotomous approach (literate and illiterate) to recognition of the existence of a continuum of literacy levels, is reflected in the notion of 'good-quality literacy'.

This notion tries to take into account the range of functional skills applicable in a variety of situations (*e.g.* reading a legal contract or a newspaper or using a computer) and the fact that what ultimately matters is the ability to grasp the meaning(s) of a text and develop critical judgement. Most discussions of literacy emphasize reading, but the ability to write correctly is as important, and complementary numeracy skills should not be overlooked. The literacy data currently available are too narrowly focused to reflect a set of skills that includes much more than the ability to decipher a text. One of the practical difficulties met with when assessing literacy is that different methods may yield different literacy rates.

Sometimes a test is administered in which respondents have to read a sentence from a printed card and the interviewer judges whether they can read it aloud correctly. Most available data sets, however, rely on the respondent's answer to a question regarding his or her own literacy. Often the head of the household responds for all members of the household. Significant distortions may arise because, for instance, respondents consider themselves literate since they can write their name or are reluctant to admit they cannot read. In a study in rural Bangladesh, more than half of those who asserted that they could write were not recognized as being able to do so according to a minimum standard. Many countries do not collect national literacy data, but use educational attainment levels as a proxy. For example, in some countries, all those who have completed a certain number of years of school or reached a particular grade are considered literate. Using attainment as a proxy for literacy, however, can result in a sharp underestimation of illiteracy levels, since it is not uncommon for residents of countries with weak education systems to attend or even complete primary school without acquiring lasting literacy skills. The case of Ghana illustrates the difficulty of reaching an unambiguous measure of literacy. Not only do census- and survey-based figures pertaining to the early 1990s and 2000s differ from each other, but self-reported literacy also differs from grade 5 completion and a language test.

Both sources suggest that self-reported literacy is higher than the actual figure, and the language test, which may be considered the most accurate of the three measures, yields the lowest literacy levels. The measured increase in literacy over the 1990s is also highly dependent on the method used; by self-reporting on the census the increase is 3 percentage points, compared with 8 percentage points according to a language test in the household survey. The examples illustrate the diversity of current definitions and measurements, which contributes to the difficulties in making comparisons and drawing conclusions about the global state of literacy.

GLOBAL ESTIMATES OF ADULT AND YOUTH LITERACY

Patterns of Adult Literacy

There are nearly 800 million adult illiterates in the world, representing 18 per cent of the adult population. Two facts stand out. First, 64 per cent of adult illiterates are women. The proportion varies widely by region, from 55 per cent in Latin America and the Caribbean to 77 per cent in Central and Eastern Europe and close to the world average in sub-Saharan Africa, the Arab States and South and West Asia. Absolute numbers may be influenced by demographic characteristics, however; the ratio of the literacy rate for females to that for males (*i.e.* the gender parity index) is a better measure of gender disparities. It ranges from 0.63 to 0.77 in South and West Asia, the Arab States and sub-Saharan Africa, and is above 0.90 in the rest of the world.

Indeed, the GPI is lowest where average literacy is also lowest, *e.g.* 0.53 in Pakistan and below 0.50 in countries such as Benin, Burkina Faso, Mali, Nepal, the Niger and Yemen, where total adult literacy is below 50 per cent. Given the impact of literacy on female well-being, autonomy and empowerment, actions aimed at achieving gender parity are urgently needed. They would yield comprehensive benefits in the long run as well, given the relationship between women's education, their fertility and the development of their children. About a quarter of the adult population of the developing world is illiterate. Latin America and the Caribbean and East Asia and the Pacific both have literacy rates in the neighbourhood of 90 per cent but, as relatively populous regions, they account for 22 per cent of the world's illiterates. Truly severe illiteracy is concentrated in the three regions whose school systems have been shown in previous sections to be the weakest: sub-Saharan Africa, the Arab States and South and West Asia, which have literacy rates of around 60 per cent. These regions account for three-quarters of the world's illiterates. South and West Asia alone, with its very large population, accounts for more than half.

Literacy rates below 60 per cent are found in 22 of the 119 countries for which data are available. With the exception of Haiti, all are located in those three regions. The lowest rates are found in Burkina Faso (13 per cent), the Niger (17 per cent) and Mali (19 per cent), in sub-Saharan Africa. Note that some sub-national entities in South and West Asia have populations and literacy rates comparable to those of these entire countries. Of the world's adult illiterates, over 70 per cent, or 562 million persons, live in only nine countries with some 34 per cent in India alone. The other countries are either countries of sub-Saharan Africa, the Arab States or South and West Asia with low literacy rates (below 70 per cent) and sizeable populations (Bangladesh, Egypt, Pakistan, Nigeria, Ethiopia), or populous countries of Latin America and the Caribbean and East Asia and the Pacific with high literacy rates but large absolute numbers of illiterates (mostly China, with a literacy rate of 91 per cent, but also Indonesia and Brazil, both with a literacy rate of 88 per cent).

There has been significant progress in levels of literacy over the 1990s, as exemplified by census results available for five countries that account for 46 per cent of the world's population and 56 per cent of the world's adult illiterates. China has dramatically reduced female illiteracy through early and sustained efforts promoting school for girls and women, and the gender gap has shrunk from 18.9 to 8.6 percentage points. It has started narrowing in India, where male and female literacy rates increased quickly between the last two censuses. Yet a striking contrast remains between, on the one hand, Pakistan (where literacy essentially stagnated, especially among men) and, on the other, Brazil, China and Indonesia, with literacy now above 80 per cent for both sexes.

Youth Literacy

The literacy rate among the population aged 15 to 24 is another indicator of progress towards Education for All and the Millennium Development Goals. Youth literacy reflects the education system's ability to deliver basic literacy skills, as well as the extent of literacy-related activities and other forms of support that children and youth receive at home. In general, literacy rates tend to be higher among youth than adults, because of recent expansion of access to basic education. The latest available estimates indicate that there are nearly 137 million illiterate youths in the world (17 per cent of all adult illiterates), 85 million of them (63 per cent) female.

Youth literacy rates are above 70 per cent in all regions, though individual countries fall below the average. In developing regions, youth illiteracy rates range from 2 per cent in East Asia and the Pacific to 28 per cent in South and West Asia. Gender disparities are generally less pronounced in youth literacy than in adult literacy, but regional variations follow the same line as for adults, with gaps between men and women still notable among youth in South and West Asia, the Arab States and sub-Saharan Africa. While national literacy rates vary widely by region and country, even greater variation exists in their distribution within countries.

In small island states such as Sao Tome and Principe and Comoros, there are very minor differences in the literacy status of young women and men, particularly in urban areas. In larger, more heterogeneous countries, the gaps between women and men and between rural and urban are considerable. In the six countries with relatively high primary enrolment ratios (Cameroon, Comoros, Equatorial Guinea, Madagascar, Rwanda, Sao Tome and Principe, with GER close to, or above, 90 per cent), the differences in literacy rates by gender are relatively minor. Nevertheless, there are enormous rural-urban differences, *e.g.* in Madagascar, Cameroon and Rwanda. In the remaining six countries, overall youth literacy rates are lower and the rates by gender and rural residence are startlingly different, except in Burundi.

There are more likely to be differences between urban youth by gender. For instance: literacy rates are 10 to 20 percentage points less for urban girls than for urban boys. In the Central African Republic, Sierra Leone, Chad and the Niger, fewer than one in four rural youths are literate, compared to one in ten young women, or fewer. These data reflect narrow, stratified access to learning opportunities and underline the importance of going beyond national averages to identify populations that are marginalized by low literacy skills.

SKILLS DEVELOPMENT IN FOUR COUNTRIES

Goal 3 of the Dakar Framework for Action addresses the learning needs of all young people and adults, especially those who missed out on a good basic education. It concerns various sorts of skills: the generic skills, more context-specific skills (including livelihood skills) and vocational skills, which are usually acquired in more formal settings. Efforts to systematically enhance these skills are increasingly referred to collectively as skills development. Literacy is not always seen as part of skills development. Four countries recently reviewed their skills development activities. Assisted by UNESCO and its International Institute for Educational Planning (IIEP), the Lao People's

Democratic Republic, Mali, Nepal and Senegal have developed a common framework to assess youth and adult learning needs and the provision of relevant learning opportunities. The aim is to identify gaps between the two and, after consultative meetings, prepare an Education for All Skills Development Plan.

This approach is intended to be applied in the near future in other countries, in the first instance the Pacific subregion, so that a more or less standardized instrument emerges for the monitoring of goal 3. In all four countries, national review teams found that governments tend to give little attention to disadvantaged and vulnerable young people who are not in school.

Their needs are commonly left to NGOs. Many initiatives exist to reach and empower the marginalized through non-formal vocational skills training, but they are often locally based, may be short-lived and are not part of a comprehensive national strategy. Government-sponsored skills training is often scattered in nature and not well coordinated, involving not only the ministry dealing with education but also those handling other sectors and issues (*e.g.* labour, agriculture, women, youth).

Defining Skills Development Programmes

The four countries looked at the following issues:

- Who are the target groups?
- What skills are relevant in specific contexts?
- What programmes are being provided in formal and non-formal settings, public and private?
- Which training methods work best in centrebased programmes, which in communitybased programmes and which in distance education?
- What are the roles of government and NGOs?
- Who are the trainers? How can they be better recruited, trained and supported?
- What languages should be used?
- What are the financing sources and mechanisms for skills development?
- How can skills development strategies and programmes best be monitored and evaluated?

Young people who drop out of primary school or never attended one are a major target group for skills development (although in countries or regions where most children complete primary school, secondary-school dropouts can have a relative disadvantage). Irrespective of educational background, certain groups have been identified as vulnerable. These mainly include those living in a difficult environment (Lao People's Democratic Republic); sensitive occupational groups, *e.g.* apprentices in the informal sector (Mali and Senegal); marginalized minority groups (low-caste persons in Nepal); various ethnic minorities (Lao People's Democratic Republic and Nepal); street children (Mali and Senegal) and disabled youth (all four countries). Only scattered indications of the size of these out-of-school groups are available, as reliable data are scarce. In Nepal, some 80 per cent of adolescents are neither in school nor in a training institution.

In the Lao People's Democratic Republic, about 53 per cent of 15-year-olds, 67 per cent of 16-year-olds and 75 per cent of 17-year-olds are out of school. In each country, the review teams identified a set of skills important for social inclusion and poverty reduction in the local context. Agricultural and artisan skills were particularly emphasized. In many cases, especially in poor rural areas, wage employment is rare so skills development must focus on livelihoods – the activities and means by which individuals make a living independently. Household and community needs have to be taken into account. In an effort to improve the impact of skills development programmes, countries (*e.g.* the Lao People's Democratic Republic) sometimes include posttraining microcredit initiatives, which pose additional challenges for programme management and the development of monitoring and evaluation tools.

Countries can begin to design national skills development strategies only if there is adequate information on programme providers, course content and duration, enrolment, costs and fees. Among the many ministries that may be involved, those in charge of education tend to have the best data on skills development. As regards NGO participation, some programmes are supported by large international organizations and others by local, community-based groups. In all four countries, the latter type makes up the larger part of the NGO sector, but data are usually scarce. The former type, while smaller, is generally more transparent. In Mali and Senegal, contracting to NGOs is an important means of implementing skills development programmes, particularly those aimed at reaching apprentices in the informal sector. Nepal is considering this approach, possibly via a skills development fund. The involvement of subcontractors increases the need for tight monitoring. The allocation of public resources to private providers normally necessitates the establishment of mechanisms to assure quality, efficiency and transparency.

Such control is easier when some support functions are publicly provided, such as funding or training of trainers. Locating the most vulnerable groups is another challenge, especially in large and culturally diverse countries with strong disparities between richer and poorer areas. The Lao People's Democratic Republic is using a geographical information system to chart the areas where poverty, school dropout rates and gender disparities need most urgently to be addressed and where there is a risk of learning opportunities being insufficient.

Assessing Skills Development Programmes

As with other educational programmes, efficiency of skills development programmes can be measured by dropout and completion rates, while effectiveness should be measured through direct assessment of the skills and knowledge acquired. However, as with literacy programmes, such data are seldom available. Short skills programmes are rarely followed by an exam, and where they are, the results are not often recorded. Nevertheless, in Mali and Nepal there is increasing interest in awarding certificates for successful completion of longer programmes, and the Lao People's Democratic Republic is also interested in defining the equivalence of such certificates to formal qualifications.

Equivalence policies should allow learners to build their own pathways, for instance by first attending nonformal learning and then making a transition (back) to school (an option that is mainly realistic for younger members of target groups). Discussions in the Lao People's Democratic Republic and Nepal on establishing a national qualification framework suggest that eventually more systematic data collection on achievement will be possible. Non-formal skills development programmes tend to cost less than formal vocational education, though precise information about costs is difficult to obtain, because such programmes are often subsidized by external donors and not covered by national statistics.

Furthermore, the diversity of programmes offered by a given provider (long-term/shortterm, centre-based/community-based, agricultural skills/ industrial skills) often makes it difficult to assess unit cost. The government of Nepal estimates that 47,000 students are enrolled in training programmes offered by ministries other than the Ministry of Education.

Although cost data are available, they are not related to course length and thus are difficult to compare with costs in formal education. The Lao Ministry of Education has estimated the unit costs of non-formal basic vocational skills programmes, vocational programmes delivered by community learning centres and outreach programmes conducted by technical and vocational schools.

These estimates are being used in an EFA simulation model that allows various policy options' cost implications and likely results to be assessed. Skills development represents a marginal share of national education budgets in the four countries. In Mali and Nepal, non-formal education accounts for less than 1 per cent of public current expenditure on education. Technical and vocational education constitutes 2.6 per cent of the education budget in the Lao People's Democratic Republic and 1.4 per cent in Nepal. As in most countries, this segment of educational provision continues to be very much a junior partner of the formal system. Decentralization is under way in the four countries, and the provincial and district levels enjoy increasing responsibilities.

Given the contextual nature of many learning needs, there is every reason to differentiate skills development programmes at local level. Information systems at the grass roots, however, do not easily provide the summary information that national policymakers need for effective monitoring, evaluation and policy development. Locally relevant data need to be aggregated to be of use in analytical and diagnostic tools at the national level. The Lao People's Democratic Republic and Senegal are working on this step.

12

Morale, Motivation and Performance in the School Organization

THE NATURE AND MEANING OF ENVIRONMENT

We have seen that a community or social group sustains itself through continuous self-renewal, and that this renewal takes place by means of the educational growth of the immature members of the group. By various agencies, unintentional and designed, a society transforms uninitiated and seemingly alien beings into robust trustees of its own resources and ideals. Education is thus a fostering, a nurturing, a cultivating, process. All of these words mean that it implies attention to the conditions of growth. We also speak of rearing, raising, bringing up — words which express the difference of level which education aims to cover.

Etymologically, the word education means just a process of leading or bringing up. When we have the outcome of the process in mind, we speak of education as shaping, forming, molding activity — that is, a shaping into the standard form of social activity. In this chapter we are concerned with the general features of the way in which a social group brings up its immature members into its own social form. Since what is required is a transformation of the quality of experience till it partakes in the interests, purposes, and ideas current in the social group, the problem is evidently not one of mere physical forming. Things can be physically transported in space; they may be bodily conveyed.

Beliefs and aspirations cannot be physically extracted and inserted. How then are they communicated? Given the impossibility of direct contagion or literal inculcation, our problem is to discover the method by which the young assimilate the point of view of the old, or the older bring the young into like-mindedness with themselves. The answer, in general formulation, is: By means of the action of the environment in calling out certain responses. The required beliefs cannot be hammered in; the needed attitudes cannot be plastered on. But the particular medium in which an individual exists leads him to see and feel one thing rather than another; it leads him to have certain plans in order that he may act successfully with others; it strengthens some beliefs and weakens others as a condition of winning the approval of others. Thus it gradually produces in him a certain system of behaviour, a certain disposition of action. The words "environment," "medium" denote something more than surroundings which encompass an individual. They denote the specific continuity of the surroundings with his own active tendencies. An inanimate being is, of course, continuous with its surroundings; but the environing circumstances do not, save metaphorically, constitute an environment.

For the inorganic being is not concerned in the influences which affect it. On the other hand, some things which are remote in space and time from a living creature, especially a human creature, may form his environment even more truly than some of the things close to him. The things with which a man varies are his genuine environment. Thus the activities of the astronomer vary with the stars at which he gazes or about which he calculates. Of his immediate surroundings, his telescope is most intimately his environment. The environment of an antiquarian, as an antiquarian, consists of the remote epoch of human life with which he is concerned, and the relics, inscriptions, etc., by which he establishes connections with that period.

In brief, the environment consists of those conditions that promote or hinder, stimulate or inhibit, the characteristic activities of a living being. Water is the environment of a fish because it is necessary to the fish's activities — to its life. The north pole is a significant element in the environment of an arctic explorer, whether he succeeds in reaching it or not, because it defines his activities, makes them what they distinctively are. Just because life signifies not bare passive existence but a way of acting, environment or medium signifies what enters into this activity as a sustaining or frustrating condition.

THE SOCIAL ENVIRONMENT

A being whose activities are associated with others has a social environment. What he does and what he can do depend upon the expectations, demands, approvals, and condemnations of others. A being connected with other beings cannot perform his own activities without taking the activities of others into account. For they are the indispensable conditions of the realization of his tendencies. When he moves he stirs them and reciprocally. We might as well try to imagine a business man doing business, buying and selling, all by himself, as to conceive it possible to define the activities of an individual in terms of his isolated actions.

The manufacturer moreover is as truly socially guided in his activities when he is laying plans in the privacy of his own counting house as when he is buying his raw material or selling his finished goods. Thinking and feeling that have to do with action in association with others is as much a social mode of behaviour as is the most overt cooperative or hostile act. What we have more especially to indicate is how the social medium nurtures its immature members. There is no great difficulty in seeing how it shapes the external habits of action. Even dogs and horses have their actions modified by association with human beings; they form different habits because human beings are concerned with what they do.

Human beings control animals by controlling the natural stimuli which influence them; by creating a certain environment in other words. Food, bits and bridles, noises, vehicles, are used to direct the ways in which the natural or instinctive responses of horses occur. By operating steadily to call out certain acts, habits are formed which function with the same uniformity as the original stimuli. If a rat is put in a maze and finds food only by making a given number of turns in a given sequence, his activity is gradually modified till he habitually takes that course rather than another when he is hungry. Human actions are modified in a like fashion.

A burnt child dreads the fire; if a parent arranged conditions so that every time a child touched a certain toy he got burned, the child would learn to avoid that toy as automatically as he avoids touching fire. So far, however, we are dealing with what may be called training in distinction from educative teaching. The changes considered are in outer action rather than in mental and emotional dispositions of behaviour. The distinction is not, however, a sharp one. The child might conceivably generate in time a violent antipathy, not only to that particular toy, but to the class of toys resembling it. The aversion might even persist after he had forgotten about the original burns; later on he might even invent some reason to account for his seemingly irrational antipathy. In some cases, altering the external habit of action by changing the environment to affect the stimuli to action will also alter the mental disposition concerned in the action. Yet this does not always happen; a person trained to dodge a threatening blow, dodges automatically with no corresponding thought or emotion.

We have to find, then, some differentia of training from education. A clew may be found in the fact that the horse does not really share in the social use to which his action is put. Some one else uses the horse to secure a result which is advantageous by making it advantageous to the horse to perform the act — he gets food, etc. But the horse, presumably, does not get any new interest. He remains interested in food, not in the service he is rendering. He is not a partner in a shared activity. Were he to become a copartner, he would, in engaging in the conjoint activity, have the same interest in its accomplishment which others have. He would share their ideas and emotions. Now in many cases — too many cases — the activity of the immature human being is simply played upon to secure habits which are useful. He is trained like an animal rather than educated like a human being. His instincts remain attached to their original objects of pain or pleasure. But to get happiness or to avoid the pain of failure he has to act in a way agreeable to others. In other cases, he really shares or participates in the common activity. In this case, his original impulse is modified. He not merely acts in a way agreeing with the actions of others, but, in so acting, the same ideas and emotions are aroused in him that animate the others. A tribe, let us say, is warlike. The successes for which it strives, the achievements upon which it sets store, are connected with fighting and victory.

The presence of this medium incites bellicose exhibitions in a boy, first in games, then in fact when he is strong enough. As he fights he wins approval and advancement; as he refrains, he is disliked, ridiculed, shut out from favourable recognition. It is not surprising that his original belligerent tendencies and emotions are strengthened at the expense of others, and that his ideas turn to things connected with war. Only in this way can he become fully a recognized member of his group. Thus his mental habitudes are gradually assimilated to those of his group. If we formulate the principle involved in this illustration, we shall perceive that the social medium neither implants certain desires and ideas directly, nor yet merely establishes certain purely muscular habits of action, like "instinctively" winking or dodging a blow. Setting up conditions which stimulate certain visible and tangible ways of acting is the first step. Making the individual a sharer or partner in the associated activity so that he feels its success as his success, its failure as his failure, is the completing step.

As soon as he is possessed by the emotional attitude of the group, he will be alert to recognize the special ends at which it aims and the means employed to secure success. His beliefs and ideas, in other words, will take a form similar to those of others in the group. He will also achieve pretty much the same stock of knowledge since that knowledge is an ingredient of his habitual pursuits. The importance of language in gaining knowledge is doubtless the chief cause of the common notion that knowledge may be passed directly from one to another. It almost seems as if all we have to do to convey an idea into the mind of another is to convey a sound into his ear.

Thus imparting knowledge gets assimilated to a purely physical process. But learning from language will be found, when analyzed, to confirm the principle just laid down. It would probably be admitted with little hesitation that a child gets the idea of, say, a hat by using it as other persons do; by covering the head with it, giving it to others to wear, having it put on by others when going out, etc. But it may be asked how this principle of shared activity applies to getting through speech or reading the idea of, say, a Greek helmet, where no direct use of any kind enters in. What shared activity is there in learning from books about the discovery of America?

Since language tends to become the chief instrument of learning about many things, let us see how it works. The baby begins of course with mere sounds, noises, and tones having no meaning, expressing, that is, no idea. Sounds are just one kind of stimulus to direct response, some having a soothing effect, others tending to make one jump, and so on. The sound h-a-t would remain as meaningless as a sound in Choctaw, a seemingly inarticulate grunt, if it were not uttered in connection with an action which is participated in by a number of people. When the mother is taking the infant out of doors, she says "hat" as she puts something on the baby's head. Being taken out becomes an interest to the child; mother and child not only go out with each other physically, but both are concerned in the going out; they enjoy it in common.

By conjunction with the other factors in activity the sound "hat" soon gets the same meaning for the child that it has for the parent; it becomes a sign of the activity into which it enters. The bare fact that language consists of sounds which are mutually intelligible is enough of itself to show that its meaning depends upon connection with a shared experience. In short, the sound h-a-t gains meaning in precisely the same way that the thing "hat" gains it, by being used in a given way.

And they acquire the same meaning with the child which they have with the adult because they are used in a common experience by both. The guarantee for the same manner of use is found in the fact that the thing and the sound are first employed in a joint activity, as a means of setting up an active connection between the child and a grownup. Similar ideas or meanings spring up because both persons are engaged as partners in an action where what each does depends upon and influences what the other does. If two savages were engaged in a joint hunt for game, and a certain signal meant "move to the right" to the one who uttered it, and "move to the left" to the one who heard it, they obviously could not successfully carry on their hunt together.

Understanding one another means that objects, including sounds, have the same value for both with respect to carrying on a common pursuit. After sounds have got meaning through connection with other things employed in a joint undertaking, they can be used in connection with other like sounds to develop new meanings, precisely as the things for which they stand are combined. Thus the words in which a child learns about, say, the Greek helmet originally got a meaning by use in an action having a common interest and end. They now arouse a new meaning by inciting the one who hears or reads to rehearse imaginatively the activities in which the helmet has its use.

For the time being, the one who understands the words "Greek helmet" becomes mentally a partner with those who used the helmet. He engages, through his imagination, in a shared activity. It is not easy to get the full meaning of words. Most persons probably stop with the idea that "helmet" denotes a queer kind of headgear a people called the Greeks once wore. We conclude, accordingly, that the use of language to convey and acquire ideas is an extension and refinement of the principle that things gain meaning by being used in a shared experience or joint action; in no sense does it contravene that principle.

When words do not enter as factors into a shared situation, either overtly or imaginatively, they operate as pure physical stimuli, not as having a meaning or intellectual value. They set activity running in a given groove, but there is no accompanying conscious purpose or meaning. Thus, for example, the plus sign may be a stimulus to perform the act of writing one number under another and adding the numbers, but the person performing the act will operate much as an automaton would unless he realizes the meaning of what he does.

THE SOCIAL MEDIUM AS EDUCATIVE

Our net result thus far is that social environment forms the mental and emotional disposition of behaviour in individuals by engaging them in activities that arouse and strengthen certain impulses, that have certain purposes and entail certain consequences. A child growing up in a family of musicians will inevitably have whatever capacities he has in music stimulated, and, relatively, stimulated more than other impulses which might have been awakened in another environment. Save as he takes an interest in music and gains a certain competency in it, he is "out of it"; he is unable to share in the life of the group to which he belongs. Some kinds of participation in the life of those with whom the individual is connected are inevitable; with respect to them, the social environment exercises an educative or formative influence unconsciously and apart from any set purpose. In savage and barbarian communities, such direct participation furnishes almost the sole influence for rearing the young into the practices and beliefs of the group.

Even in present-day societies, it furnishes the basic nurture of even the most insistently schooled youth. In accord with the interests and occupations of the group, certain things become objects of high esteem; others of aversion. Association does not create impulses or affection and dislike, but it furnishes the objects to which they attach themselves. The way our group or class does things tends to determine the proper objects of attention, and thus to prescribe the directions and limits of observation and memory. What is strange or foreign tends to be morally forbidden and intellectually suspect. It seems almost incredible to us, for example, that things which we know very well could have escaped recognition in past ages. We incline to account for it by attributing congenital stupidity to our forerunners and by assuming superior native intelligence on our own part.

But the explanation is that their modes of life did not call for attention to such facts, but held their minds riveted to other things. Just as the senses require sensible objects to stimulate them, so our powers of observation, recollection, and imagination do not work spontaneously, but are set in motion by the demands set up by current social occupations. The main texture of disposition is formed, independently of schooling, by such influences. What conscious, deliberate teaching can do is at most to free the capacities thus formed for fuller exercise, to purge them of some of their grossness, and to furnish objects which make their activity more productive of meaning. While this "unconscious influence of the environment" is so subtle and pervasive that it affects every fibre of character and mind, it may be worth while to specify a few directions in which its effect is most marked. First, the habits of language. Fundamental modes of speech, the bulk of the vocabulary, are formed in the ordinary intercourse of life, carried on not as a set means of instruction but as a social necessity.

The babe acquires, as we well say, the mother tongue. While speech habits thus contracted may be corrected or even displaced by conscious teaching, yet, in times of excitement, intentionally acquired modes of speech often fall away, and individuals relapse into their really native tongue. Secondly, manners. Example is notoriously more potent than precept. Good manners come, as we say, from good breeding or rather are good breeding; and breeding is acquired by habitual action, in response to habitual stimuli, not by conveying information. Despite the never ending play of conscious correction and instruction, the surrounding atmosphere and spirit is in the end the chief agent in forming manners.

And manners are but minor morals. Moreover, in major morals, conscious instruction is likely to be efficacious only in the degree in which it falls in with the general "walk and conversation" of those who constitute the child's social environment. Thirdly, good taste and esthetic appreciation. If the eye is constantly greeted by harmonious objects, having elegance of form and colour, a standard of taste naturally grows up. The effect of a tawdry, unarranged, and over-decorated environment works for the deterioration of taste, just as meagre and barren surroundings starve out the desire for beauty. Against such odds, conscious teaching can hardly do more than convey second-hand information as to what others think.

Such taste never becomes spontaneous and personally engrained, but remains a labored reminder of what those think to whom one has been taught to look up. To say that the deeper standards of judgments of value are framed by the situations into which a person habitually enters is not so much to mention a fourth point, as it is to point out a fusion of those already mentioned. We rarely recognize the extent in which our conscious estimates of what is worth while and what is not, are due to standards of which we are not conscious at all. But in general it may be said that the things which we take for granted without inquiry or reflection are just the things which determine our conscious thinking and decide our conclusions. And these habitudes which lie below the level of reflection are just those which have been formed in the constant give and take of relationship with others.

13

Education and Human Values: Dalits Perspectives

INTRODUCTION AND PURPOSE STATEMENT

From the moment a Hindu child is born in India, his or her opportunities for social and religious freedom are shaped through the influence of the caste system despite laws passed 50 years ago to abolish such discriminatory practices. Many children at the bottom of this caste system face a future of poverty, unemployment, illiteracy, abuse, sickness, and for girls, even rape and prostitution. Stemming from its 3000-year-old origins, the caste system is one of the world's longest surviving forms of social stratification. People are divided by birth just as to one of four main castes, with yet another estimated 200 million categorized beneath this caste system.

Many in society consider these people to be unclean and unworthy of basic human rights and label them "The Untouchables" or Dalits. In 1955, the Indian Parliament passed the Untouchability Offences Act, making the practice of castes illegal, however, it may take generations to remove the stigma and change the views and traditions of an entire society. This lack of social justice for many, coupled with the desire to promote fair and equal treatment of the people within a country that is quickly gaining influence in the global market and economy, has made this topic one of extreme interest. Although many of these longstanding traditions continue to hold fast, India has also experienced significant changes during the last several decades. With the advancement of technology, some researchers no longer consider India to be classified as a developing country, but as a newly industrialized country.

This classification includes several nations, such as Mexico and Thailand, with economies more advanced and developed than those in the developing world, yet without the full indicators that would classify it as a developed country. With the rapid increase of major global corporations choosing to outsource large portions of high technology jobs to India, the need for quality English medium education is vital if the country intends to continue to compete in that particular market. Yet India continues to struggle with the needs of its individuals, especially in rural areas, with limitations that inhibit the ability to make the desired changes in a timely manner. Not only has the current government been unable to increase the number of schools and teachers needed to rectify the situation, but society itself has been resistant in some areas to the change of the social order embedded in the caste system.

In an effort to affect change in a social structure that consists of an interdependent set of roles and norms, Dalit leaders have joined forces to demand what they refer to as a holistic reformation for their own people. They describe this as a concern for the whole individual's physical, mental, emotional and spiritual development through education, economic support, health aid, and legal advocacy. By accepting the outside resources of International Non-Governmental Organizations, they feel they can make the changes necessary to reduce the educational and socioeconomic gap between the castes. The Dalit Empowerment International, a Non-Government Organization based in the United States, formed in 2002 in response to this corporate uprising of the Dalit people. The Dalit leaders at that time challenged the organization with a twofold request: to offer their children an English medium education, and to include Christian principles in the hope of transforming their worldview to one based on human dignity and self-worth, in an effort to create a new future. Working together with the already established All India Christian Council and other partners, the DEI uses its resources from the United States, Canada and the United Kingdom, to educate the western world about the situation of the Dalits and to gather financial and human resources to support ongoing work in India.

The AICC is a coalition of over 3,000 Indian organizations and federations and proactively protects the interests of Christians, Muslims, Dalits, Tribals and Backward communities. Also, by joining together with AICC as well as another national overhead organization with four decades of educational experience, they feel they can use the expertise and experience to make a significant impact. Having volunteered with several non-profit and faith-based organizations, studying education and its societal role around the world has become an area of extreme interest for me. I chose to study the field of international comparative education in order to examine the effectiveness of such programmes in diverse cultural contexts. Having met the president of the DEI at a symposium in the United States, I was intrigued by the overall approach and methods of their model.

The organization situates the educational component within a framework of three other elements, human rights advocacy, health and medical needs, and economic development. I wanted to study in depth the effectiveness of this approach, and specifically this programme, and its religious implications within the established caste system. A substantial amount of research has been done to define quality education to confirm the educational inequities within the caste system and to acknowledge the addition of many INGOs in the global effort to create access to quality education for all. However, little research examines the effectiveness of faith-based INGOs and their impact on an educational situation that is affected by another religious system. This study will add to the current literature by providing an evaluative look at one particular programme, which can add to our understanding of how such educational faith-based programmes could aid disadvantaged and stigmatized groups. In order to gain insight into the strategies of this organization, I used qualitative research methods including ethnographic evaluative techniques to conduct a formative programme evaluation.

A programme evaluation of this sort seeks to appraise the quality of the education and the achievement of the stated goals, which is not only useful to the DEI programme administrators, but to other programmes as well. The purpose of a formative evaluation is to examine each of the components of a programme in such a way that specific changes could be made to enhance the programme, not to judge the overall worth or value of the programme. My role as an evaluator is to present the specific findings to the leaders of the organization such that the appropriate stakeholders and decision makers can use it to guide future implementation.

Using the following questions, I evaluated four out of the DEI's 62 schools:

- How does this education programme plan to improve the future quality of life for Dalits?
- Does the DEI programme meet its proposed goals?
- What further areas of research will address the long term societal change that will be necessary for this programme and others to be effective?

To be as objective in my evaluation as possible, given the timeframe, resources and the fact that I would be the only evaluator, I used methodological triangulation by inter-viewing administrators, teachers and students, reviewing the program's literature and observing in the classroom. This process allowed me to compare the goals with the actual implementation practices in order to examine effectiveness of the programme in the schools observed. This study focuses on both the practical application and logistics of this education as well as the religious aspect.

Introducing educational practices which promote religious choice and enhance India's efforts towards a worldview of human dignity may be of key importance in providing information for future aid in the urgent educational needs within India today. The following parts present the research and the findings. To begin with, the background surrounding the disparity in education for the Dalit child, as well as the governmental policy, anti-conversion laws, and the specific goals of the DEI are described. Next, a series of questions that guided the research are discussed. Following this is a review of current literature on subjects that formed the foundation for this evaluation.

This includes topics such as the inequities in education, NGO involvement, the use of English medium, the future implications of education for the Dalits, the paucity of similar studies evaluating other programmes, and finally educational programme evaluation theories. This is followed by a detailed explanation of the data collection and methods that were used to gather the information to evaluate the programme. The findings are then analysed and the results of the evaluation are discussed. In the conclusion, the findings are summarized such that programme developers can use this material in the future to benefit the programme, as well as to inform readers of the issues and future implications of this research.

BACKGROUND

UNDERSTANDING CASTES

The plight of the Dalits must be understood, in order to have the cultural sensitivity needed to bring in an outside organization and use the resources effectively. The goal of closing the gap in education, so entrenched in thousands of years of religious or cultural practices will require time and skill, and much of it will have to do with teaching from a platform of education based on human rights. As I began this study, it quickly became obvious that I could not ignore the religious element of the education, as it is so enmeshed in the cultural differences and discriminatory practices which lead to such a gap in achievement and attainment in the first place.

As one director in India said:

- In the United States, you had discrimination between blacks and whites, and it was a social justice issue, which can be changed by laws over time. People were free to choose to be Christians, but were discriminated against because of their colour. In India, though, it is far deeper. It is a religious issue, if people remain Hindu, they are discriminated against, if they convert, they are fined and even persecuted. To try to change the discrimination, one must face the religious issue of caste.

It is historically understood that Hinduism was first established by an amalgamation of three different religious sects, Arayanism, Dravidianism and Animism and the four caste levels were a method of establishing social order, whereby each person had an occupational function. Traditionally, for example, the top level, the Brahmins, were considered the highest level and held the positions of priests and teachers. The next group included the Kshatriyas, who held positions as the warriors and royalty. Then, the Vaisyas were given positions as moneylenders and traders. Finally, considered the lowest of the four levels, the Sudras carried out the menial jobs in society. The Dalits, or untouchables, or ati-Sudras were actually considered beneath all of these levels, performing the jobs that other members of society would not. To be touched or even crossed by the shadow of a Dalit made any other caste member unclean and ritualistic cleansing was required. Though much of this structure has changed over time, as governmental order and economic models changed, the concept of social stratification has remained, in some areas more so than others.

Through several grass roots efforts to empower individuals, the Dalits are now seeking societal change. The DEI, as one of these efforts, feels that by eliminating discriminatory practices in the classroom, and changing the beliefs within the family and the community, there can eventually be actual change at the government and societal level.

From their literature, they intend to be involved at all of these levels:

- Serving as an international advocate for Dalit rights is the heartbeat of the Dalit Empowerment International. Beginning with the United States government in Washington DC, DEI seeks to bring an end to caste-based discrimination and the resulting oppression the Dalit community experiences. DEI also represents Dalits inter-nationally in the United Nations and at major conferences on human rights and religious liberties. Additionally, DEI seeks funding to underwrite legal fees for Dalits actively pursuing political and social change through the Indian legal system and all necessary constitutional means.

Therefore, educational practices can become a crucial part in this path towards change.

GOVERNMENTAL VIEWS

The people of India respect Gandhi as the founding father of the modern Indian nation. However, there is controversy as to his approach to try to abolish the caste system. Some feel that he merely tried to eradicate the practice of untouchability but did not do enough to touch the foundations of the stratification of caste. He believed that "caste as it exists today is no doubt a travesty of the original fourfold division which only defined men's different calling". Gandhi attempted to teach by example that doing the menial labour of a Dalit should be considered as honourable as any other trade. It was actually Dr. Bhim Rao Babasaheb Ambedkar, a former Dalit, who founded the Indian Constitution in 1949 and attempted to abolish the foundation of the caste system itself in an effort to bring about the commitments made in the Constitution to promote equality. Despite the strong beginnings, Dr. Ambedkar expressed his concerns that such an undertaking may seem impossible without a change in the thinking established by caste when he stated:

- There is no doubt; in my opinion, that unless you change your social order you can achieve little by way of progress. You cannot mobilize

> the community either for defence or for offence. You cannot build anything on the foundations of caste. You cannot build up a nation, you cannot build up a morality. Anything that you will build on the foundations of caste will crack and will never be whole. The only question remains to be considered is ... How to abolish caste? This is the question of supreme importance

Other countries, though not affected by caste, also recognized the need to change societal norms and in 1974, UNESCO began to lay the foundations for human rights education.

By 1978, the participants in the International Congress on the Teaching of Human Rights created specific and practical definitions by stating that human rights education and teaching must aim at:

- Fostering the attitudes of tolerance, respect and solidarity inherent in human rights
- Providing knowledge about human rights, in both their national and international dimensions, and the institutions established for their implementation
- Develop the individual's awareness of the ways and means by which human rights can be translated into social and political reality at both the national and international levels.

Following these efforts more than forty years after the creation of India's constitution, the UN Decade for Human Rights Education began in 1995 and has been influential in raising global awareness of educational inequities. It will continue to take time, however, to create curriculum based on practices that will change the thinking of the individual as well as the society. The DEI intends to support his effort. India has become a central focus as various countries attempt to eradicate discriminatory practices through these educational efforts.

For example, the United States House of Representatives just passed House Concurrent Resolution 139 on July 23, 2007, that addresses the ongoing problem of untouchability in India. The resolution is the first of its kind from the United States Congress and the DEI has been involved at several levels of global awareness. Juxtaposed with this global awareness, however, is the continued effort by the Indian government to implement more anti-conversion laws in order to protect people from coercion and manipulation by what is considered any minority religion in India.

Anti-conversion laws have been passed through much controversy in eight of the 28 states and the specific language states:

- No person shall convert or attempt to convert, either directly or otherwise, any person from one religion to another by use of force or by inducement or by any fraudulent means, nor shall any person abet any such conversion.

Although these protective efforts are well founded due to past practices by different religious groups pressuring people to convert by way of inducement through education or medical aid, they create a dichotomous message that goes against the Constitution's Article 25 that promises free choice:

- Freedom of conscience and free profession, practice and propagation of religion.- Subject to public order, morality and health and to the other provisions of this Part, all persons are equally entitled to freedom of conscience and the right freely to profess, practice and propagate religion.

Though it is too complex a topic to discuss in this document, as the debate over coercion and choice through new knowledge can be subjective, one must be aware of the conflict in attempting to use any other religious educational foundation within various states in India.

GOALS OF DALIT EMPOWERMENT INTERNATIONAL

From the literature established by the DEI and through interviews with individuals involved in the education, it is clear that their goal is to accomplish each of the human rights agendas by including the egalitarian practices of Christianity as they build their curriculum. With this in mind, this study will attempt to compare the following mission statement and all of its underlying elements with the actual practices.

Their holistic efforts focus on four main areas:

- Education through English-based curriculum with trained national teachers
- Medical resources of vaccinations, health care, and medical interventions
- Economic Development by offering micro-loans and vocational training programmes
- Human Rights and Social Justice by serving as an international advocate for social change and new governmental policies

To incorporate each of these areas into the development of a community, the DEI establishes what it calls Community Education Centres as a central location for all four aspects of their charter. Though each of these areas is crucial to the advancement of developing societies, this document will focus specifically on the educational efforts. For the purpose of this document, the term CEC or DEI school will be interchangeable. To date, 62 CECs have been established in 13 states, serving over 10,000 students, through DEI's efforts to coordinate a global interest in the situation of the Dalit people. The DEI provides an excellent example to use for this study, because, unlike several other faith-based organizations such as World Vision and Compassion

International, the DEI focuses strictly on the needs of the Dalit people. The DEI also has many collaborative sources with churches and other organizations within India.

These organizations are in agreement as to the strategic importance that an English and faith-based education brings to the Dalits, as a gateway to eradicating injustice, illiteracy and overcoming poverty. They have determined that some of the greatest opportunities for education and employment within India and around the world are given to those who are literate in English as well as their own state language. Also, since one of their main charters is to teach from a worldview based on human dignity and self-worth, the issue of faith is a key component in this study. Dalits are choosing to convert primarily to the egalitarian beliefs of Buddhism, Islam and Christianity as a way out of a system that still holds great power, not only in India, but in other countries as well. The regions for developing schools are selected through careful research conducted by the DEI national leaders to locate areas of Dalit majority with the greatest needs, where no other comparable facilities exist, and no other full time holistic development projects are functioning.

The schooling is subsidized by the organization, but a nominal fee is charged to create a sense of ownership and accountability for the students and their families. DEI's child sponsorship programme brings in funds from around the world to provide the uniforms, books, a meal where needed, and to cover the teacher's salaries, the cost of the facility and other administrative costs. I was told that, "Many of these children are introduced to education for the first time, and the enthusiasm spreads as they take home what they have learned and share it with their families."

A statement from the literature given to me by the director explains:

- To teach a Dalit is social service, but to destroy the social structure which made him illiterate, is social transformation. To open a new school in a Dalit village is a social service, but to motivate the Dalit hungry and illiterate parent to send his child to school even if it meant less income for the household is social transformation. To provide free food to a Dalit is a social service, but to educate and empower him to earn his own food is social transformation.

This document will evaluate the DEI's approach of holistic transformation within a group of people in order to shed light on the goal of accomplishing global awareness and support for the struggle for freedom through education.

CRITICAL LITERATURE REVIEW

In order to lay the foundation that guided the planning and design of this research, the following part will review current literature on four essential subjects. First, it discusses established discrimination and inequities in education for Dalits and the need for human rights education. This is followed by studies about involvement of INGOs and their participation in education or social justice worldwide, as well as the paucity of studies evaluating similar programmes. Third, it discusses global debates over whether to teach from an English medium of instruction. Finally, it establishes the framework of educational ethnography and programme evaluation theories that were used as the foundation of this study.

DISCRIMINATORY PRACTICES AND THE NEED FOR HUMAN RIGHTS EDUCATION

Numerous studies have been done to understand the level of disparity between the treatment of the Dalits and their upper caste peers. Education inequality is merely a portion of the complex nature of what Prime Minister Singh acknowledges as "India's hidden apartheid". Despite the Constitutional Directive of universal elementary education and Education for All goals, the gap in educational access and achievement between the Dalits and the general population in India is still quite large and continues to increase, which is of great concern in the globalizing world today. Dalits, also referred to in the Constitution as the Scheduled Castes make up approximately 16.2 per cent of the population of India, yet only 41.5 per cent of Dalits in rural India were considered literate compared to the national literacy rate of 64.8 per cent. Using econometric estimates on data gathered from 16 states and 33,000 rural households, in 1765 villages, Borooah and Iyer found that Dalit enrollment was lower than for Hindus for various reasons such as income, psychological factors, and access.

For Hindu boys and girls, the enrollment rates were 84 per cent and 68 per cent respectively, but for Dalit boys and girls it was 70 per cent and 55 per cent. Parent and community attitude, as well as religion and caste, are intertwined and have much to do with a child's education. Even though states such as Kerala have been involved for years with anti-caste reform, findings show that there is still statistically significant disparity between the Scheduled Caste and Scheduled Tribe groups and all other groups, suggesting the continued existence of an elite group despite years of effort to eradicate the discrepancies. In an effort to uncover the reasons behind the continued disparities, a group of researchers began a first-ever study examining the practice of untouchability in 11 states, specifically in 565 rural villages between 2001 and 2002.

Investigators conducted an 18 month survey, spending several days in each village using observations, interviews and focus groups to gather their data. Though there has been improvement over the past decades, they found that practices of untouchability and discrimination do indeed still exist, though at different levels in each state and region. For example, one third of the villages still keep separate glasses and plates for Dalits, and refuse them entry into the shops. Purchases must be made from outside, without touching or examining the merchandise. They found that 64 per cent are not allowed in public places of worship, and 48 per cent are not permitted to use the village water facilities for fear of their contamination. In order to understand the level of degradation many of the Dalits still face today, it must be noted that investigators found that "in every state, despite legal bans, Dalits continue to manually remove human excreta from public and private latrines, often with their bare hands". Most often, they are required to perform tasks that relate to human waste, and death, all without pay, as an expected role in their existence.

In terms of educational practices, Nambissan and Sedwell state that "the perspective within which the educational concerns of Dalit communities should be addressed must be one of social justice as Dalit communities have suffered from social discrimination and have traditionally been denied access to learning." They contend that unless the discrimination is acknowledged, and confronted by teachers, parents, community leaders and educational institutions, the gap will continue to widen. For example, currently 38 per cent of the village schools practiced separate eating arrangements, and 22 per cent separate seating arrangements in the classroom.

Shah found that "rural schools impress upon young minds and bodies the principles of segregation and discrimination, reproducing the hierarchies of caste and untouchability." Many feel that these practices must stop in order for the message of equality to be heard and incorporated into the thinking of the individuals. If the community, and society at large, does not change this way of thinking about Dalits and other marginalized groups, merely creating more sensitized teaching practices and more educational opportunities may not be enough.

Studies show that despite the increased sense of dignity that education alone can bring, many still have a difficult time converting this cultural capital into actual long term employment due to discrimination within the job market. These studies depict a new crisis, where Dalit youth are becoming frustrated due to their lack of opportunities, even if they are educated, and parents are becoming less willing to invest in the education they thought would make a difference for their whole family. If education access does increase, yet society does not accept the change in thinking of these Dalits, then developmental initiatives simply focusing on increased formal education may not be as successful as hoped in raising the social standing of the Dalits.

Therefore, if outside organizations enter into a community, some find that it may be important that they teach not only with a cultural sensitivity, but with the goal of diffusing egalitarian thinking and practice throughout the entire community in order for long term effects to take place. Although such debate over the best approach cannot be examined fully in this document, these issues do become foundational in this programme evaluation as it examines both the implementation of the goals of the DEI schools, as well as how these schools are situated within the current efforts for societal changes. Analysing the efforts towards creating quality education, taught with a holistic approach through a faith-based egalitarian foundation of human rights could be an important starting point as India attempts to educate the next generation.

NON-GOVERNMENTAL ORGANIZATION

As a newly industrialized country, India's government has found it difficult to keep up with the demand for quality education. Each state within India has widely disparate needs in educational funding, but for most, bringing in outside resources by working together with NGOs becomes a key factor in advancement for the people. Obtaining additional sources of financial aid, as well as creating effective ways of expending them, becomes even more critical if a society is expected to improve and develop.

This especially becomes significant with the growing trend of dissatisfaction with the poor quality of education offered through the existing government schools. Dalit parents have dreams for their children to become engineers, doctors and government officials, yet they realise that quality education is necessary to achieve these dreams. Many are turning to an alternate private schooling for their children.

In this "differentiated demand" for education that is considered of "good quality" this began a mushrooming increase in private unaided schools in the past decade alone. However, quality becomes difficult to maintain here as well, as many of these private schools hire poorly trained teachers, with lower pay, creating schools for the Dalits that are of substandard nature with a poor reputation.

It is also difficult to gain official statistics on private schools in India, and the affects of NGO involvement, as many private schools are not granted official recognition by the government for a variety of reasons. Singh's initial studies show through preliminary tests of achievement, that performance of children in the PUA unrecognized schools did not differ much from the scores of children studying in the government schools. Current research is needed to examine these trends and possible progress over time. With both international and national NGOs willing to step in to help fill this demand, evaluating specific programmes to determine the quality and type of education provided and whether it is effectively implemented is essential if funds are to be used to their fullest potential.

Although there is plenty of literature discussing the need and involvement or NGOs, there is a paucity of literature studying the effectiveness of specific programmes and practices. With India's goals of Education For All, NGOs will continue to play an important role, working along with the government to come up with creative ways to motivate people towards further education, with a holistic approach, but without creating dependency, ultimately effecting a change in society.

ENGLISH MEDIUM OF INSTRUCTION

Even if funding and other resources are available, however, there is still much debate over the pedagogy and curriculum that must be chosen by the key actors. Currently, there is global discussion over whether classes should be taught in the more traditional style of rote learning and classroom order, or in the more recent trend towards child centered pedagogies, with interactive classroom involvement. Also included in this debate for India is the question of whether classes should be taught through an English medium of instruction, the native language of each state, or the national language, Hindi.

These decisions are being made on a state-by-state basis within India, which has 22 state languages, and continued controversy over whether Hindi should still be considered the national language as the Constitution allows for the use of both Hindi and English in varying circumstances. As an example of the difficulties in these decisions, the state of Kerala began to make some of these changes in style and curriculum in 1998. The state planned to adopt a new experimental approach that was designed to be "child-friendly and to deemphasize rote learning lectures in favour of guided learning and playful interaction". This District Primary Education programme met with controversy, however, as people feared even further stratification between the Kerala students: those who would be able to afford to choose private schools, or those who would become "guinea pigs" in the government schools under this new method.

Along with changes in style not English. Although the native tongue of Malayalum was already being used for instruction after a controversial decision to drop the universal English medium in 1987, it was still a difficult transition to make. Some continue to pose that teaching in the mother tongue or first language for most of the day with English being taught as a separate subject is the most effective method, as children will understand the subject matter better.

Others feel that by starting English younger, the children will become more proficient and will catch up with the subject matter as needed. Although the controversy continues, it must be noted that Kerala, due to a variety of factors, does hold the highest literacy rate in the country at 90.9 per cent compared to the national rate of 64.8 per cent. The dilemma in this decision is that although each state is requiring that all government schools will teach using the local language up through the 10th grade, all testing and education after that is in English. Thus, children who go to the local government schools, especially in rural areas where no English is used, are by default eliminated from attending upper education that would qualify them for the jobs being reserved for them under affirmative action laws. Also, without quality English education, these children cannot compete for the jobs in the rapidly growing sectors of the Indian economy, such as technical support and sales for major corporations.

Although it is not within the purview of this document to determine the positive and negative ramifications of these decisions, it helps to provide a foundation for the decisions that organizations such as the DEI must wrestle with in determining what they consider to be best educational practices for the Dalit children.

EDUCATIONAL ETHNOGRAPHIES AND PROGRAMME EVALUATION

In order to evaluate an educational programme, such as the DEI provides, it is important to understand first the terminology as well as the overall intent. Popham to evaluate something is to appraise its quality and ultimately, to determine its worth. One approach in educational research is to focus on quantitative measures, such as achievement, assessments, levels of attainment, and so on.

Although I did query these particular areas, and future long term studies would be necessary to discern improvement and success, this study will use qualitative ethnographic methods, focusing on the purpose of the education, the effectiveness, and its position within a view towards societal change. Using ethnographic methods allows a more descriptive approach, seeking to understand actual situations in context, providing the reader with a far more "meaningful picture of educational undertakings than would be possible from a more traditional scientific paradigm". As Cronbach so eloquently puts it, "Intensive local observation goes beyond discipline to an open-eyed, open-minded appreciation of the surprises nature deposits in the investigative net". It is understood that, with the ethnographer as the human instrument, there will be some influence by the personality and background of the ethnographer. Being able to study a situation in its natural context, and gather data from a range of sources such as observations, and conversations with key actors to gain their perspective, brings together a valuable collection of information.

This approach is usually accomplished in a less structured way, and the analysis of the data involves interpretation through descriptions and explanations, with any form of quantifiable analysis taking a supportive role. One of the differences in most ethnographic educational evaluations, is that there is less time spent on site than a typical ethnographic study because so much is already known about the expectations of an educational environment. Also, for the purpose of this study, there are a few differences between research and evaluation that require clarification. Although both seek to gain new or additional knowledge, a researcher aims to reach a conclusion, and evaluators are more interested in affecting decisions, whether made by the evaluators themselves, or those who have requested the evaluation. Also, generalizability is a crucial difference between the two. Ideally, results from research can be generalized to fit a larger scope of similar situations that are being studied. However, educational evaluations tend to focus on a specific educational programme with no intent to generalize to others. The gathered knowledge can be useful to the stakeholders and key decision makers as they seek to improve the programme. Since DEI, working with the AICC, intends to expand these 62 schools to 1,000, placed all over India, the information gathered in this method, can be useful to a larger scope within the organizations and even other organizations evaluating similar issues in their programmes. One difficulty in any kind of evaluation stems from determining the level of judgement the evaluative ethnographer can or should make in assessing the results of his or her study, what Scriven refers to as the recommendation problem. Theorists do not agree as to whether an evaluator should simply present the findings and leave it up to the programme administrators and decision makers to take it to the next step of modifying policy or implementing change, or whether the evaluators should be the ones to lay out a series of recommendations based on their findings.

Cronbach's approach would be that of a minimalist, holding to the first view that an evaluator should collect the facts about the programme being evaluated, but not place any sort of value on the results, leaving that to the programme administrators. Others, such as Scriven, would take it further, making actual judgements on "value, merit or worth" and using a team of experts to make specific recommendations that could be implemented. Finally, the term formative evaluation must be clarified. Once again, different theorists disagree on the role of the evaluator. In 1967, Scriven created the terms formative and summative that are currently used today to distinguish two specific roles in educational evaluation. Formative evaluations apply to programmes that are still capable of being modified. That is, they are still malleable, and even slight modifications to different components can be made as the programme continues to be implemented.

If there are some components that are considered deficient, they can be improved upon towards a better overall programme. Summative evaluations on the other hand are generally focused on more complete and established programmes and are being assessed as to the overall worth of the programme and whether it should continue. This type of evaluation has more of a final judgement approach, versus the modification approach of formative evaluations. This concept is useful in understanding the overall intent and expectation in any particular evaluation. Having reviewed the various approaches, I have chosen to use qualitative ethnographic methods to conduct an educational formative programme evaluation using a minimalist approach. To begin with, though I have background in education, and have studied the situation with the Dalits, I am not an expert nor am I fully knowledgeable in the cultural context.

As such, the value judgements should be made by both the national and international elected and paid officials of the programme who are held accountable to the budgetary considerations as well as overall strategy and outcomes. Also, there is not enough time in this study to delve fully into the data gathering phase in the field to make necessary recommendations. This study can be useful however, as I am coming in with as objective an eye as possible, knowing that I am not a stakeholder, but am interested in the global efforts to affect change in a society through education. With this approach, I can collect data at the micro level and present this information to the programme developers of the DEI to discuss some of the changes that could be made, and how these changes would affect the overall programme.

In summary, there has been much research on the educational gap, and discriminatory practices against the Dalits, and the need for quality education based on equality and human rights. However, little research exists that specifically evaluates the various approaches of NGOS such that best approaches and methods can be implemented by others. Specifically, there is little research, if any, that evaluates faith-based NGOs as they work within a delicate balance between conflicting worldviews, societal norms and government policy. This document will add to the future foundation for such in depth research on various programmes that could aid other organizations in the continued quest to eradicate the gap in education for the Dalit children.

DATA AND METHODS

The purpose of this formative educational programme evaluation is to examine each element of the programme, focusing on individual aspects of the intended goals and actual implementation. Looking at these elements at each of the four individual sites allows for separate examination as well as some comparison and vision towards future implementation. Even though the time frame was limited to only ten days in Andhra Pradesh, I used qualitative methods, drawing largely from the ethnographic tradition of in-field research, gathering documentation, conducting interviews and observing the situation in context.

Ideally, I would have had access to some of the typical quantitative information such as test scores, attainment, and teachers' experience levels that can be used to support the findings. However, due to time constraints at each site, I had to limit the investigation to the self-report of the participants, combined with my own observations, understanding that much of this involves individual perceptions. As an evaluator, I will present the findings in such a way that they can be used by the programme developers for the purpose of shaping and refining the programme, as well as guiding further research.

Many of these findings will involve fiscal decisions, and strategic plans for future implementation, which are beyond the role of the evaluator in this case. The following four parts clarify the various points of how the data was collected as well as the methods used. The first part describes the preparation prior to departure which is followed by the in-field set up and constraints.

The third part describes the interviews and limitations of this process, followed by an explanation of the observation methods.

PRIOR TO DEPARTURE

Several months prior to departure, in preparation to conduct this evaluation, I briefly outlined the intended purpose for my study and contacted the DEI in the United States to discuss feasibility of this type of research over a ten day period in the spring. The United States based administrators contacted the programme directors in India and gained permission for me to travel to Andhra Pradesh in March, 2007, to observe in classrooms and interview various programme participants at multiple sites.

Although the DEI has established schools in 13 states, this location was purposely selected by the DEI for its easy access to transportation and lodging as this area contains a college campus of a partner organization, as well a medical clinic. It was also centrally located to four different schools, one in an urban setting, and three others in surrounding rural villages which added to the diversity of the sample. I recognize that this is just one region and these schools may not be indicative of the overall programme, however, safety, cost and time were constraints that made some of the other schools too difficult to consider. The DEI was supportive and eager to have this programme evaluated. Even though they clearly believe in the effectiveness of their programme, they encouraged having an outside observer review it from an academic perspective.

Also, these particular schools have been established for at least three years, and they felt that they were stable enough to be implementing the original objectives, yet far enough along to look for continued improvement, creating a perfect opportunity for a formative approach. One of the constraints that I faced was the confidentiality issues that needed to be addressed before permission could be granted to conduct interviews and, more importantly, write up the findings to be available on the internet. Along with the typical anonymity of the participants, I needed to commit to the leaders of the DEI schools in India that they would have permission to read the material before it became available to others to help avoid any risk of exposure to individuals. Although each school is recognized by the government and has permission to function in full academic capacity, families in these Dalit communities still suffer from discrimination and outright persecution from those in society who either do not want them to receive equal rights and quality education, or to be attending a school with faith-based ideology.

Thus, any identifying details of the organization, leaders, students and locations had to be removed, including references to their web site. To begin the evaluation process, I reviewed the goals as stated in the DEI documentation and on their web site and then formed semistructured interview questions that would allow the programme implementers and participants the opportunity to confirm effective implementation, and suggest improvement. This would also allow flexibility in the interview process to follow up on topics that the participants found important to discuss. Due to the time constraints and expense, I was not able to conduct a pilot study, so I discussed and revised the questions several times with the DEI administrators, as well as colleagues who received their prior education in India.

Both suggested adjustments to the questions that would help the participants better understand the questions without my leading them to certain answers. Next, a particular advantage in programme evaluation is for the evaluator to have background knowledge and some level of expertise in order to more accurately observe and document what is seen, as well as probe deeper through the interview process.

To prepare for this, I read a collection of essays and written by the president of the organization to better understand the background and issues that the families face, as well as the overall goals of this organization, and its partnership with established organizations in India. I watched their DVD and read newsletters, and other documentation. Reading news articles about current discriminatory practices as well as academic journal articles discussing the educational gaps faced by Dalits also helped to gain corroborative evidence of current difficulties that are not just the opinions of the DEI leaders.

To gain a better understanding of India's historical context and current practices, I also read parts of the Indian Constitution, the Affirmative Action Laws and Anti-Conversion Laws. Rounding out this preparation was my own background teaching and volunteering in classrooms from kindergarten to 12th grades in the United States, observing first-hand the classroom environment and the expected ability levels of each age group. As Wolcott states, "we know the school setting so well that, unknowingly, we become our own best informants".

IN THE FIELD: INTENTIONS AND PRACTICAL CONSTRAINTS

Having prepared through readings and communication with the field, I then traveled to India to begin the interviews and observations. Originally, the DEI coordinator in India had committed to introducing me to the principals of the schools for interviews followed by a "snowball method" to select further participants. That is, the staff would ask for volunteers, and those who participated would recommend more volunteers, and so on. In order to maintain as much validity as possible, I had intended to interview both students and their parents as well.

Also, to avoid selecting only avid supporters, I intended to ask to interview people who may have some negative views about the education, teachers and school, as this could lead to clarification and a balance of perspectives. Typical of many evaluations, things did not go smoothly in the field. When I arrived in Andhra Pradesh, I found that the key actors who would be coordinating all of the interviews had not been notified of my plans, or the purpose of the study. However, one advantage of the individual sites not being notified in advance was that it added a level of credibility to what I observed in that they did not have time to prepare or alter the situations in any way that would place them in a more favourable light. This lack of preparation, coupled with the fact that a school holiday was suddenly added to the schedule by the Ministry of Education, something that apparently happens periodically without prior notice, as well as the shift in schedules to a half day summer schedule that week, led to several changes in plans.

So despite the number of days allocated for this evaluation, five days were lost due to logistical problems alone. Also, having to travel four to five hours each way to two of the schools made it such that I could only spend one or two hours at each, making it impossible to schedule meetings with the parents. For greater validity, this study should have included several days at the same site, with the opportunity to interview parents as well as community leaders involved in establishing the programme. While waiting for the coordinators to establish plans to visit the sites, I immersed myself in the daily life of the campus, finding as many opportunities to meet with people in the community, travel in the area, experience life in India, and observe activities that would create a better cultural context for my study.

I attended a college graduation which was especially interesting as many of these students had spent their internships teaching in the DEI schools and had earned their credentials with the goal of becoming full time teachers at various locations throughout India in the following year. Next, a pastor who volunteers with some of the local youth who attend the DEI schools, and one of the school managers, took me to visit an area they commonly refer to as "the slums," where a large number of Dalit families live in abject poverty. They also took me to what they call the "pipe village" where approximately 150 families live in concrete pipes joined together. Although there was not enough time to start any interviews at this point, it gave me insight about their living conditions, and when I observed some of these children days later in their classroom, they had met me before with men they already trusted. This is extremely important in participant observer research.

14

Effects of Educational Experiences on Personality Trait Development

Education is one of the most critical determinants of success for both individuals and society. Individuals who are highly educated earn more, are healthier, and are more likely to contribute to civic organizations, whereas individuals with lower amounts of education are more likely to commit crimes, suffer unemployment, default on loans, and be incarcerated. As such, education is associated with economic growth and progress and is considered one of the main sources of prosperity for both individuals and nations.

The benefits from education are thought to be attributable to gains in knowledge and skills. Borrowing from the economic literature, these skills are used in the labour market and life to garner better and higher paying occupations, stability in one's life, and access to health care. Education, traditionally, is thought to lead to the accrual of information that can be applied to problems, while also contributing to independent thinking. In psychological terms, educational experiences are thought to impact cognitive skills, such as critical reasoning and crystallized intelligence.

The focus on cognitive abilities can be seen in the evaluation of the current American school system. Success for both individuals and institutions is judged by achievement tests that assess knowledge of facts and the ability to think critically. One idea that has not been given much attention is that schooling experiences also change non-cognitive factors, such as personality traits. Recent findings from the Perry Preschool Project provide an example of this possibility. The Perry Preschool Project intervention programme was intended to promote cognitive skill development in at-risk children. While the intervention had little long- term effect on academic or cognitive skills, intervention participants outperformed non-participants on a number of important life outcomes, such as employment and low criminal behaviour – suggesting that the benefits of the Perry Preschool Project were associated with personality factors, rather than cognitive abilities. Thus, psychological factors other than cognitive ability, such as personality traits, are potentially influenced by experiences within an educational context.

It is surprising that the effect of educational experiences on personality development has not received more attention. In terms of sheer time and resources, education can be considered one of the longest and most intense efforts created by societies to change psychological functioning. Moreover, since the educational system is in place to provide skills and abilities to navigate the world, school experiences should influence the development of personality. In fact, one of the main emphases of education during the middle of the 19th century was the development of "character" and a "mature personality"

The present study investigates the effect of educational experiences on personality traits. Personality traits are defined as neurophysiological structures, underlying relatively enduring patterns of thoughts, feelings, and behaviours that represent a readiness to respond in particular ways to specific environmental cues. By now, it is well established that personality traits are not set in stone but are prone to change throughout the lifespan. Late adolescence and early adulthood is the time when personality traits tend to change the most. Specifically, individuals tend to increase in the personality traits of social dominance, conscientiousness, agreeableness, emotional stability, and openness. The most salient environment during this time period, the educational environment, is thus likely to contribute to these changes in personality. The present study sought to identify what specific educational experiences were related to personality trait change during late adolescence and early adulthood.

The research described here will rely on a longitudinal data set from Germany and will focus on two goals at the interface of personality and educational experiences. First, the present study will examine the predictive relationship between personality assessed in high school and a number of educational experiences. Personality traits are thought to guide individuals into specific experiences through a variety of selection processes. These selection processes, however, may bias estimates of personality trait change because not everyone will encounter the same experience. Accordingly, it is necessary to examine and account for these selection biases to examine changes in personality traits.

Second, the present study will test the associations between a wide array of educational experiences and personality changes that occur during the transition into and throughout the university experience. Furthermore, this study will employ advanced longitudinal models that permit the combination of latent growth models with autoregressive structures that better examine the influence of educational environments on personality development. This allows for a stronger test of the hypothesis that educational experiences can lead to or promote changes in personality traits, by examining the direction of relationship between changes in educational and changes in personality traits.

HOW DO EXPERIENCES CHANGE PERSONALITY TRAITS

Changes in personality traits are thought to involve transactional processes, where certain experiences have the power to affect changes in personality traits. A prevailing difficulty, however, is identifying what types of experiences are important and how these experiences are able to change personality traits. A recently proposed model of personality trait change, the sociogenomic model of personality traits describes the type of experiences the may change personality traits. The sociogenomic model differs from past models of personality traits by focusing on the state-level manifestations of personality traits.

Traits are manifest through stable, enduring patterns of states and are responsible for future states. Of course, traits are not the only cause of our state level behaviours, thoughts and feelings. These states may be partly due to the specific situation or experience that a person is embedded in, such as an extraverted person not talking as much because they are in class. As a result, the focus on states due to both traits and experiences provides a straightforward explanation for variability in behaviour.

Importantly, such variability in states does not invalidate the existence of a trait because the experiences do not directly influence personality traits. Instead, experiences can affect personality traits only indirectly, mediated through personality states. Specifically, experiences can only affect personality traits if changes in state level manifestations exist for a prolonged period of time. Trait change is thus thought to occur by relatively consistent experiences that lead to lasting changes in the way one behaves, thinks, or feels. If these shifts in states are prolonged, changes in the neurophysiology of personality traits may occur through a bottom up fashion.

That is, by observing one perform behaviours different than normal, these behaviours become internalized and may lead to changes in personality traits. Moreover, long-term shifts in states may not even occur consciously. For example, being around industrious colleagues may act as a contagion, where your productivity increases due to ones desire to fit in and not stand out. An example of this type of change process due to persistent states is found in the effects of stress and the neurophysiological structures associated with memory. Interestingly, continued stressful experiences over time lead to changes in the actual structure of the hippocampus and the amygdala, which results in changes in memory processes.

In contrast to prevailing views about changes in personality traits, the sociogenomic model suggests that life transitions or life events are not the main catalysts of change. Much like one stressful experience would not change memory processes, a single or short term event likely will not lead to changes in personality traits. As such, the sociogenomic model is able to integrate findings from longitudinal studies that demonstrate changes in personality traits occur in a relatively slow manner over long periods of time and that a major life transitions, such as leaving home to go to college, does not drastically shape one's personality. Thus, in terms of educational experiences, it is unlikely that a single experience say, being bullied once or going to a specific party, would greatly shape personality trait development. Instead, the model suggests that long-standing changes in trait-related states should lead to changes in the trait.

That is, having sustained thoughts feelings and behaviours associated with the trait over a long period of time, and likely at levels that are greater than your latent trait level, will lead to changes in personality traits. An important relationship exists between experiences and traits, however, where individuals with certain traits are more likely to enter into particular experiences. These experiences, because they are related to the trait can, in turn, lead to greater trait-related thoughts, feelings and behaviours. This third path is identified and suggests that not all people are likely to end up in the same experience. As a consequence these experiences lead to prolonged changes in states; states that are related to the personality traits because the personality trait was partially responsible for bringing someone to the experience in the first place. Overtime, these prolonged changes in states may eventually lead to changes in personality traits. The sociogenomic model suggests two important characteristics of personality trait change that will guide the current study's examination of educational experiences and personality trait change. First, this model suggests a reciprocal path where personality traits predict experiences and that these experiences are the ones most likely to lead to changes in personality traits. Secondly, the model suggests that the important experiences for personality trait development are closely aligned to trait-related states.

That is, experiences that change one's behaviours, thoughts and feelings overtime are the most likely experiences to change personality traits. As such, a focus on the typical behaviours and emotional experiences that students have will be stressed, as well as broader experiences that likely reflect changes in these state-level variables.

SELECTION EFFECTS IN EDUCATIONAL EXPERIENCES

Individuals often seek out, create, evoke, respond to, or are selected into experiences that are compatible and correlated with their personality. This pattern, generally referred to as selection effects, is consistent with a life-course perspective that suggests early emerging personality traits influence the experiences that people encounter in adolescence and young adulthood. Niche-building processes such as these are thought to exist for a broad range of personality traits and experiences. For example, highly conscientious people are more likely to prefer conventional jobs, and individuals higher in extraversion prefer, and obtain, more social jobs

Selection effects for personality traits are quite pervasive, spanning many different educational contexts and continuing to exist even after controlling for other important psychological factors. Conscientiousness is the Big Five trait most closely associated with achievement experiences. Specifically, childhood levels of conscientiousness are associated with academic achievement across educational levels both concurrently and prospectively. For example, conscientiousness assessed at age 10 by parental reports is associated with academic performance both concurrently and prospectively 10 years later. Additionally, conscientiousness is associated with SAT scores and college grades.

The remaining Big Five traits are also associated with academic achievement in adolescence and young adulthood though not always. A recent meta-analysis indicates that high levels of conscientiousness, agreeableness, and openness are positively associated with academic achievement. In contrast, emotional stability and extraversion demonstrate more complex relationships, such that extraversion appears to be positively associated with better performance in elementary school but decreased levels of performance during college. Similarly, emotional stability is helpful early on but is not predictive of achievement during college.

The effect of personality on academic performance is likely mediated by specific school experiences that help promote better academic performance. For example, conscientiousness predicts early completion of assignments, better attendance and study habits, and better teamwork skills that, in turn are associated with higher grades. Agreeableness is also associated with these academic experiences such that individuals higher in agreeableness are more likely to attend class and spend more time studying. Additionally, agreeableness is associated with following teacher instructions and staying focused on learning tasks. Studying harder and attending to instructions are, in turn, associated with better achievement. These studies suggest that personality is related to better grades and performance through greater involvement in the school process, as well as performing behaviours in accordance with teacher expectations.

In addition to achievement-related experiences, experiences within interpersonal relationships are also associated with personality traits. For example, people with high levels of agreeableness tend to have better interpersonal relations with peers and teachers which lead to fewer behavioural problems in school. Similar to agreeableness, extraversion is also associated with interpersonal experiences. Extraverts tend to have larger peer groups and are more accepted by their peers, which lead them to have lower levels of peer victimization and less overall interpersonal conflict. In contrast to these predominantly positive effects, high levels of extraversion may also lead to negative outcomes. For example, extraversion is associated with difficulties paying attention in class and more behavioural problems.

Individuals higher in neuroticism are less able to cope with difficulties that arise in the school and have a greater likelihood of getting along with teachers. Neuroticism also tends to be associated with greater exam-related and school- related stress. However, low levels of neuroticism are not always positive. Individuals low on neuroticism tend to study less and procrastinate more than people high in neuroticism. Overall, it appears that low levels of neuroticism safeguard against school stressors, but low levels of neuroticism might also lead to neglecting responsibilities.

The studies reviewed above leave little doubt that personality traits reflect a niche-building process wherein people tend to select into, create, evoke, and respond to experiences that are associated with their personality. These selection effects are found to exist across the Big Five personality traits and predict a variety of educational experiences. However, a number of important educational experiences have yet to be investigated.

Currently, it is not clear if personality traits play a role in the decision to switch majors, drop out of college, or the balance of time spent between academic, extra-curricular, and job-related activities. Moreover, most of these reported selection effects reviewed above are cross-sectional rather than prospective. As such, the first goal of this study will examine prospective selection effects of personality across a number of educational experiences. Specifically, does personality assessed in high school lead to specific educational experiences in college? Moreover, selection effects are especially important to assess because they provide clues as to what experiences are likely to result in trait related thoughts, feelings and behaviours, which can lead to changes in personality traits.

EDUCATIONAL EXPERIENCES AND PERSONALITY TRAIT CHANGE

In no other period of the lifespan do greater changes in personality traits occur than during late adolescence and young adulthood. During the college period, young adults become more dominant, more conscientious, and more emotionally stable. There is also evidence that agreeableness, social vitality, and openness to experience increase during young adulthood. However, not everyone undergoes changes in personality traits during this time period. The general trends for personality trait change come about because a disproportionate number of individuals change in the direction found in the overall pattern of mean-level change. The existence of a large number of individuals that do not undergo personality trait change opens up that possibility that changes in personality traits may result from having life experiences that pull for changes in personality.

If a large number of people go through an experience that change personality traits, then normative mean level changes will occur. Similarly, not having the experiences will also lead to individual differences in personality trait change compared to people that do have those experiences. This pattern of normative and individual differences in personality trait change invites the question of what experiences are associated with personality trait change in young adulthood.

Presumably, life experiences impart some change in the personalities of individuals living through those experiences—a process typically described as socialization. Past research suggests that socialization and selection effects are intimately related. There is a strong overlap between the experiences selected through personality traits and the changes that result from those same experiences. That is, life experiences do not impinge themselves on people in a random fashion causing widespread transformation. Rather, selection effects set in motion socialization effects, wherein the personality traits that people already possess are deepened and elaborated by trait-correlated experiences. This pattern is described as the corresponsive principle and has been proposed as the most probable type of personality change that occurs over the life course. Specifically, experiences that are in line with one's dispositions will be viewed as validating and rewarding, thus resulting in changes in the traits that brought the person to the experience in the first place.

For example, individuals who behave counterproductively in their jobs are low in conscientiousness. In turn, engagement in these counterproductive behaviours is associated with changes in conscientiousness such that people become less conscientious over time when performing these behaviours. A number of studies have attempted to link life experiences with changes in personality traits. For example, being fired from a job is associated with increases in neuroticism, whereas positive work experiences are associated with decreases in neuroticism. However, these studies predominantly focused on life events associated with work and marriage. The relation between educational experiences and personality trait change has not received similar attention.

Specifically, only a handful of studies have examined the relationship between *educational* experiences and personality trait change. These studies offer a starting point for identifying educational experiences that may play a role in personality trait change. For example, one study found that college students who received higher grades were initially higher in conscientiousness in a longitudinal study across four years of college. In turn, students who achieved higher grades increased more in conscientiousness between their freshman and senior years. Presumably, individuals were rewarded for their behaviour, and this led to further deepening of the characteristics first responsible for the grades. Interestingly, the subjective responses people had about their grades were also related to changes in personality. Feeling good about one's grades was related to increases in extraversion, agreeableness, conscientiousness, and emotional stability. Changes in perceptions of the university from freshman to senior year were also related to changes in personality. Individuals who had a more positive view of the university increased in agreeableness and emotional stability. In contrast, if students' interactions with the university environment worsened over time, this was associated with decreases in emotional stability and extraversion. Other variables not directly related to academic achievement were also associated with changes in personality. For example, individuals who went to the doctor more often during college were more likely to decrease in extraversion and emotional stability.

Similarly, students who had good friends and were popular tended to increase in extraversion. Also, higher overall levels of well-being were associated with increases in extraversion, agreeableness, conscientiousness, emotional stability, and openness. Increases in well-being over time were, in turn, also associated with increases in these traits. This suggests, albeit indirectly, that being happy with one's educational role, which likely relates to personality at baseline, is associated with further positive personality trait change—in a cyclical fashion.

A second study that examined the relationship between educational experiences and personality trait change used the same sample used in the current study. In this study, a broad list of life experiences were examined, which also included a few experiences related to education. A number of specific life experiences, such as taking a trip abroad, starting or breaking off a relationship, and changes in one's social circle, were associated with changes in personality. In terms of educational experiences, failing an important academic exam was associated with increases in neuroticism. These initial studies suggest that grades, performance on exams, and satisfaction with one's university are all associated with changes in personality traits.

Given that these initial studies only identify a small number of salient educational experiences, the current study will examine a number of additional experiences associated with personality traits change. Specifically, the experiences that are subject to selection effects are especially likely to be associated with changes in personality, due to the corresponsive principle. For example, given that personality traits are associated with class attendance, class attendance is likely to be associated with subsequent changes in personality traits.

DO EDUCATIONAL EXPERIENCES CAUSE PERSONALITY CHANGE

Based on studies reviewed above, personality trait change should be associated with educational experiences. There are at least two possible interpretations for these hypothesized findings. First, life experiences may actually lead to changes in personality traits. For example, working hard in school *is* the reason why changes in conscientiousness occur; without the experience there would be no change. The second interpretation is changes in personality may be leading people to receive good grades, for example. That is, the experiences themselves do not cause changes in personality but are merely associated with personality changes. For example, becoming more conscientious may lead to working harder through increased studying and, therefore, be associated with good grades. Unfortunately, this distinction is difficult to disentangle due to the designs that the previous research has employed.

A recent statistical model has been proposed to be better able to tease apart these different interpretations to get at the direction of the association. The ALT model builds upon two partially distinct traditions of longitudinal data analysis: latent trajectory models and auto-regressive models. Each of these methods of longitudinal data analysis conceptualizes development differently and has different shortcomings in disentangling the causes of development. However, by combining these two traditions, the ALT model is able to capture the strengths of the different methods. By doing so, the ALT model provides a much stronger test of whether educational experiences actually cause personality change or are merely associated with changes.

The latent trajectory model that makes up one half of the ALT model identifies individual growth trajectories for each participant. Latent factors that represent an intercept and a growth factor are modeled to capture the development of a construct. The intercept can be modeled to represent the starting value for the first occasion of measurement or the average value over time, whereas the growth factor represents the rate of change over time. The latent trajectory model can also be easily extended to incorporate multiple constructs over time to test for different developmental phenomena. Intercepts are used to address selection effects, whereas growth factors may be used to examine socialization effects.

A number of difficulties arise when using latent trajectory models to examine whether or not experience causes changes in personality traits. First, there is a tendency to treat experiences as single events or average levels of experience. Often this is done to obtain a more valid assessment of the experience, as experiences are, ironically, more difficult to measure than psychological constructs. In support of this practice, the continuity of experiences across time is somewhat high. However, despite moderate test-retest correlations, general day to day experiences may, of course, change. Moreover, evidence suggests that changes in these experiences are related to personality trait change above and beyond average levels.

These findings imply that the development of both experience and personality must be simultaneously incorporated. Secondly, and most importantly, while the latent trajectory model can include the development of both constructs simultaneously, it cannot address the direction of association. That is, do changes in the experience precede changes in personality or vice versa? In a latent growth model where changes are estimated across all repeated measures, correlating the growth factor with an experience addresses only associations with the experience. Thus, testing a causal effect of experience on personality change necessitates a more proximal measurement of the process of change in which the experience is antecedent to change in personality. This type of data structure is typically captured and examined using auto-regressive approaches.

The second half of the ALT model – the auto-regressive model – at first blush appears to be better suited to examine time-specific relations between two different constructs and thereby better suited to draw causal inferences from these relations. In contrast to the latent trajectory models, the auto-regressive model only depends on the immediately preceding time point (*t*-1). In a multivariate sample, this results in cross-lagged paths that allow for the prediction of one construct, above and beyond the preceding value. An interpretation of these findings is that changes in *y* are attributable to *z*. Thus, the auto-regressive approach allows a more time specific analysis of when changes occur.

For example, a recent study examined the joint development of personality traits and adjustment in a classroom setting across four waves in middle school using an auto-regressive cross-lagged design. Increases in conscientiousness and agreeableness were associated with increases in teacher reported student adjustment for all waves. Teacher reported student adjustment was also associated with future levels of conscientiousness and agreeableness. The reciprocal influence of personality and educational experiences in this study, suggests that students evoked responses from the teacher based on their behaviour, which, in turn, led to a reinforcement of that trait overtime.

Reciprocal processes between personality and experiences such as these are consistent with the corresponsive principle and highlight the need to study experiences over time. Selection effects lead a person to have an experience whereby the experience then leads to changes in personality traits. However, as a person changes in response to an experience, they are likely to select into and evoke different experiences consistent with their personality. The bi-directional development seen here reflects a process where changes in one construct leads to changes in another, and then back again.

Though the auto-regressive approach better captures this bi-directional development compared to latent trajectories, a number of limitations prevent the explicit interpretation that *z* causes changes in *y*. For example, even if the environmental experience occurred prior to growth, the relationship may be spurious because of unmeasured experiences or unmeasured growth processes. In addition to these third variable confounds, the auto-regressive model assumes that the *t*-1 measurement point is a meaningful point in time. Because the model is unable to examine whether changes in one variable predict changes in another, this initial point in time may reflect an arbitrary starting point in a more complex bi-directional process. Some researchers have suggested that embedding the auto-regressive approach in a broader model that accounts for these shortcomings offers a stronger test of causal relations. The ALT model accomplishes this goal by merging the latent trajectory and autoregressive approaches. Doing so offers a stronger test of experiential influences on the development of personality traits by capitalizing on the advantages of both types of models. Specifically, the ALT model can be used to examine cross-lagged influences of personality traits and educational experiences while simultaneously estimating growth. It is therefore possible to separate the influence of educational experiences on personality trait change from the overall growth trajectory, which may be the result of other, unmeasured variables.

Testing intercepts and growth parameters with cross-lagged effects simultaneously provides stronger causal inferences to be made when using correlation data structures. The ALT model is able to examine discrete life events while controlling for average environmental experiences and growth across time, thereby controlling for a common underlying shared trajectory between education and personality traits. Controlling for overall level and growth over time provides a much stronger test by which to examine how educational experiences cause changes in personality. Despite the potential contributions of this method, the ALT model has yet to be applied to the development of personality traits.

CURRENT STUDY

Given the recent evidence that educational experiences impart not only cognitive skills but also skills that fall under the rubric of personality traits, the current study examines the effect of educational experiences on personality trait development. In doing so, two different dynamics will be examined. First, this study will examine selection processes that create an association between personality and educational experiences. Second, this study will also examine socialization processes in order to identify experiences associated with personality change. Finally, through advanced statistical models, the directionality of socialization processes will be examined. That is, do changes in personality occur in response to educational experiences or merely along with them?

This study will build upon and extend previous studies of personality development and educational experiences in a number of ways. First, the proposed study will utilize a 4-wave study that tracks students from high school to college using sophisticated modeling techniques to better understand the causal pathways between personality and educational experiences. Previous research linking life experiences and personality development has relied disproportionately on 2-wave designs. Two waves of data are not well suited to distinguish true changes from measurement error. As such, the current study will utilize four waves of data spanning from high school to university. Second, this study will focus on the joint development of personality traits and educational experiences. Past studies have tended to treat experiences as single, static variables that do not themselves change. In contrast, this study incorporates the development of both the environment and personality overtime. Doing so makes it possible to test a reciprocal model between environmental experiences and personality traits that is closer to the proposed processes underlying personality trait development. Furthermore, while it is difficult to infer causality using passive longitudinal designs, the ALT model is able to examine cross-lagged influences of personality and educational experiences while simultaneously estimating growth. Testing overall intercepts and growth parameters with cross-lagged effects simultaneously helps to increase confidence in the potential causal relationships one identifies in correlational data.

Given that these methods have not been used with personality trait data in the past, the current study will examine change in a number of separate analyses that reflect each component of the overall ALT model. Specifically, after testing for selection effects, analyses will test whether growth in personality traits are associated with static forms of educational experiences. This set of analyses will allow the examination of a large set of educational experiences, some of which were not measured more than once. Then, multivariate latent growth models estimating intercepts and growth parameters for both changes in educational experiences and personality traits will examine the effect of changes in educational experiences on personality trait change. Third, auto-regressive cross-lagged models will be used to test the reciprocal relation between educational experiences and personality change over time, as this reflects the most common approach when researchers desire to infer causal associations.

Finally, I will test the full ALT model, which combines the multivariate latent growth and auto-regressive models into a single model. By necessity, the ALT models will be tested on a limited set of variables as, at a minimum, the ALT model requires four waves of high quality data in order to converge. The latter restriction eliminated a number of variables from being examined. By progressing through the various ways of testing change, the results across techniques can be compared to see if specific approaches provide biased or problematic conclusions.

15

National Policy on Education

INTRODUCTORY

Education has continued to evolve, diversify, and extend its reach and coverage since the dawn of human history. Every country develops its system of education to express and promote its unique socio-cultural identity and also to meet the challenges of the times. There are moments in history when a new direction has to be given to an age-old process. That moment is today. The country has reached a stage in its economic and technical development when a major effort must be made to derive the maximum benefit from the assets already created and to ensure that the fruits of change reach all sections. Education is the highway to that goal. With this aim in view, the Government of India announced in January 1985 that a new Education Policy would be formulated for the country. A comprehensive appraisal of the existing educational scene was made followed by a countrywide debate. The views and suggestions received from different quarters were carefully studied.

THE 1968 EDUCATION POLICY AND AFTER

The National Policy of 1968 marked a significant step in the history of education in post- Independence India. It aimed to promote national progress, a sense of common citizenship and culture, and to strengthen *national* integration. It laid stress on the need for a radical reconstruction of the education system, to improve its quality at all stages, and gave much greater attention to science and technology, the cultivation of moral values and a closer relation between education and the life of the people.

Since the adoption of the 1968 Policy, there has been considerable expansion in educational facilities all over the country at all levels. More than 90 per cent of the country's rural habitations now have schooling facilities within a radius of one kilometre. There has been sizeable augmentation of facilities at other stages also. Perhaps the most notable development has been the acceptance of a common structure of education throughout the Country and the introduction of the 10+2+3 system by most States. In the school curricula, in addition to laying down a common scheme of studies for boys and girls, science and mathematics were incorporated as compulsory subjects and work experience assigned a place of importance. A beginning was also made in restructuring of courses at the undergraduate level. Centres of Advanced Studies were set up for post-graduate education and research. And we have been able to meet our requirements of educated manpower.

While these achievements are impressive by themselves, the general formulations incorporated in the 1968 Policy did not, however, get translated into a detailed strategy of implementation, accompanied by the assignment of specific responsibilities and financial and organisational support. As a result, problems of access, quality, quantity, utility and financial outlay, accumulated over the years, have now assumed such massive proportions that they must be tackled with the utmost urgency.

Education in India stands at the crossroads today. Neither normal linear expansion nor the existing pace and nature of improvement can meet the needs of the situation. In the Indian way of thinking, a human being is a positive asset and a precious national resource, which needs to be cherished, nurtured and developed with tenderness, and care, coupled with dynamism. Each individual's growth presents a different range of problems and requirements, at every stage from the womb to the tomb. The catalytic action of Education in this complex and dynamic growth process needs to be planned meticulously and executed with great sensitivity. India's political and social life is passing through a phase, which poses the danger of erosion to long-accepted values. The goats of secularism, socialism, democracy and professional ethics are coming under increasing strain.

The rural areas, with poor infrastructure and social services, will not get the benefit of trained and educated youth, unless rural-urban disparities are reduced and determined measures are taken to promote diversification and dispersal of employment opportunities. The growth of our population needs to be brought down significantly over the coming decades. The largest single factor that could help achieve this is the spread of literacy and education among women. Life in the coming decades is likely to bring new tensions together with unprecedented opportunities. To enable the people to benefit in the new environment will require new designs of human resource development. The coming generations should have the ability to internalise new ideas constantly and creatively. They have to be imbued with a strong commitment to humane values and to social justice. All this implies better education.

THE ESSENCE AND ROLE OF EDUCATION

In our national perception, education is essentially for all. This is fundamental to our allround development, material and spiritual. Education has an acculturating role. It refines sensitivities and perceptions that contribute to national cohesion, a scientific temper and independence of mind and spirit - thus furthering the goals of socialism, secularism and democracy enshrined in our Constitution. Education develops manpower for different levels of the economy. It is also the substrate on which research and development flourish, being the ultimate guarantee of national self-reliance. In sum, Education is a unique investment in the present and the future. This cardinal principle is the key to the National Policy on Education.

NATIONAL SYSTEM OF EDUCATION

The Constitution embodies the principles on which the National System of Education is conceived of. The concept of a National System of Education implies that, up to a given level, all students, irrespective of caste, creed, location or sex, have access to education of a comparable quality. To achieve this, the Government will initiate appropriately funded programmes. Effective measures will be taken in the direction of the Common School System recommended in the 1968 Policy. The National System of Education envisages a common educational structure.

The 10+2+3 structure has now been accepted in all parts of the country. Regarding the further break-up of the first 10 years efforts will be made to move towards an elementary system comprising 5 years of primary education and 3 years of upper primary, followed by 2 years of High School. Efforts will also be made to have the +2 stage accepted as a part of school education throughout the country]. The National System of Education will be based on a national curricular framework which contains a common core along with other components that are flexible.

The common core will include the history of India's freedom movement, the constitutional obligations and other content essential to nurture national identity. These elements will cut across subject areas and will be designed to promote values such as India's common cultural heritage, egalitarianism, democracy and secularism, equality of the sexes, protection of the environment, removal of social barriers, observance of the small family norm and inculcation of the scientific temper. All educational programmes will be carried on in strict conformity with secular values. India has always worked for peace and understanding between nations, treating the whole world as one family. True to this hoary tradition, Education has to strengthen this world view and motivate the younger generations for international co-operation and peaceful co-existence.

This aspect cannot be neglected. To promote equality, it will be necessary to provide for equal opportunity to all not only in access, but also in the conditions for success. Besides, awareness of the inherent equality of all will be created through the core curriculum. The purpose is to remove prejudices and complexes transmitted through the social environment and the accident of birth. Minimum levels of learning will be laid down for each stage of education. Steps will also be taken to foster among students an understanding of the diverse cultural and social systems of the people living in different parts of the country. Besides the promotion of the link language, programmes will also be launched to increase substantially the translation of books from one language to another and to publish multi-lingual dictionaries and glossaries. The young will be encouraged to undertake the rediscovery of India, each in his own image and perception.

In higher education in general, and technical education in particular, steps will be taken to facilitate inter-regional mobility by providing equal access to every Indian of requisite merit, regardless of his origins. The universal character of universities and other institutions of higher education is to be underscored. In the areas of research and development, and education in science and technology, special measures will be taken to establish network arrangements between different institutions in the country to pool their resources and participate in projects of national importance. The Nation as a whole will assume the responsibility of providing resource support for implementing programmes of educational transformation, reducing disparities, universalisation of elementary education, adult literacy, scientific and technological research, etc. Life-long education is a cherished goal of the educational process. This presupposes universal literacy. Opportunities will be provided to the youth, housewives, agricultural and industrial workers and professionals to continue the education of their choice, at the pace suited to them.

The future thrust will be in the direction of open and distance learning. The institutions which will be strengthened to play an important role in giving shape to the National System of Education are the University Grants Commission, the All India Council of Technical Education, the Indian Council of Agricultural Research and the Indian Medical Council. Integrated planning will be instituted among all these bodies so as to establish functional linkages and reinforce programmes of research and post graduate education. These, together with the National Council of Education Research and Training, the National Institute of Educational Planning and Administration, the National Council of Teacher Education and the National Institute of Adult Education will be involved in implementing the Education Policy].

A MEANINGFUL PARTNERSHIP

The Constitutional Amendment of 1976, which includes Education in the Concurrent List, was a far-reaching step whose implications-substantive, financial and administrative-require a new sharing of responsibility between the Union Government and the States in respect of this vital area of national life. While the role and responsibility of the States in regard to education will remain essentially unchanged, the Union Government would accept a larger responsibility to reinforce the national and integrative character of education, to maintain quality and standards (including those of the teaching profession at all levels), to study and monitor the educational requirements of the country as a whole in regard to manpower for development, to cater to the needs of research and advanced study, to look after the international aspects of education, culture and Human Resource Development and, in general, to promote excellence at all levels of the educational pyramid throughout the country. Concurrency signifies a partnership, which is at once meaningful and challenging; the National Policy will be oriented towards giving effect to it in letter and spirit.

EDUCATION FOR EQUALITY

DISPARITIES

The new Policy will lay special emphasis on the removal of disparities and to equalise educational opportunity by attending to the specific needs of those who have been denied equality so far.

EDUCATION FOR WOMEN'S EQUALITY

Education will be used as an agent of basic change in the status of woman. In order to neutralise the accumulated distortions of the past, there will be a well-conceived edge in favour of women. The National Education System will play a positive, interventionist role in the empowerment of women. It will foster the development of new values through redesigned curricula, textbooks, the training and orientation of teachers, decision-makers and administrators, and the active involvement of educational institutions. This will be an act of faith and social engineering. Women's studies will be promoted as a part of various courses and educational institutions encouraged to take up active programmes to further women's development. The removal of women's illiteracy and obstacles inhibiting their access to, and retention in, elementary education will receive overriding priority, through provision of special support services, setting of time targets, and effective monitoring. Major emphasis will be laid on women's participation in vocational, technical and professional education at different levels. The policy of non-discrimination will be pursued vigourously to eliminate sex stereo-typing in vocational and professional courses and to promote women's participation in non-traditional occupations, as well as in existing and emergent technologies.

THE EDUCATION OF SCHEDULED CASTES

The central focus in the SCs' educational development is their equalisation with the non-SC population at all stages and levels of education, in all areas and in all the four dimensions -rural male, rural female, urban male and urban female.

The measures contemplated for this purpose include:

- Incentives to indigent families to send their children to school regularly till they reach the age of 14;
- Pre-matric Scholarship scheme for children of families engaged in occupations such as scavenging, flaying and tanning to be made applicable from Class I onwards. All children of such families, regardless of incomes, will be covered by this scheme and time-bound programmes targeted on them will be undertaken;
- Constant micro-planning and verification to ensure that the enrolment, retention and successful completion of courses by SC students do not fall at any stage, and provision of remedial courses to improve their prospects for further education and employment.
- Recruitment of teachers from Scheduled Castes;
- Provision of facilities for SC students in students' hostels at district headquarters, according to a phased programme;
- Location of school buildings, Balwadis and Adult Education Centres in such a way as to facilitate full participation of the Scheduled Castes;
- The utilisation of Jawahar Rozgar Yojana resources so as to make substantial educational facilities available to the Scheduled Castes; and
- Constant innovation in finding new methods to increase the participation of the Scheduled Castes in the educational process.

THE EDUCATION OF SCHEDULED TRIBES

The following measures will be taken urgently to bring the Scheduled Tribes on par with others:

- Priority will be accorded to opening primary schools In tribal areas. The construction of school buildings will be undertaken in these areas on a priority basis under the normal funds for education, as well as under the Jawahar Rozgar Yojana, Tribal Welfare schemes, etc.
- The socio-cultural milieu of the STs has its distinctive characteristics Including, in many cases, their own spoken languages. This underlines the need to develop the curricula and devise Instructional materials in tribal languages at the initial stages, with arrangements for switching over to the regional language.
- Educated and promising Scheduled Tribe youths will be encouraged and trained to take up teaching in tribal areas.

- Residential schools, including Ashram Schools, will be established on a large scale.
- Incentive schemes will be formulated for the Scheduled Tribes, keeping in view their special needs and life styles. Scholarships for higher education will emphasise technical, professional and para-professional courses. Special remedial courses and other programmes to remove psycho-social impediments will be provided to improve their performance in various courses.
- Anganwadis, Non-formal and Adult Education Centres will be opened on a priority basis in areas predominantly inhabited by the Scheduled Tribes.
- The curriculum at all stages of education will be designed to create an awareness of the rich cultural identity of the tribal people as also of their enormous creative talent.

OTHER EDUCATIONALLY BACKWARD SECTIONS AND AREAS

Suitable incentives will be provided to all educationally backward sections of society, particularly in the rural areas. Hill and desert districts, remote and inaccessible areas and islands will be provided adequate institutional infrastructure.

MINORITIES

Some minority groups are educationally deprived or backward. Greater attention will be paid to the education of these groups in the interests of equality and social justice. This will naturally include the Constitutional guarantees given to them to establish and administer their own educational institutions, and protection to their languages and culture. Simultaneously, objectivity will be reflected in the preparation of textbooks and in all school activities, and all possible measures will be taken to promote an integration based on appreciation of common national goals and ideals, in conformity with the core curriculum.

HANDICAPPED

The objective should be to integrate the physically and mentally handicapped with the general community as equal partners, to prepare them for normal growth and to enable them to face life with courage and confidence.

The following measures will be taken in this regard:

- Wherever it is feasible, the education of children with motor handicaps and other mild handicaps will be common with that of others.

- Special schools with hostels will be provided, as far as possible at district headquarters, for the severely handicapped children.
- Adequate arrangements will be made to give vocational training to the disabled.
- Teachers' training programmes will be reoriented, in particular for teachers of primary classes, to deal with the special difficulties of the handicapped children; and
- Voluntary effort for the education of the disabled, will be encouraged in every possible manner.

ADULT EDUCATION

Our ancient scriptures define education as that which liberates— *i.e.,* provides the instruments for liberation from ignorance and oppression. In the modern world, it would naturally include the ability to read and write, since that is the main instrument of learning. Hence the crucial importance of adult education, including adult literacy. The whole nation has pledged itself, through the National Literacy Mission, to the eradication of illiteracy, particularly in the 15-35 age group through various means, with special emphasis on total literacy campaigns.

The Central and State Governments, political parties and their mass organisations, the mass media and educational institutions, teachers, students, youth, voluntary agencies, social activist groups, and employers, must reinforce their commitment to mass literacy campaigns, which include literacy and functional knowledge and skills, and awareness among learners about the socio-economic reality and the possibility to change it]. * Since involvement of the participants of the literacy campaigns in the development programmes is of crucial importance, the National Literacy Mission will be geared to the national goals such as alleviation of poverty, national integration, environmental conservation, observance of the small family norm, promotion of women's equality, universalisation of primary education, basic health-care, etc. It will also facilitate energisation of the cultural creativity of the people and their active participation in development processes]. * Comprehensive programmes of post-literacy and continuing education will be provided for neo-literates and youth who have received primary education with a view to enabling them to retain and upgrade their literacy skills, and to harness it for the improvement of their living and working condition.

These programmes would include:

- Establishment of continuing education centres of diverse kind to enable adults to continue their education of their choice;
- Workers' education through the employers, trade unions and government;

- Wider promotion of books, libraries and reading rooms;
- Use of radio, TV and films ~ as mass as well as group learning media;
- Creation of learners' groups and organisations; and
- Programmes of distance learning.

A critical development issue today is the continuous upgradation of skills so as to produce manpower resources of the kind and the number required by the society. Special emphasis will, therefore, be laid on organisation of employment/self-employment oriented, and need and interest based vocational and skill training programmes.

REORGANISATION OF EDUCATION AT DIFFERENT STAGES: EARLY CHILDHOOD CARE AND EDUCATION

The National Policy on Children specially emphasises investment in the development of young child, particularly children from sections of the population in which first generation learners predominate. Recognising the holistic nature of child development, *viz.*, nutrition, health and social, mental, *physical, moral and emotional development, Early Childhood Care and Education (ECCE) will* receive high priority and be suitably integrated with the Integrated Child Development Services programme, wherever possible. Day-care centres will be provided as a support service for universalisation of primary education, to enable girls engaged in taking care of siblings to attend school and as a support service for working women belonging to poorer sections.

Programmes of ECCE will be child-oriented, focused around play and the individuality of the child. Formal methods and introduction of the 3 R's will be discouraged at this stage. The local community will be fully involved in these programmes. A full integration of child care and pre-primary education will be brought about, both as a feeder and a strengthening factor for primary education and for human resource development in general. In continuation of this stage, the School Health Programme will be strengthened.

ELEMENTARY EDUCATION

The new thrust in elementary education will emphasise three aspects:

1. *Universal access* and enrolment,
2. Universal retention of children upto 14 years of age; and
3. A substantial improvement in the quality of education to enable all children to achieve essential levels of learning.

CHILD-CENTRED APPROACH

A warm, welcoming and encouraging approach, in which ail concerned share a solicitude for the needs of the child, is the best motivation for the child to attend school and learn. A childcentred and activity-based process of learning should be adopted at the primary stage. First generation learners should be allowed to set their own pace and be given supplementary remedial instruction. As the child grows, the component of cognitive learning will be increased and skills organised through practice. The policy of non-detention at the primary stage will be retained, making evaluation as disaggregated as feasible. Corporal punishment will be firmly excluded from the educational system and school timings as well as vacations adjusted to the convenience of children.

SCHOOL FACILITIES

Provision will be made of essential facilities in primary schools. The scope of Operation Blackboard will be enlarged to provide three reasonably large rooms that are usable in all weather, and black boards, maps, charts, toys, other necessary learning aids and school library. At least three teachers should work in every school, the number increasing, as early as possible, to one teacher per class. At least 50 per cent of teachers recruited in/future should be women. The Operation Blackboard will be extended to upper primary stage also. Construction of school buildings will be a priority charge on JRY funds.

NON-FORMAL EDUCATION

The Non-formal Education Programme, meant for school dropouts, for children from habitations without schools, working children and girls who cannot attend whole-day schools, will be strengthened and enlarged Modern technological aids will be used to improve the learning environment of NFE Centres. Talented and dedicated young men and women from the local community will be chosen to serve as instructors, and particular attention paid to their training.

All necessary measures will be taken to ensure that the quality of non-formal education is comparable with the formal education. Steps will be taken to facilitate lateral entry into the formal system of children passing out of the non-formal system]. * Effective steps will be taken to provide a framework for the curriculum on the lines of the national core curriculum, but based on the needs of the learners and related to the local environment. Learning material of high quality will be developed and provided free of charge to all pupils.

NFE programmes will provide participatory learning environment, and activities such as games and sports, cultural programmes, excursions, etc. The Government will take over-all responsibility for this vital sector. Voluntary agencies and Panchayati Raj institutions will take much of the responsibility of running NFE programmes. Theprovision of funds to these agencies will be adequate and timely]. *

A RESOLVE

The New Education Policy will give the highest priority to solving the problem of children dropping out of school and will adopt an array of meticulously formulated strategies based on micro-planning, and applied at the grass roots level all over the country, to ensure children's retention at school. This effort will be fully co-ordinated with the network of non-formal education. It shall be ensured that free and compulsory education of satisfactory quality is provided to all children upto 14 years of age before we enter the twenty-first century. A national mission will be launched for the achievement of this goal]. *

SECONDARY EDUCATION

Secondary education begins to expose students to the differentiated roles of science, the humanities and social sciences. This is also an appropriate stage to provide children with a sense of history and national perspective and give them opportunities to understand their constitutional duties and rights as citizens. Access to secondary education will be widened with emphasis on enrolment of girls, SCs and STs, particularly In science, commerce and vocational streams.

Boards of Secondary Education will be reorganised and vested with autonomy so that their ability to improve the quality of secondary education is enhanced. Effort will be made to provide computer literacy in as many secondary level institutions as possible so that the children are equipped with necessary computer skills to be effective In the emerging technological world. A proper understanding of the work ethos and of the values of a humane and composite culture will be brought about through appropriately formulated curricula.

Vocationalisation through specialised institutions or through the refashioning of secondary education will, at this stage, provide valuable manpower for economic growth]. * It is universally accepted that children with special talent or aptitude should be provided opportunities to proceed at a faster pace, by making good quality education available to them, irrespective of their capacity to pay for it.

Pace-setting residential schools, Navodaya Vidyalayas, intended to serve this purpose have been established in most parts of the country on a given pattern, but with full scope for innovation and experimentation. Their broad aim will continue to be to serve the objective of excellence coupled with equity and social justice (with reservation for the rural areas, SCs and STs), to promote national integration by providing opportunities to talented children from different parts of the country, to live and learn together, to develop their full potential, and, most importantly, to become catalysts of a nation-wide programme of school improvement.

VOCATIONALISATION

The introduction of systematic, well planned and rigourously implemented programmes of vocational education is crucial in the proposed educational reorganisation. These elements are meant to develop a healthy attitude amongst students towards work and life, to enhance individual employability, to reduce the mis-match between the demand and supply of skilled manpower, and to provide an alternative for those intending to pursue higher education without particular interest or purpose. Efforts will be made to provide children at the higher secondary level with generic vocational courses which cut across several occupational fields and which are not occupation specific]. * Vocational Education will also be a distinct stream, intended to prepare students for identified occupations spanning several areas of activity.

These courses will ordinarily be provided after the secondary stage, but keeping the scheme flexible, they may also be made available after class VIII]. * Health planning and health service management should optimally interlock with the education and training of appropriate categories of health manpower through health-related vocational courses. Health education at the primary and middle levels will ensure the commitment of the individual to family and community health, and lead to health-related vocational courses at the +2 stage of higher secondary education.

Efforts will be made to devise similar vocational courses based on Agriculture, Marketing, Social Services, etc. An emphasis in vocational education will also be on development of attitudes, knowledge, and skills for entrepreneurship and self-employment. The establishment of vocational courses or institutions will be the responsibility of the Government as well as employers in the public and private sectors; the Government will, however, take special steps to cater to the needs of women, rural and tribal students and the deprived sections of society.

Appropriate programmes will also be started for the handicapped. Graduates of vocational courses will be given opportunities, under predetermined conditions, for professional growth, career improvement and lateral entry into courses of general, technical and professional education through appropriate bridge courses. Non-formal, flexible and need-based vocational programmes will also be made available to neoliterates, youth who have completed primary education, school drop outs, persons engaged in work and unemployed or partially employed persons. Special attention in this regard will be given to women. Tertiary level courses will be organised for the young who graduate from the higher secondary courses of the academic stream and may also require vocational courses. It is proposed that vocational courses cover 10 per cent of higher secondary students by 1995 and 25 per cent by 2000. Steps will be taken to see that a substantial majority of the products of vocational courses are employed or become self-employed. Review of the courses offered would be regularly undertaken. Government will also review its recruitment policy to encourage diversification at the secondary level.

HIGHER EDUCATION

Higher education provides people with an opportunity to reflect on the critical social, economic, cultural, moral and spiritual issues facing humanity. It contributes to national development through dissemination of specialised knowledge and skills. It is therefore a crucial factor for survival. Being at the apex of the educational pyramid, it has also a key role in producing teachers for the education system. In the context *of the* unprecedented explosion *of* knowledge, higher education has to become dynamic as never before, constantly entering uncharted areas.

There are around 150 universities and about 5,000 colleges in India today. In view of the need to effect an all round improvement in the institutions, it is proposed that, in the near future, the main emphasis will be on the consolidation of, and expansion of facilities in, the existing institutions. Urgent steps will be taken to protect the system from degradation. In view of mixed experiences with the system of affiliation, autonomous colleges will be helped to develop in large numbers until the affiliating system is replaced by a freer and more creative association of universities with colleges. Similarly, the creation of autonomous departments within universities on a selective basis will be encouraged. Autonomy and freedom will be accompanied by accountability. Courses and programmes will be redesigned to meet the demands of specialisation better. Special emphasis will be laid on linguistic competence. There will be increasing flexibility in the combination of courses. State level planning and.co-ordination of higher education will be done through Councils of Higher Education.

The UGC and these Councils will develop coordinative methods to keep a watch on standards. Provision will be made for minimum facilities and admission will be regulated according to capacity. A major effort will be directed towards the transformation of teaching methods. Audiovisual aids and electronic equipment will be introduced; development.of science and technology curricula and material, *research, and* teacher orientation will receive attention. This will require preparation of teachers at the beginning of the service as well as continuing education thereafter. Teachers' performance will be systematically assessed. All posts will be filled on the basis of merit.

Research in the universities will be provided enhanced support and steps will be taken to ensure its high quality. Suitable mechanisms will be set up by the UGC for co-ordinating research in the universities, particularly in thrust areas of science and technology, with research undertaken by other agencies. An effort will be made to encourage the setting up of national research facilities within the university system, with proper forms of autonomous management.

Research in Indology, the humanities and social sciences will receive adequate support. To fulfil the need for the synthesis of knowledge, inter-disciplinary research will be encouraged.

Efforts will be made to delve into India's ancient fund of knowledge and to relate it to contemporary reality. This effort will imply the development of facilities for the intensive study of Sanskrit and other classical languages. An autonomous Commission will be established to foster and improve teaching, study and research in Sanskrit and other classical languages. In the interest of greater co-ordination and consistency in policy, sharing of facilities and developing inter-disciplinary research, a national body covering higher education in general, agricultural, medical, technical, legal and other professional fields will be set up.

OPEN UNIVERSITY AND DISTANCE LEARNING

The open learning system has been initiated in order to augment opportunities for higher education, as an instrument of democratising education and to make it a lifelong process. The flexibility and innovativeness of the open learning system are particularly suited to the diverse requirements of the citizens of our country, including those who had joined the vocational stream.

The Indira Gandhi National Open University, established in 1985 in fulfilment of these objectives, will be strengthened. It would also provide support to establishment of open universities in the States. The National Open School will be strengthened and open learning facilities extended in a phased manner at the secondary level in all parts of the country].

DELINKING DEGREES FROM JOBS

A beginning will be made in de-linking degrees from jobs in selected areas. The proposal cannot be applied to occupation-specific courses like Engineering, Medicine, Law, Teaching, etc. Similarly, the services of specialists with academic qualifications in the humanities, social sciences, sciences, etc. will continue to be required in various job positions.

De-linking will be applied in services for which a university degree need not be a necessary qualification. Its implementation will lead to a re-fashioning of job-specific courses and afford greater justice to those candidates who, despite being equipped for a given job, are unable to *get it because of an unnecessary preference for graduate candidates.* Concomitant with de-linking, an appropriate machinery, such as National Evaluation Organisation, will be established to conduct tests on a voluntary basis to determine the suitability of candidates for specific jobs, to pave the way for the emergence of norms of comparable competencies across the nation, and to bring about an over-all improvement in testing and measurement.

RURAL UNIVERSITY

The new pattern of the Rural University will be consolidated and developed on the lines of Mahatma Gandhi's revolutionary ideas on education so as to take up the challenges of microplanning at grassroots levels for the transformation of rural areas. Institutions and programmes of Gandhian basic education will be supported.

TECHNICAL AND MANAGEMENT EDUCATION

Although the two streams of technical and management education are functioning separately, it is essential to look at them together, in view of their close relationship and complementary concerns. The reorganisation of Technical and Management Education should take into account the anticipated scenario by the turn of the century, with specific reference to the likely changes in the economy, social environment, production and management processes, the rapid expansion of knowledge and the great advances in science and technology. The infrastructure and services sectors as well as the unorganised rural sector also need a greater induction of improved technologies and a supply of technical and managerial manpower.

This will be attended to by the Government. In order to improve the situation regarding manpower information, the recently set up Technical Manpower Information System will be further developed and strengthened. Continuing education, covering established as well as emerging technologies, will be promoted. As computers have become important and ubiquitous tools, a minimal exposure to computers and a training in their use will form part of professional education. Programmes of computer literacy will be organised on wide scale from the school stage. In view of the present rigid entry requirements to formal courses restricting the access of a large segment of people to technical and managerial education, programmes through a distancelearning process, including use of the mass media will be offered. Technical and management education programmes, including education in polytechnics, will also be on a flexible modular pattern based on credits, with provision for multi-point entry A strong guidance and counselling service will be provided. In order to increase the relevance of management education, particularly in the noncorporate and under-managed sectors, the management education system will study and document the Indian experience and create a body of knowledge and specific educational programmes suited to these sectors. Appropriate formal and non-formal programmes of technical education will be devised for the benefit of women, the economically and socially weaker sections, and the physically handicapped.

The emphasis of vocational education and its expansion will need a large number of teachers and professionals in vocational education, educational technology, curriculum development, etc. Programmes will be started to meet this demand. To encourage students to consider "self-employment" as a career option, training in entrepreneurship will be provided through modular or optional courses, in degree or diploma programmes. In order to meet the continuing needs of updating curriculum, renewal should systematically phase out obsolescence and introduce new technologies of disciplines.

INSTITUTIONAL THRUSTS

Some polytechnics in the rural areas have started training weaker groups in those areas for productive occupations through a system of community polytechnics. The community polytechnic system will be appropriately strengthened to increase its quality and coverage.

INNOVATION, RESEARCH AND DEVELOPMENT

Research as a means of renovation and renewal of educational processes will be undertaken by all higher technical institutions. It will primarily aim at producing quality manpower capable of taking up R&D functions. Research for development will focus on improving present technologies, developing new indigenous ones and enhancing production and productivity. A suitable system for watching and forecasting technology will be set up. The scope for co-operation, collaboration and networking relationships between institutions at various levels and with the user systems will be utilised. Proper maintenance and an attitude of innovation and improvement will be promoted systematically.

PROMOTING EFFICIENCY AND EFFECTIVENESS AT ALL LEVELS

As technical and management education is expensive, the following major steps will be taken for cost-effectiveness and to promote excellence:

- High priority will be given to modernisation and removal of obsolescence. However, modernisation will be undertaken to enhance functional efficiency and not for its own sake or as a status symbol.
- Institutions will be encouraged to generate resources using their capacities to provide services to the community and industry. They will be equipped with up-to-date learning resources, library and computer facilities.
- Adequate hostel accommodation will be provided, specially for girls. Facilities for sports, creative work and cultural activities will be expanded.
- More effective procedures will be adopted in the recruitment of staff. Career opportunities, service conditions, consultancy norms and other perquisites will be improved.

- Teachers will have multiple roles to perform: teaching, research, development of learning resource material, extension and managing the institution. Initial and in-service training will be made mandatory for faculty members and adequate training reserves will be provided. Staff Development Programmes will be integrated at the State, and coordinated at Regional and National levels.
- The curricula of technical and management programmes will be targeted on current as well as the projected needs of industry or user systems. Active interaction between technical or management institutions and industry will be promoted in programme planning and implementation, exchange of personnel, training facilities and resources, research and consultancy and other areas of mutual interest.
- Excellence in performance of institutions and individuals will be recognised and rewarded. The emergence of substandard and mediocre institutions will be checked. A climate conducive to excellence and innovation will be promoted with full involvement of the faculty.
- Select institutions will be awarded academic, administrative and financial autonomy of varying degrees, building in safeguards with respect to accountability.
- Networking systems will have to be established between technical education and industry, R&D organisations, programmes of rural and community development, and with other sectors of education with complementary characteristics.

MANAGEMENT FUNCTIONS AND CHANGE

In view of the likely emergence of changes in management systems and the need to equip students with the ability to cope with them, effective mechanisms will be devised to understand the nature and direction of change per se and to develop the important skill of managing change. In view of the integrated nature of the task, the Ministry of Human Resource Development will co-ordinate the balanced development of engineering, vocational and management education as well as the education of technicians and craftsmen. Professional societies will be encouraged and enabled to perform their due role in the advancement of technical and management education. The All India Council for Technical Education, which has been given statutory status, will be responsible for planning, formulation and the maintenance of norms and standards, accreditation, funding of priority areas, monitoring and evaluation, maintaining parity of certification and awards and ensuring the co-ordinated and integrated development of technical and management education.

Mandatory periodic evaluation will be carried out by a duly constituted Accreditation Board. The Council will be strengthened and it will function in a decentralised manner with greater involvement of State governments and technical institutions of good quality. In the interests of maintaining standards and for several other valid reasons, the commercialisation of technical and professional education will be curbed. An alternative system will be devised to involve private and voluntary effort in this sector of education, in conformity with accepted norms and goals.

MAKING THE SYSTEM WORK

It is obvious that these and many other new tasks of education cannot be performed in a state of disorder. Education needs to be managed in an atmosphere of utmost intellectual rigour, seriousness of purpose and, at the same time, of freedom essential for innovation and creativity. While far-reaching changes will have to be incorporated in the quality and range of education, the process of introducing discipline into the system will have to be started, here and now, in what exists. The country has placed boundless trust in the educational system. The people have a right to expect concrete results. The first task is to make it work. All teachers should teach and all students study.

The strategy in this behalf will consist of:

- Better deal to teachers with greater accountability;
- Provision of improved students services and insistence on observance of acceptable *norms of* behaviour;
- Provision of better facilities to institutions; and
- Creation of a system of performance appraisals of institutions according to standards and norms set at the National or State levels.

REORIENTING THE CONTENT AND PROCESS OF EDUCATION

THE CULTURAL PERSPECTIVE

The existing schism between the formal system of education and the country's rich and varied cultural traditions need to be bridged. The preoccupation with modern technologies cannot be allowed to sever our new generations from the roots in India's history and culture. De-culturisation, de-humanisation and alienation must be avoided at all costs. Education can and must bring about the fine synthesis between change-oriented technologies and the country's continuity of cultural tradition. The curricula and processes of education will be enriched by cultural content in as many manifestations as possible. Children will be enabled to develop sensitivity to beauty, harmony and refinement. Resource persons in the community, irrespective of their formal educational qualifications, will be invited to contribute to the cultural enrichment of education, employing both the literate and oral traditions of communication.

To sustain and carry forward the cultural tradition, the role of old masters, who train pupils through traditional modes will be supported and recognised. Linkages will be established between the university system and institutions of higher learning in art, archaeology, oriental studies, etc. Due attention will also be paid to the specialised disciplines of Fine Arts, Museology, Folklore, etc. Teaching, training and research in these disciplines will be strengthened so as to replenish specialised manpower in them.

VALUE EDUCATION

The growing concern over the erosion of essential values and an increasing cynicism in society has brought to focus the need for readjustments in the curriculum in order to make education a forceful tool for the cultivation of social and moral values. In our culturally plural society, education should foster universal and eternal values, oriented towards the unity and integration of our people.

Such value education should help eliminate obscurantism, religious fanaticism, violence, superstition and fatalism. Apart from this combative role, value education has a profound positive content, based on our heritage, national and universal goals and perceptions. It should lay primary emphasis on this aspect.

LANGUAGES

The Education Policy of 1968 had examined the question of the development of languages in great detail; its essential provisions can hardly be improved upon and are as relevant today as before. The implementation of this part of the 1968 Policy has, however, been uneven. The Policy will be implemented more energetically and purposefully.

BOOKS AND LIBRARIES

The availability of books at low prices is indispensable for people's education. Effort will be made to secure easy accessibility to books for all segments of the population. Measures will be taken to improve the quality of books, promote the reading habit and encourage creative writing. Authors' interests will be protected.

Good translations of foreign books into Indian languages will be supported. Special attention will be paid to the production of quality of books for children, including text books and work books. Together with the development of books, a nation-wide movement for the improvement of existing libraries and the establishment of new ones will be taken up. Provision will be made in all educational institutions for library facilities and the status of librarians improved.

MEDIA AND EDUCATIONAL TECHNOLOGY

Modern communication technologies have the potential to bypass several stages and sequences in the process of development encountered in earlier decades. Both the constraints of time and distance at once become manageable. In order to avoid structural dualism, modern educational technology must reach out to the most distant areas and the most deprived sections of beneficiaries simultaneously with the areas of comparative affluence and ready availability. Educational technology will be employed in the spread of useful information, the training and re-training of teachers, to improve quality, sharpen awareness of art and culture, inculcate abiding values, etc., both in the formal and non-formal sectors.

Maximum use will be made of the available infrastructure. In villages without electricity, batteries or solar packs will be used to run the programme. The generation of relevant and culturally compatible educational programmes will form an important component of educational technology, and all available resources in the country will be utilised for this purpose. The media have a profound influence on the minds of children as well as adults; some of them tend to encourage consumerism, violence, etc., and have a deleterious effect, Radio and T.V. programmes, which clearly militate against proper educational objectives, will be prevented. Steps will be taken to discourage such trends in films and other media also. An active movement will be started to promote the production of children's films of high quality and usefulness.

WORK EXPERIENCE

Work experience, viewed as purposive and meaningful manual work, organised as an integral part of the learning process and resulting in either goods or services useful to the community, is considered as an essential component at all stages of education, to be provided through well-structured and graded programmes. It would comprise activities in accord with the interests, abilities and needs of students, the level of skills and knowledge to be upgraded with the stages of education. This experience would be helpful on his entry into the workforce. Prevocational programmes provided at the lower secondary stage will also facilitate the choice of the vocational courses at the higher secondary stage.

EDUCATION AND ENVIRONMENT

There is a paramount need to create a consciousness of the environment. It must permeate *all ages* and *all sections of* society, beginning with the child.

Environmental consciousness should inform teaching in schools and colleges. This aspect will be integrated in the entire educational process.

POPULATION EDUCATION

Population education must be viewed as an important part of the nation's strategy to contain the growth of population. Starting at the primary and secondary levels with inculcation of consciousness about the looming crisis due to expansion of population, educational programmes should actively motivate and inform youth and adults about family planning and responsible parenthood.}*

MATHEMATICS TEACHING

Mathematics should be visualised as the vehicle to train a child to think, reason, analyse and to articulate logically. Apart from being a specific subject, it should be treated as a concomitant to any subject involving analysis and reasoning. With the recent introduction of computers in schools, educational computing and the emergence of learning through the understanding of cause-effect relationships and the interplay of variables, the teaching of mathematics will be suitably redesigned to bring it in line with modern technological devices.

SCIENCE EDUCATION

Science education will be strengthened so as to develop in the child well defined abilities and values such as the spirit of Enquiry, creativity, objectivity, the courage to question, and an aesthetic sensibility. Science education programmes will be designed to enable the learner to acquire problem solving and decision making skills and to discover the relationship of science with health, agriculture, industry and other aspects of daily life. Every effort will be made to extend science education to the vast numbers who have remained outside the pale of formal education.

SPORTS AND PHYSICAL EDUCATION

Sports and physical education are an integral part of the learning process, and will be included in the evaluation of performance. A nation-wide infrastructure for physical education, sports and games will be built into the educational edifice. The infrastructure will consist of playfields, equipment, coaches and teachers of physical education as part of the School Improvement Programme. Available open spaces in urban areas will be reserved for playgrounds, if necessary by legislation. Efforts will be made to establish sports institutions and hostels where specialised attention will be given to sports activities and sports-related studies, along with normal education.

Appropriate encouragement will be given to those talented in sports and games. Due stress will be laid on indigenous traditional games.

YOGA

As a system, which promotes an integrated development of body and mind, Yoga will receive special attention. Efforts will be made to introduce Yoga in all schools. To this end, it will be introduced in teacher training courses.

THE ROLE OF YOUTH

Opportunities will be provided for the youth to Involve themselves in national and social development through educational institutions and outside them. Students will be required to participate In one or the other of existing schemes, namely, the National Service Scheme, National Cadet Corps, etc. Outside the Institutions, the youth will be encouraged to take up programmes of development, reform and extension. The National Service Volunteer Scheme will be strengthened.

THE EVALUATION PROCESS AND EXAMINATION REFORM

Assessment of performance Is an Integral part of any process of learning and teaching. As part of sound educational strategy, examinations should be employed to bring about qualitative Improvements In education. The objective will be to re-cast the examination system so as to ensure a method of assessment that is a valid and reliable measure of student development and a powerful instrument for improving teaching and learning; in functional terms, this would mean:

- The elimination of excessive element of chance and subjectivity;
- The de-emphasis of memorisation;
- Continuous and comprehensive evaluation that incorporates both scholastic and nonscholastic aspects of education, spread over the total span of instructional time;
- Effective use of the evaluation process by teachers, students and parents;
- Improvement in the conduct of examination;
- The introduction of concomitant changes in instructional materials and methodology;
- Instruction of the semester system from the secondary stage in a phased manner; and
- The use of grades in place of marks.

The goals are relevant both for external examinations and evaluations within educational institutions. Evaluation at the institutional level will be streamlined and the predominance of external examinations reduced. A National Examination Reform Framework would be prepared to serve as a set of guidelines to the examining bodies, which would have the freedom to innovate and adapt the framework to suit the specific situations.

THE TEACHER

The status of the teacher reflects the socio-cultural ethos of a society; it is said that no people can rise above the level of its teachers. The Government and the community should endeavour to create conditions, which will help motivate and inspire teachers on constructive and creative lines. Teachers should have the freedom to innovate, to devise appropriate methods of communication and activities relevant to the needs and capabilities of and the concerns of the community. The methods of recruiting teachers will be reorganised to ensure merit, objectivity and conformity with spatial and functional requirements. The pay and service conditions of teachers have to be commensurate with their social and professional responsibilities and with the need to attract talent to the profession. Efforts will be made to reach the desirable objective of uniform emoluments, service conditions and grievance-removal mechanisms for teachers throughout the country. Guidelines will be formulated to ensure objectivity in the postings and transfers of teachers.

A system of teachers evaluation ~ open, participative and data-based - will be created and reasonable opportunities of promotion to higher grades provided. Norms of accountability will be laid down with incentives for good performance and disincentives for non-performance. Teachers will continue to play a crucial role in the formulation and implementation of educational programmes. Teachers' associations must play a significant role in upholding professional integrity, enhancing the dignity of the teacher and in curbing professional misconduct. National level associations of teachers, could prepare a Code of Professional Ethics for Teachers and see to its observance.

TEACHER EDUCATION

Teacher Education is a continuous process, and its pre-service and in-service components are inseparable. As the first step, the system of teacher education will be overhauled. The new programmes of teacher-education will emphasise continuing education and the need for teachers to meet the thrusts envisaged in this Policy. District Institutes of Education and Training (DIET) will be established with the capability to organise pre-service and in-service courses for elementary school teachers and for the personnel working in non-formal and adult education. As DIETs get established, sub-standard institutions will be phased out. Selected Secondary Teacher Training Colleges will be upgraded to complement the work of State Councils of Educational Research and Training. The National Council of Teacher Education will be provided the necessary resources and capability to accredit institutions of teacher-education and provide guidance regarding curricula and methods. Networking arrangements will be created between institutions of teacher education and university departments of education.

THE MANAGEMENT OF EDUCATION

An overhaul of the system of planning and the management of education will receive high priority.

The guiding considerations will be:

- Evolving a long-term planning and management perspective of education and its integration with the country's developmental and manpower needs;
- Decentralisation and the creation of a spirit of autonomy for educational institutions;
- Giving pre-eminence to people's involvement, including association of non-governmental agencies and voluntary effort;
- Inducting more women in the planning and management of education;
- Establishing the principle of accountability in relation to given objectives and norms.

NATIONAL LEVEL

The Central Advisory Board of Education will play a pivotal role in reviewing educational development, determining the changes required to improve the system and monitoring implementation. It will function through appropriate Committees and other mechanisms created to ensure contact with, and co-ordination among, the various areas of Human Resource Development. The Departments of Education at the Centre and in the States will be strengthened through the involvement of professionals.

INDIAN EDUCATION SERVICE

A proper management structure in education will entail the establishment of the Indian Education Service as an All-India Service. It will bring a national perspective to this vital sector. The basic principles, functions and procedures of recruitment to this service will be decided in consultation with the State Governments.

STATE LEVEL

State Governments may establish State Advisory Boards of Education on the lines of CABE. Effective measures should be taken to integrate mechanisms in the various State departments concerned with Human Resource Development. Special attention will be paid to the training of educational planners, administrators and heads of institutions. Institutional arrangements for this purpose should be set up in stages.

DISTRICT AND LOCAL LEVEL

District boards of Education will be created to manage education up to the higher secondary level. State Governments will attend to this aspect with all possible expedition. Within a multilevel framework of educational development, Central, State and District and Local level agencies will participate in planning, co-ordination, monitoring and evaluation.

A very Important role must be assigned to the head of an educational institution. Heads will be specially selected and trained. School complexes will be promoted on a flexible pattern so as to serve as networks of institutions and synergic alliances to encourage professionalism among teachers to ensure observance of norms of conduct and to enable the sharing of experiences and facilities. It is expected that a developed system of school complexes will take over much of the inspection functions in due course. Local communities, through appropriate bodies, will be assigned a major role in programmes of school improvement.

VOLUNTARY AGENCIES AND AIDED INSTITUTIONS

Non-government and voluntary effort including social activist groups will be encouraged, subject to proper management, and financial assistance provided. At the same time, steps will be taken to prevent the establishment of institutions set up to commercialise education.

REDRESS OF GRIEVANCES

Educational tribunals, fashioned after Administrative Tribunals, will be established at the national and state levels.

RESOURCES AND REVIEW

The Education Commission of 1964-66, the National Education Policy of 1968 and practically all others concerned with education have stressed that the egalitarian goals and the practical, development-oriented objectives of Indian society can be realised only by making investments in education of an order commensurate with the nature and dimensions of the task. Resources, to the extent possible, will be raised by mobilising donations, asking the beneficiary communities to maintain school buildings and supplies of some consumables, raising fees at the higher levels of education and effecting some savings by the efficient use of facilities.

Institutions involved with research and the development of technical and scientific manpower should also mobilize some funds by levying a *cess* or charge on the user agencies, including Government departments, and entrepreneurs. All these measures will be taken not only to reduce the burden on State resources but also for creating a greater sense of responsibility within the educational system. However, such measures will contribute only marginally to the total funding. The Government and the community in general will find funds for such programmes as: the universalisation of elementary education; liquidating illiteracy; equality of access to educational opportunities to all sections throughout the country; enhancing the social relevance, quality and functional effectiveness of educational programmes; generating knowledge and developing technologies in scientific fields crucial to self-sustaining economic development and creating a critical consciousness of the values and imperatives of national survival.

The deleterious consequences of non-investment or inadequate investment in education are indeed very serious. Similarly, the cost of neglecting vocational and technical education and of research is also unacceptable. Sub-optimal performance in these fields could cause irreparable damage to the Indian economy. The network of institutions set up from time to time since Independence to facilitate the application of science and technology would need to be substantially and expeditiously updated, since they are fast becoming obsolete. In view of these imperatives, education will be treated as a crucial area of investment for national development and survival.

The National Policy on Education, 1968, had laid down that the investment on education be gradually increased to reach a level of 6 per cent of the national income as early as possible. Since the actual level of investment has remained far short of that target, it is important that greater determination is shown now to find the funds for the programmes laid down in this Policy. While the actual requirements will be computed from time to time on the basis of monitoring and review, the outlay on education will be stepped up to ensure that during the Eighth Five Year Plan and onwards it will uniformly exceed 6 per cent of the national income. The implementation of the various parameters of the New Policy must be reviewed every five years. Appraisals at short Intervals will also be made to ascertain the progress of implementation and the trends emerging from time to time.

THE FUTURE

The future shape of education in India is too complex to envision with precision. Yet, given our tradition, which has almost always put high premium on intellectual and spiritual attainment, we are bound to succeed in achieving our objectives. The main task is to strengthen the base of the pyramid, which might come close to a billion people at the turn of the century. Equally, it is important to ensure that those at the top of the pyramid are among the best in the world. Our cultural well springs had taken good care of both ends in the past; the skew set in with foreign domination and influence. It should now be possible to further intensify the nation-wide effort in Human Resource Development, with Education playing its multifaceted role.

NATIONAL POLICY ON EDUCATION, 1968

Education has always been accorded an honoured place in Indian society. The great leaders of the Indian freedom movement realised the fundamental role of education and throughout the nation's struggle for independence, stressed its unique significance for national development. Gandhiji formulated the scheme of basic education, seeking to harmonise intellectual and manual work. This was a great step forward in making education directly relevant to the life of the people. Many other national leaders likewise made important contributions to national education before independence. In the post-independence period, a major concern of the Government of India and of the States has been to give increasing attention to education as a factor vital to national progress and security. Problems of educational reconstruction were reviewed by several commissions and committees, notably the University Education Commission (1948-49) and the Secondary Education Commission (1952-53). Some steps to implement the recommendations of these Commissions were taken; and with the passing of the Resolution on Scientific Policy under the leadership of Jawaharlal Nehru, the development of science, technology and scientific research received special emphasis.

Towards the end of the third Five Year Plan, a need was felt to hold a comprehensive review of the educational system with a view to initiating a fresh and more determined effort at educational reconstruction; and the Education Commission (1964-66) was appointed to advise Government on " the national pattern of education and on the general principles and policies for the development of education at all stages and in all aspects." The Report of the Education Commission has since been widely discussed and commented upon. Government is happy to note that a consensus on the national policy on education has emerged in the course of these discussions. The Government of India is convinced that a radical reconstruction of education on the broad lines recommended by the education commission is essential for economic and cultural development of the country, for national integration and for realising the ideal of a socialistic pattern of society.

This will involve a transformation of the system to relate it more closely to life of the people; a continuous effort to expand educational opportunity; a sustained and intensive effort to raise the quality of education at all stages; an emphasis on the development of science and technology; and the cultivation of moral and social values. The educational system must produce young men and women of character and ability committed to national service and development. Only then will education be able to play its vital role in promoting national progress, creating a sense of common citizenship and culture, and strengthening the national integration. This is necessary if the country is to attain its rightful place in the comity of nations in conformity with its great cultural heritage and its unique potentialities.

The Government of India accordingly resolves to promote the development of education in the country in accordance with the following principles:

- *Free and Compulsory Education:* Strenuous efforts should be made for the early fulfilment of the Directive principle under Article 45 of the Constitution seeking to provide free and compulsory education for all children up to the age of 14. Suitable programmes should be developed to reduce the prevailing wastage and stagnation in schools and to ensure that every child who is enrolled in schools successfully completes the prescribed course.
- Status, Emoluments and Education of Teachers:
  - Of all the factors which determine the quality of education and its contribution to national development, the teacher is undoubtedly the most important. It is on his personal qualities and character, his educational qualifications and professional competence that the success of all educational endeavours must ultimately depend. Teachers must, therefore, be accorded an honoured place in society, Their emoluments and other service conditions should be adequate and satisfactory having regard to their qualifications and responsibilities.
  - The academic freedom pf teachers to, pursue and publish independent studies and researches and to speak and write about significant national and international issues should be protected.
  - Teacher education, particularly in-service education, should receive due emphasis.
- Development of languages:
  - *Regional Languages:* The energetic development of Indian Languages and literature is a *sine qua non* for educational and cultural development. Unless this is done, the creative energies of the people will not be released, standards of education will not improve, knowledge will not spread to the people and the gulf between the intelligentsia and masses will remain if not widen further. The regional languages are already in use as media of education at the primary and secondary stages. Urgent steps should now be taken to adopt them as media of education at the university stage.
  - *Three-Language Formula:* At the secondary stage, the State

Governments should adopt, and vigourously implement, the three-language formula which includes the study of a modern Indian language, preferably one of the southern languages, apart from Hindi and English in the Hindi-speaking States, and of Hindi along with the regional *language and* English *in* the Non-Hindi-speaking States. Suitable courses in Hindi and/or English should also be available in universities and colleges with a view to improving the proficiency of students in these languages up to the prescribed university standards.

- *Hindi.* Every effort should be made to promote the development of Hindi. In developing Hindi as the link language, due care should be taken to ensure that it will serve, as provided for in Article 351 of the Constitution, as a medium of expression for all the elements of the composite culture of India. The establishment, in non-Hindi States, of colleges and other institutions of higher education which use Hindi, as the medium of education should be encouraged.
- *Sanskrit* Considering the special importance of Sanskrit to the growth and development of Indian languages and its unique contribution to the cultural unity of the country, facilities for its teaching at the school and university stages should be offered on a more liberal scale. Development of new methods of teaching the language should be encouraged, and the possibility explored of including the study of Sanskrit in those courses (such as modern Indian languages, ancient Indian history, Indology and Indian philosophy) at the first and second degree stages, where such knowledge is useful.
- *International Languages:* Special emphasis needs to be laid on the study of English and other international languages. World knowledge is growing at a tremendous pace, especially in science and technology. India must not only keep up this growth but should also make her own significant contribution to it. For this purpose, study of English deserves to be specially strengthened.

- *Equalisation of Educational Opportunity:* Strenuous efforts should be made to equalise educational opportunity.
  - Regional imbalances in the provision of educational facilities should be corrected and good educational facilities should be provided in rural and other backward areas.
  - To promote social cohesion and national integration the Common School System as recommended by the Education Commission should be adopted. Efforts should be made to improve the standard of education in general schools. All special schools like

public schools should be required to admit students on the basis of merit and also to provide a *prescribed* proportion of free-studentships to prevent segregation of social classes. This will not, however, affect the rights of minorities under Article 30 of the Constitution.

- The education of girls should receive emphasis, not only on grounds of social justice, but also because it accelerates social transformation.
- More intensive efforts are needed to develop education among the backward classes and especially among the tribal people.
- Educational facilities for the physically and mentally handicapped children should be expanded and attempts should be made to develop integrated programmes enabling the handicapped children to study in regular schools.

- *Identification of Talent:* For the cultivation of excellence, it is necessary that talent in diverse fields should be identified at as early an age as possible, and every stimulus and opportunity given for its full development.
- *Work - Experience and National Service:* The school and the community should be brought closer through suitable programmes of mutual service and support. Work-experience and national service including participation in meaningful and challenging programmes of community service and national reconstruction should accordingly become an integral part of education. Emphasis in these programmes should be on self-help, character formation and on developing a sense of social commitment.
- *Science Education and Research:* With a view to accelerating the growth of the national economy, science education and research should receive high priority. Science and mathematics should be an integral part of general education till the end of the school stage.
- *Education for Agriculture and Industry:* Special emphasis should be placed on the development of education for agriculture and industry.
  - There should be at least one agricultural university in every State. These should, as far as possible, be single campus universities; but where necessary, they may have constituent colleges on different campuses. Other universities may also be assisted, where the necessary potential exists, to develop strong departments for the study of one ore more aspects of agriculture.
  - In technical education, practical training in industry should form an integral part of such education. Technical education and

research should be related closely to industry, encouraging the flow of personnel both ways and providing for continuous cooperation in the provision, design and periodical review of training programmes and facilities.

- There should be a continuous review of the agricultural, industrial and other technical manpower needs of the country and efforts should be made continuously to maintain a proper balance between the output of the educational institutions and employment opportunities.

- *Production of Books:* The quality of books should be improved by attracting the best writing talent through a liberal policy of incentives and remuneration. Immediate steps should be taken for the production of high quality textbooks for schools and universities. Frequent changes of textbooks should be avoided and their prices should be low enough for students of ordinary means to buy them. The possibility of establishing autonomous book corporations on commercial lines should be examined and efforts should be made to have a few basic textbooks common throughout the country. Special attention should be given to books for children and to university level books in regional languages.
- *Examinations:* A major goal of examination reforms should be to improve the reliability and validity of examinations and to make evaluation a continuous process aimed at helping the student to improve his level of achievement rather than at 'certifying' the quality of his performance at a given moment of time.
- Secondary Education:
  - Education opportunity at the secondary (and higher) level is a major instrument of social change and transformation. Facilities for Secondary education should accordingly be extended expeditiously to areas and classes, which have been denied these in the past.
  - There is need to increase facilities for technical and vocational education at this stage. Provision of facilities for secondary and vocational education should conform broadly to requirements of the developing economy and real employment opportunities. Such linkage is necessary to make technical and vocational education at the secondary stage effectively terminal. Facilities for technical and vocational education should be suitably diversified to cover a large number of fields such as agriculture, industry, trade and commerce, medicine and public health, home management, arts and crafts, secretarial training, etc.

- University Education:
  - The number of whole-time students to be admitted to a college or university department should be determined with reference to the laboratory, library and other facilities and to the strength of the staff.
  - Considerable care is needed in establishing new universities. These should be started only after an adequate provision of funds has been made for the purpose and due care has been taken to ensure proper standards.
  - Special attention should be given to the organisation of postgraduate courses and to the improvement of standards of training and research at this level.
  - Centres of advanced study should be strengthened and a small number of 'cluster of centres' aiming at the highest possible standards in research and training should be established.
  - There is need to give increased support to research in universities generally. The institutions for research should, as far as possible, function within the fold of universities or in intimate association with them.
- *Part-time Education and Correspondence Courses:* Part time education and correspondence courses should be developed on a large scale at the university stage. Such facilities should also be developed for secondary school students, for teachers and for agricultural, industrial and other workers. Education through part-time and correspondence courses should be given the same status as full-time education. Such facilities will smoothen transition from school to work, promote the cause of education and provide opportunities to the large number of people who have the desire to educate themselves further but cannot do so on a full-time basis.
- Spread of Literacy and Adult Education:
  - The liquidation of mass illiteracy is necessary not only for promoting participation in the working of democratic institutions and for accelerating programmes of production, especially in agriculture, but for quickening the tempo of national development in general. Employees in large commercial, industrial and other concerns should be made functionally literate as early as possible. A lead in this direction should come from the industrial undertakings in the public sector. Teachers and students should be actively involved in organising literacy campaigns, especially as part of the Social and National Service Programme.

  - Special emphasis should be given to the education of young practising farmers and to the training of youth for self-employment.
- Games and Sports: Games and sports should be developed on a large scale with the object of improving the physical fitness and sportsmanship of the average student as well as of those who excel in this department. Where playing field and other facilities for developing a nation-wide programme of physical education do not exist, these should be provided on a priority basis.
- Education of Minorities: Every effort should be made not only to protect the rights of minorities but to promote their educational interests as suggested in the statement issued by the Conference of the Chief Ministers of States and Central Ministers held in August, 1961.
- The Educational Structure: It will be advantageous to have a broadly uniform educational structure in all parts of the country. The ultimate objective should be to adopt the 10+2+3 pattern, the higher secondary stage of two years being located in schools, colleges or both according to local conditions.
  - The reconstruction of education on the lines indicated above will need additional outlay. The aim should be gradually to increase the investment in education so as to reach a level of expenditure of 6 per cent of the national income as early as possible.
  - The Government of India recognises that reconstruction of education is no easy task. Not only are the resources scarce but the problems are exceedingly complex. Considering the key role which education, science and research play in developing the material and human resources of the country, the Government of India will, in addition to undertaking programmes in the Central sector, assist the State Governments for the development of programmes of national importance where co-ordinated action on the part of the States and the Centre is called for.
  - The Government of India will also review, every five years; the progress made and recommend guidelines for future development.

Index

L

M

O

P

R

S

T

U

Y